Second Language Learning in t
School Years: Trends and Cont

Published in this series

Second Language Learning in the Early School Years: Trends and Contexts

VICTORIA A. MURPHY

OXFORD
UNIVERSITY PRESS

OXFORD
UNIVERSITY PRESS

Great Clarendon Street, Oxford, OX2 6DP, United Kingdom

Oxford University Press is a department of the University of Oxford.
It furthers the University's objective of excellence in research, scholarship,
and education by publishing worldwide. Oxford is a registered trade
mark of Oxford University Press in the UK and in certain other countries

First published in 2014
2018 2017 2016 2015 2014
10 9 8 7 6 5 4 3 2 1

No unauthorized photocopying

ISBN: 978 0 19 434885 0

Printed in China

This book is printed on paper from certified and well-managed sources

ACKNOWLEDGEMENTS
*The author and publisher are grateful to those who have given permission to
reproduce the following extracts and adaptations of copyright material*: pp.77–8
Figures from OECD (2006), *Where Immigrant Students Succeed: A Comparative
Review of Performance and Engagement in PISA 2003*, PISA, OECD Publishing,
http://dx.doi.org/10.1787/9789264023611-en. Reproduced by permission.
pp.105–6 Figures from *Dual Language Development & Disorders: A Handbook
on Bilingualism & Second Language Learning, Second Edition* (2011) by
J. Paradis, F. Genesee, and M.B. Crago, Paul H Brookes Publishing Co., Inc.,
Baltimore. Reprinted by permission.

For Robin

Acknowledgements

I have hugely enjoyed the process of preparing this volume, and have learned a tremendous amount. I have been so inspired by all the exciting research that is being conducted around the world addressing key issues in the area of child L2 learning and I feel very privileged to be a part of such a vibrant research community.

Most things worth doing are rarely possible without the help and support of a number of people, and writing a book is by no means an exception. There are so many people to thank who supported me throughout the process of putting this volume together that I fear the acknowledgements section itself could be as long as one of the chapters! However, there are some individuals who absolutely must be identified, for without them this book would never have been completed.

I would first like to thank Julia Bell, Sophie Rogers, and Ann Hunter from the Oxford University Press for the enormous support they have given to me throughout the entire process of getting this volume to print. Julia in particular has been a constant source of encouragement, from the earliest stages and throughout, and I have very much enjoyed our discussions. I am exceedingly grateful for Ann's patience and skill, not to mention her positive words of wisdom. Other friends and colleagues to whom I owe a debt of gratitude and who have been generally supportive include Ernesto Macaro, Kathy Sylva, Robert Vanderplank, Catherine Walter, Robert Woore, and the lovely Kate Nation. I cannot express adequately the appreciation I feel towards Janet Enever, Fred Genesee, Johanne Paradis, and Silvina Montrul, all of whom kindly reviewed chapters and offered excellent advice and critical commentary (though of course all errors are my own!). Additionally, I owe a great debt to Nick Ellis, Patsy Lightbown, Nina Spada, and Lydia White for setting me on my current path and generally being both positively influential and supportive.

On a more personal note, I would like to thank my friends and family for being a steady source of encouragement; Miles Davis, Bill Evans, Oscar Peterson, and Nina Simone who were constant companions throughout the writing; and lastly but most importantly, Evan and Cameron who have taught me the most important lessons of all, and Robin, the breath of my life.

Preface

One of the tasks in my professional life is to act as Course Director of the MSc in Applied Linguistics/Second Language Acquisition at the University of Oxford. I teach a module on that course entitled 'L1 and Bilingualism', which covers what we know about how children learn language, both when it is their native (only) language and when they are developing bilingually. I have been teaching this module for nine years; through this graduate seminar, in conjunction with the inspiring PhD students I have been fortunate enough to work with over the years, I have been able to enjoy many lively, informative discussions and debates with some very talented students. These interactions, together with the research I have been engaged in for the past 20 years, have had a profound impact on the way I conceive of the research outcomes on L2 learning in children and I am very grateful to all of the students who have inspired my thinking. However, in the course of teaching and researching these topics, over and over again I have had students ask me to recommend a volume that reviews research evidence on L2 learning in childhood—a volume that would provide them with a 'bird's eye view' of what has been going on in the research investigating different aspects of how children learn more than one language in childhood. While I was certainly able to draw up impressive reading lists, given the fantastic research available on numerous different aspects of research on these subjects, I was not able to identify a single volume which I thought provided such a general review. A number of years ago, one student suggested that I might write such a book myself. This planted the initial seed in my mind—that I might perhaps one day prepare such a review. That day has now arrived and this volume is the product.

Research on child bilingualism and L2 learning, like a well-cut diamond, is multi-faceted. As a result, in writing this book I have had to necessarily make decisions about what facets would be included and, perhaps more notably, which would not. Undoubtedly some will argue that I have erred in my judgment on areas of research I have included. Given that I have had a prolonged interest in language development in education, I decided to focus on contexts of learning in children that intersect and interact with educational provision. This is also particularly important internationally, as increasingly children are becoming bi- or multilingual through their experiences with languages in the context of primary education. The only exception to this general approach is Chapter 2 on simultaneous bilingualism, which sets the scene for the remaining chapters and illustrates that very young children are more than capable of learning multiple languages without any adverse consequences to their linguistic development in either language. However, I am fully aware that there are gaps in this book, as I found it challenging to address everything I felt was important, both in terms of which contexts to include, and which research to include within each. I hope that minimally this volume provides a good starting point for the interested reader to delve more deeply into the multi-faceted subject of child L2 learning through education.

While the 'seed' of the idea to write this book was germinating, I began to notice various emerging trends in relation to teaching foreign languages to young learners that also guided the thinking and writing of this book. Having been educated in Canada, where it is standard practice to learn French at young ages in primary school, I was shocked when I came to England in the mid 1990s and discovered that foreign language instruction was not part of the primary curriculum. I learned that it once had been, but had been withdrawn for a variety reasons, notably that the government of the day had decided it was not effective. A number of issues are related here, not the least of which includes the fact that a decision to withdraw FL learning would have been less likely in a non-Anglophone country and reflects a view that English is the most important language for our young global citizens. I was concerned that there might be an underlying belief along the lines of: If our children are already native speakers of English then, while FL learning might be nice, it does not deserve any prominence within a primary curriculum in an English-speaking country. Additionally, I was concerned by some of the approaches to FL learning that I came to read and learn about, those which demotivate an inherently motivated and interested population of learners. As someone who learned quite a lot of a second language through primary education, I felt a significant sense of loss for the generation of children in the UK who did not have the benefit of learning a FL properly through school.

I was most heartened, however, to learn that around the world, including in the UK, governments began to consider FL learning in childhood more seriously by making policy decisions about either introducing FL into the curriculum or even lowering the starting age at which FL instruction begins (see Chapter 6). However, like many other researchers with an interest in child L2 learning, I began to wonder what was motivating the decision to lower these starting ages, when I realized that it did not always appear that these initiatives were made on the basis of evidence. As I discuss in Chapter 6, policy documents in the UK, for example, speak to the 'ease' with which children learn languages. However, those of us who research children learning an L2 have been aware for some time that age is not likely to be the critical variable here—that the nature of the child's exposure to the L2/FL is equally or indeed perhaps even more important than the age of the learner.

I decided, therefore, that in taking up my student's suggestion to write the review of research on child L2 learning, I would focus the discussion on a comparison of L2 outcomes across contexts within the overarching population of young learners. I felt this would be useful for a wide variety of individuals (such as graduate students from a range of disciplines, practitioners, policy makers, etc.), and that it would be constructive to identify the diversity of contexts, and outcomes within contexts. Given that all the learners across each of the contexts in this volume are young learners, the discussion highlights that age is arguably not the most significant variable in predicting successful L2/bilingual outcomes. In so doing, I hope too that I have been able to highlight the multiplicity of different factors which contribute to the variability both within and across contexts, so that in examining L2 outcomes these can be taken into account. To illustrate, the fact that simultaneous bilinguals rarely develop with fully balanced proficiency in both of their languages (Chapter 2); that heritage language learners often lose or fail to completely develop their knowledge of their home language (Chapter 3); the difficulties that many minority language learners experience with literacy development (Chapter 4); and the slow progress made by young FL learners (Chapter 6); can all be understood when factoring in a range of different contextual variables. As but one example, it would be gratifying if future evaluations of FL learning outcomes in input-limited environments (as in the UK, for example) would take note of some of these contextual variables, such as the nature of the provision and the kinds of support for FL learning outside of the classroom. Perhaps with these sorts of contextual issues in mind, future policy makers might make more evidence-based decisions about educational provision that best supports multilingual development. I live in hope!

Contents

I

A typology of contexts

Introduction

Children seem to learn languages easily, without apparent effort, regardless of their parents' level of education, literacy skills, or socioeconomic status[1]. A child living in a yurt in central Asia will learn his/her language as readily as a prince in castle. Anyone who has been around young children as they develop their linguistic proficiency can observe the remarkable facility with which children develop knowledge of something as complex as language, without even seeming to try. Indeed, there is a prevailing assumption that young, developing children are little sponges who soak up everything around them, including languages. This view is exemplified by an online article about children learning languages on a popular online site for parents where it was stated that '…as children are sponges who pick up new things much more quickly than adults, learning a language comes easily to young minds'[2]. This view that children have a predisposition for learning language was originally brought to the fore with Lenneberg's (1967) influential Critical Period Hypothesis (CPH), in which he proposed that there was a biological explanation for language acquisition and that humans were predisposed to learn language more successfully in early childhood than later on in their lives. Lenneberg's CPH was temporally contiguous with Chomsky's work arguing that certain abstract aspects of linguistic knowledge were innate, given to us at birth (Chomsky, 1965; Hauser, Chomsky, and Fitch, 2002; Chomsky, 2007)—a Universal Grammar (UG) enabling children to readily acquire linguistic competence in the languages to which they are exposed. In contrast to the ease with which children learn their first languages, older individuals have long been identified as less or unsuccessful language learners in comparison to children. Adults in particular, in attempting to learn a second or foreign language, have been shown to have particular difficulties and typically fail to achieve native-like competence in the L2. Some researchers have even argued that the rare cases of successful adult foreign language (FL) learning are 'pathological' in the same sense as the rare failures to acquire a first language in children (Selinker, 1972). The very fact of being old(er) has been argued to explain the apparent difficulty adults have in learning an L2. The view is that an older learner (i.e. beyond Lenneberg's critical period) will necessarily struggle to acquire a second language because the window of opportunity has closed and access to Chomsky's UG is lost[3]. These views suggest then, that the critical variable in determining ultimate success in learning languages is the age of the learner—the younger the better.

If children learn languages easily, at least, more easily than adult (older learners), then it follows that they will learn second languages easily, and more easily in childhood than in adolescence or adulthood. In the past few decades the facility with which children can become bi- or multilingual has gained increasing prominence, both from theoretical and more applied perspectives. From a theoretical perspective, a more comprehensive understanding of how language is acquired (Ambridge and Lieven, 2011), the extent to which language development is a child-internal process (inside–out) relative to a process driven by the environment in which the child develops (outside–in) (Hirsh-Pasek and Golinkoff, 1996), and the extent to which L1 acquisition theories can account for bi- or multilingualism (Ellis, O'Connell, and Römer, 2013; Martin and Ellis, 2012; Ellis and Sagarra, 2011), has led to an increase in research investigating young children's L2 development. From more applied perspectives, increased global migration (Davis, D'Oderico, Laio, and Ridolfi, 2013), developments in educational policy and practice (Baker, 2011; García, 2009), and greater intercultural sensitivity, recognizing the need to preserve indigenous languages at risk of dying out (Cortina, 2014), have all been forces that have led to greater interest in L2 learning in childhood. However, the context in which a child becomes bi- or multilingual can vary substantially, therefore, understanding L2 learning in children necessarily entails a better understanding of the effect of context on child L2 outcomes. Children might be raised in homes or societies where multiple languages are regularly spoken and where there is consistent exposure and opportunities to interact with more than one language, as in cites such as Montréal, Barcelona, and Mumbai. Alternatively, children might receive instruction in a foreign language at some point in their formal education. This latter context of foreign language instruction in formal education is becoming a more prevalent language learning context for young learners throughout the world (see Chapter 6). As there is variability in the contexts in which children could become bilingual, there is corresponding variability in the extent to which a young child actually does become bilingual, and/or the degree of proficiency in each language. It is timely, therefore, to examine the research literature with respect to child L2 learning through formal education in the early, formative years.

The purpose of this volume is twofold. The first aim is to bring together in one book a review of the major themes and issues that have emerged from research investigating the development of L2 learning in childhood, across a range of contexts. Many of these contexts are in a formal education setting[4].

Each chapter, therefore, presents a review of a given context. These reviews, however, are selective not systematic. Consequently, there will be omissions both in terms of level of detail provided in certain discussions and also in terms of which themes or issues are included. I have included discussions of those themes that I believe are most salient, relevant, and informative for the purposes of this volume. Despite the selective nature of these reviews, each chapter should minimally provide a good beginning for the interested reader who wishes to delve in greater detail into these areas and their related research.

The second major aim of this volume is to use these reviews to investigate the notion that 'younger is better' for L2 learning. As mentioned earlier, there is a prevailing view that younger children learn languages more easily than older learners. Increasingly, this 'younger is better' idea has led educational policy makers to lower the age at which children begin learning a second language as part of the primary curriculum. For example, in the UK Modern Foreign Language (MFL) is being introduced as a curricular subject in 2014. To be more precise, it is being *re*-introduced, because MFL used to be part of the primary curriculum but was removed in part due to an influential (but methodologically flawed) study which purported to show that older learners actually were *better* learners than younger ones (Burstall, 1975). Consequently, the then government of the UK decided to remove MFL from its already overcrowded primary curriculum. The current UK government, however, has more recently decided to reintroduce MFL to primary school learners and provide taught foreign language instruction as young as seven years old. The stated aims for this decision include 'younger children learn languages more easily' (Department for Education, 2013, p. 4); 'young children have a natural disposition to learn languages'; '...pupils will benefit from a more global outlook and enhanced career prospects'; '...children benefit from learning a foreign language...' (Department for Education, 2012, p. 1). We can see, therefore, that there are underlying beliefs about the benefits of learning a foreign language at primary school in these governmental documents, many of which centre around the notion that children have a propensity to 'pick up' languages more easily in the younger years. This belief is neatly encapsulated in a quote from Tony Blair in 1999 when he was Prime Minister of the UK. At one point in delivering a speech he said 'Everyone knows that with languages the earlier you start, the easier they are' (Sharpe, 2001). It is not clear, however, whether and to what extent these beliefs concerning 'younger is better' hold across different contexts in primary school-aged learners. In order to tackle this issue, therefore, an examination of the research reviewed in each chapter of this volume will help identify the extent to which these different cases of child L2 learning is in fact 'easy'. But first, it is worthwhile taking a closer look at the 'younger is better' idea, as all the contexts included in this volume represent instances of L2 learning in childhood, a time at which many people believe language learning comes naturally. To what extent is this belief supported by evidence?

Age and L2 learning in primary school children

It is important to be clear that the focus of this book is not on evaluating the validity of the Critical Period Hypothesis (CPH), nor indeed is it intended to identify the most effective age at which to learn an L2. Nonetheless, the age of the learners is an important variable when discussing L2 outcomes and is obviously related to key discussions in the literature about both the CPH and issues of when learners should be exposed to, and taught an L2. Indeed, as indicated earlier, the notion that 'younger is better' seems to underlie a range of different policy decisions with respect to child L2 learning in primary education.

The Critical Period Hypothesis (Lenneberg, 1967) has been widely discussed in the context of both L1 and L2 development (see Bialystok and Miller, 1999; Birdsong, 1999; DeKeyser, 2000; Singleton, 2005; Nikolov, 2009; DeKeyser, Alfi-Shabtay, and Ravid, 2010; Muñoz and Singleton, 2011; DeKeyser, 2013). There is considerable variability with respect to how the CPH has been defined and the types of learner and task types that have been researched in respect of the CPH. Consequently, the results are complex and somewhat mixed (Bialystok and Miller, 1999; Singleton, 2005). One of the issues that has been difficult for researchers to pin down is the exact onset and offset of the CPH—when the CPH begins and ends. Lenneberg (1967) originally proposed the onset was around two years old, with the offset around 12 years (corresponding to puberty). This claim initiated a considerable amount of research investigating the extent to which this might be true, both for L1 and L2 (see Herschensohn, 2007). As a consequence of this research effort, almost all of Lenneberg's original ideas related to the CPH have been refuted (Herschensohn, 2007; see also Snow, 1987). Proponents of the CPH currently argue that the onset is birth, possibly even before birth (see discussion in Chapter 2 on infant speech processing) not two years, and that the offset is likely to be far earlier than puberty, possibly around the age at which typical L1 development is (almost) complete, around 5 or 6 years. Other researchers have argued that age effects in language learning should not be viewed in the constraints of a 'critical' period, but rather, opt for the term 'sensitive' period to identify that there are no exact cut-off points (Herschensohn, 2007).

There is a wide range of evidence considered supportive of the CPH for L1 development, ranging from neurological studies regarding lateralization of brain function (Penfield and Roberts, 1959), to research on age-of-acquisition effects in deaf children learning to sign, showing that children who learn to sign at younger ages tend to have higher scores on various morphological tasks (Emmorey, 2002; Newport, 1990). There are also compelling and disturbing cases of children who mature in extreme isolation and who fail to develop native-like linguistic competence (Curtiss, 1977; Curtiss, Fromkin, Krashen, Rigler, and Rigler, 2004). Despite research showing these age-of-acquisition effects, the research community has not universally accepted the view that there is a critical period for language development—for either L1 or L2 learning (Bortfield and Whitehurst, 2001; Hakuta, 2001; Snow, 2002). This is because there are a number of variables which are typically confounded with age—such as the nature of the linguistic input (both in terms of quality and quantity), the motivation and aptitude of the learner, and whether the learner receives formal instruction in the L2—where some researchers have argued that these other variables are more influential in determining differences between young and older learners (Hakuta, Bialystok, and Wiley, 2003).

The evidence for a CPH in L2 acquisition is equally mixed and there are many excellent reviews that attempt to clarify some of the problems and findings inherent in this research (Birdsong, 1999; DeKeyser and Larson-Hall, 2005; DeKeyser, 2013; Hyltenstam and Abrahamsson, 2003; Moyer, 2004; Scovel, 2000; Singleton and Ryan, 2004; Muñoz and Singleton, 2011). As indicated earlier, there are many different variables that interact with the age of the learner and contribute to L2 outcomes. DeKeyser, Alfi-Shabtay, and Ravid (2010) also highlight the fact that the learning mechanisms underlying language development in childhood are themselves qualitatively different relative to those used in adult L2 learning. Children are argued to use largely implicit mechanisms, whereas older, adult learners, have been argued to use more explicit learning mechanisms. Minimally, therefore, age of acquisition seems to interact with a range of variables. Thus age, in and of itself, may indeed be associated with L2 outcomes, but age interacts with so many other variables that it is often difficult to tease apart the effect of age, independent of the interaction of age with these other variables. Age, as a variable, is very important to understand as fully as possible because it might be assumed that as long as the child is exposed to and learns the L2 before the offset of the CPH (whenever that is), they will acquire the L2 without difficulty. This is most striking in the context of children from immigrant families who are educated through the medium of an L2. Policy makers may believe that ethnic minority children simply need to be exposed to the majority language when they are young; thus obviating the need for the development of new policy which supports minority language learners or L2 provision to be incorporated in current policy to support L2 learning in these contexts. Correspondingly, understanding age effects does not necessarily translate into educational implications, in that the notion of 'just teach earlier' is '...almost certainly wrong' (DeKeyser, 2013, p. 55). In other words, establishing that there are age-of-acquisition effects in L2 learning does not mean that we just have to teach or expose the child to the L2 when they are young to guarantee successful L2 outcomes.

In this volume the older vs. younger question is not directly assessed, as comparisons will not be made with older learners. However, what is relevant for this volume is being able to describe the extent to which context is a predictive variable in determining ultimate attainment in the L2. For example, minority language learners are approximately the same age as some FL learners when they begin to learn their L2 in an educational setting. However, the amount and nature of the L2 learned in these two populations is dramatically different, underscoring that while age may be relevant, there are many other variables (for example, type and amount of exposure, type of educational experience) that predict L2 outcomes. Young FL learners, for example, typically do not have a sufficient amount of input (being in an input-limited L2 environment) and they therefore may not have the opportunity to use their implicit learning mechanisms (DeKeyser et al., 2010; Muñoz, 2006). Minority language learners, on the other hand, having had significantly more exposure to the L2, and who are learning their L2 in an input-rich environment, are more likely to be in a position to be able to invoke such mechanisms that could subsequently lead to better developed knowledge of L2. While both populations of L2 learners may be the same age, the context is the variable that leads to differential success in these two settings.

All of the learners discussed in this volume are young learners and therefore may be operating in the 'critical' period, however that may be defined. If successful L2 learning is more likely to happen in childhood, then we can argue that all of the contexts in this volume could yield 'successful' L2 learners. Nonetheless, as Moyer stated, 'Clearly age of exposure is but one factor in ultimate attainment, and not an especially informative one...' (Moyer 2004, p. 138). She argues for the importance of 'putting age effects in context' and while for her context means either the psychological, social, or cognitive context (which undoubtedly are important contexts to consider in relation to age and L2 learning), another perhaps more obvious form of context considered in this volume is the linguistic environment and nature of experience the L2 learner has with the L2.

Why is it valuable to examine research on child L2 learning across different contexts? As mentioned earlier, increasingly around the world children are being educated either in a language that is not their home language (see Chapters 3, 4, and 5) or are offered instruction in a foreign language (Chapter 6). It is important, therefore, not only from theoretical and empirical perspectives, but also from pedagogical and policy orientations, to understand more comprehensively what the research concerning L2 learning in each of these domains actually tells us about successful L2 learning in childhood. Without doubt, developing policy is a complex business, but one would hope that policy decisions are made taking such evidence into consideration. However, it sometimes seems as if this is not always the case. For example, Burstall's (1975) study was one of the influences that led the then UK government to remove MFL from the primary curriculum. More recent and much more methodologically rigorous research has illustrated a similar finding (Muñoz, 2006)—that older children make greater L2 gains than younger learners in input-limited FL settings. This evidence, therefore, begs the question as to why governments would consider lowering the starting age at which children are taught a FL. Lowering the starting age is not necessarily a bad idea, indeed is most likely a good idea. However, the decision to do so needs to be made in the context of understanding what is reasonable in terms of realistic L2 outcomes and with greater understanding of the nature of learning in these contexts (see Chapter 6). A further example that questions policy decisions in relation to context is in the sphere of Initial Teacher Education (ITE) for primary school L2 learners. Again in the UK, it used to be possible for primary trainee teachers to specialize in English as an Additional Language (EAL)—that is, they could opt to receive specialist training and experience in educating young minority language learners who were being educated in a language (English) that was not their home language. This specialist EAL training has not been part of ITE programmes in tertiary education in the UK for some time. At the same time, however, there is a pressing need to have EAL-specific knowledge of the educational challenges faced by minority language learners, since the numbers of children with EAL in English schools is growing steadily, where at the time of writing 18.1 per cent of the primary school population in the UK are EAL learners. Yet primary trainee teachers can no longer opt to receive specialist training in EAL. There seems, therefore, to be a mismatch between certain policy decisions—both in terms of provision and training for teachers, and the evidence.

So far in this brief discussion I have provided a few examples from the UK context only. This volume, however, attempts wherever possible to take an international stance. One of the themes that will emerge from the following chapters is the substantial variability in L2 learning outcomes across the different contexts in focus in this volume. There is variability both within contexts, and across contexts. In order to better understand the extent to which policy decisions, teacher education, and curriculum development (for example) reflect the evidence (i.e. L2 outcomes), one needs to better understand the source(s) of this variability. Reviewing the evidence across a range of different contexts, therefore, should provide a good basis on which to examine this relationship more closely. As a result, in Chapters 2–6, there is a sub-section on 'the age issue', where the extent to which age predicts the outcomes discussed in each chapter is deliberated.

A typology of L2 contexts

Chapter 2 focuses on research conducted in the context of bilingual first language acquisition (BFLA). This context represents the youngest learners in this volume, examining research that addresses the development of two languages simultaneously, from birth to school age. Some of the research in this context has been carried out in settings where children have relatively equal exposure to two languages both in and outside the home from birth, and where both languages enjoy similar (high) status. Other relevant settings in the BFLA context are those where children may have a home language that is different from the language of the wider society—in cases where children come from immigrant families or speak regional minority languages in the home. In this setting, a child may be exposed to the majority language in nursery or preschool settings, on television, in the community, etc. but have a different home language, and the majority language may or may not be spoken in the home. Their bilingual development then is likely to be less balanced than in the previous example, but they are still exposed to two languages from birth. It will become apparent in Chapter 2 that there are a number of different settings in which a child can develop knowledge of two languages simultaneously, and the environment (i.e. amount and quality of exposure) is critical in determining linguistic outcomes. It is useful to begin the volume with this context because research on BFLA demonstrates that there is no biological or cognitive impediment to acquiring multiple languages and becoming multilingual. Learning two languages simultaneously does not seem to have any negative consequences on the development of the child— indeed, quite the opposite—as there are a number of studies that demonstrate certain cognitive advantages for bilingual children. Even in this context, however, there is a considerable amount of variability in the extent to which the child becomes proficient, in terms of oral language proficiency and literacy skills, in both languages. The discussion in this chapter sets the scene for the later chapters that examine L2 learning through primary education.

Chapter 3 focuses on heritage language (HL) learners, and specifically on the heritage language development of HL learners. HL learners are the same population mentioned in the paragraph above: children who speak a home language that is different from the majority language in the wider community. Often this home language is of a perceived lower status in relation to the majority language, and it will become clear from the discussion in Chapter 3 that the perceived status of languages can influence the child's bilingual development. Chapter 3 briefly describes educational policy regarding HL education in a range of countries, to identify both the similarities and differences in which various countries accommodate (or not) heritage language learners in their formal educational systems. There is also a discussion of the ways in which the HL development of HL learners is similar to or different from monolingual and L2 speakers of the HL. For many HL children there is an observed 'language shift' from a likely dominance of the HL to (majority) L2 dominance. Unfortunately, for many HL children, they either lose some of the HL knowledge they developed in childhood, or they never fully acquire a complete HL system in the first place. The evidence that speaks to the nature of their HL development and the ways in which educational programmes can support HL learning (in addition to L2 development) is discussed here.

Chapter 4 addresses the same context as Chapter 3. However, the focus is on the HL learners' (majority) L2 development. In this chapter, this population is referred to as minority language learners, to highlight the fact that the focus is on the L2, as these are children who have a minority (home) language, but who have to learn the dominant, majority L2. In examining minority language learners' L2 development, most of the research has focused on two issues: vocabulary and reading. This focus is due in part to the clearly demonstrated scholastic achievement gaps between minority and majority language learners as they progress through the primary curriculum. A number of researchers, therefore, have concentrated on trying to identify the causal variables contributing to this gap. From a linguistic perspective, a consistent finding in the literature is that minority language learners tend to lag behind their majority language peers on measures of reading comprehension—a very important skill required to access the primary curriculum. Associated with this lag in reading comprehension skill are lower scores on vocabulary assessments. Therefore, vocabulary and reading comprehension are the major focus of discussion in Chapter 4. Most of the research in this area has been carried out in North America, where there have been a number of large-scale longitudinal studies examining different aspects of minority language learners' L2 and literacy development. As a result, this chapter is decidedly less international in its scope. Considerably more work needs to be done internationally on both linguistic features and aspects of literacy (such as writing) in this population. Different educational programmes that have been developed (again, mostly in North America) to support minority language learners are also discussed here. Despite the relatively narrow focus in this chapter, it provides a good basis for further work in this globally important area.

Children fortunate enough to participate in immersion education are the focus of Chapter 5. Specifically, the spotlight is on majority language learners—those children who speak the majority language as a native language (i.e. in the home) and who are developing in majority language speaking communities, but who are able to participate in immersion programmes where academic content is taught through the medium of an L2. The chapter begins with a brief description of how immersion programmes were first developed, and the defining characteristics of immersion education. Two main immersion programmes are discussed—one-way immersion programmes where the participating children are from the same (majority) L1 background and learning the L2 through immersion, and two-way immersion where both minority and majority language learners are educated together in the same classroom, and who are educated through the medium of both the minority and majority languages. For example, there are a number of two-way immersion programmes implemented in the USA to native Spanish-speaking and native English-speaking children. Half the day is spent in Spanish, the other half is spent in English. The aim of these programmes is to develop full oral proficiency in both languages, together with biliteracy skills, at no cost to academic achievement. The extent to which these models are successful in their aims is discussed together with a snapshot of how immersion education has been adapted and extended to numerous countries throughout the world.

Chapter 6 addresses foreign language (FL) instructional contexts. As described earlier, many countries are lowering the age at which primary school children are taught a foreign language. Some of these countries and their respective policy decisions will be discussed here. Chapter 6 presents a review of the major themes that have emerged from the young learner FL context in terms of policy, provision, and outcomes. In many countries around the world, the FL of choice is English, and therefore there is discussion of English Language Teaching (ELT) threaded throughout this chapter.

FL instruction for young learners is a relatively under-researched area, though one that is increasingly important as more and more children are being taught a FL through primary school education and at younger ages. Much research across a range of different geopolitical settings still needs to be done here to get a more comprehensive understanding of the ways in which FL instruction in young learners can be best supported.

One can readily see that each of the contexts described in Chapters 2–6 vary quite substantially on a range of variables. In considering the input, for example, BFLA learners (Chapter 2), HL learners (Chapter 3), and minority language learners (Chapter 4) all receive at least one of their languages through naturalistic input. This also could be argued to be the case for the majority language learners in immersion education (Chapter 5) though their input is provided through content-based classroom discourse, which could be regarded as input-rich. FL learners, however, typically receive their input predominantly through being taught the FL, with fewer opportunities to engage and interact with the L2 outside of the classroom—in other words, an input-limited context. Clearly too, the contexts vary with respect to the extent to which the child is exposed to the L2 through formal education. In BFLA contexts, as the children are too young to be in school, the majority (or all) their input to both languages happens through the context of naturalistic exposure in the home and community. Similarly, in HL contexts, the child learns the HL through exposure to it in the home. However, as is discussed in Chapter 3, some HL children are able to participate in immersion education programmes aimed at revitalizing or maintaining (usually at-risk) heritage or indigenous languages. In which case, some HL children might also receive some level of formal education through the HL. Minority language learners (Chapter 3) are educated through the medium of the L2, and may have some Language Arts classes in the L2, where they receive explicit instruction on different aspects of the L2. However, unless they are able to participate in bilingual education programmes developed for minority language learners (such as transitional or two-way immersion programmes), they are unlikely to receive any pedagogical support for their home language[5]. Majority language learners in immersion programmes will receive some formal instruction in the L2, but the focus of immersion is not on teaching the language as a subject, rather, on using the language as the medium of instruction to allow the students to experience significant, authentic input (input-rich). Children who receive instruction in a foreign language, however, have far less naturalistic, authentic input and the significant majority of their experiences with the FL are through formal education.

There is corresponding variability in terms of pedagogical approach in those contexts where children are exposed to the L2 through formal educational settings. In the BFLA context (Chapter 2), pedagogy is not really relevant since the child becomes bilingual through naturalistic exposure to the two languages. In the HL context, children may receive some mother tongue education, and then transition to majority L2 education only, in which case, they may receive some Language Arts classes for both the L1 and L2, but in neither case is the L2 really taught as a subject. Pedagogy in immersion contexts is similar, in that there is likely to be some Language Arts classes for both the immersion language and the child's L1, but L2 pedagogy is not relevant, as the L2 is the medium, not the subject of instruction. Nonetheless, in Chapter 5 there is a discussion on how L2 immersion pedagogy might be used to ameliorate L2 outcomes from immersion settings. For students in FL settings, methodologies that have been developed to teach an L2 are employed in this setting, specifically to help develop listening, speaking, reading, and writing skills in the L2.

There are similar differences across contexts in terms of the sociopolitical motivations underlying the development of different programmes. For example, immersion education (as it is known today) was developed in Canada, in response to a desire to find more effective ways of developing L2 (French) knowledge and skills in native English-speaking children. This desire was also prompted by Canada's status as a bilingual nation, where *both* French and English have special legal status in courts, parliament, and education. Heritage (or minority) language learners may be able to participate in different educational programmes which support their home or heritage language if they:

1 speak a regional minority language that the government wishes to either maintain or revitalize, such as Indigenous languages (Mohawk in Canada; Māori in New Zealand)
2 if educational authorities provide mother-tongue education in an attempt to scaffold the child's L2 learning (in transitional bilingual programmes found throughout the world, for example, in the USA and Africa)
3 if educational authorities aim to promote bilingualism, developing both the L1 and L2 through immersion programmes, for example, in the USA and Germany.

The underlying motivations for each of these different types of provision stem from respective political and social beliefs and concerns. Similarly, the decision to lower the starting age for taught FL is motivated by sociopolitical concerns that young students develop sufficient L2 skills to compete with the rest of the world. These sociopolitical issues will be discussed where appropriate in each chapter.

Reviewing the research across each of these contexts will allow for a focused comparison identifying similarities and differences in L2 learning across each context. All the learners discussed in this volume are young learners. What will soon become apparent throughout the discussion is that despite this relative consistency in age, the outcomes from each context vary considerably. It will then be possible to begin to examine what variables might contribute to this difference. Minimally it will be clear from the cross-context comparison that it is important always to contextualize any discussion of child bilingual development or L2 learning which may be of use to policy makers, educators, and researchers.

Theoretical approaches underpinning differences in L2 outcomes

Just as the CPH is a theoretical construct that motivates the provision of some form of L2 learning or bilingual education for primary school children, it is also worth identifying theoretical approaches that might help us to understand the relationship between L2 outcomes and context. While numerous theories have attempted to explain and predict language development in children, perhaps the most relevant theoretical approach to explaining how the context or environment shapes L2 outcomes is found in 'usage-based' theories.

The term 'usage-based' theory is a general term to refer to an emphasis placed on the child's use of language in specific contexts as a driving force behind ultimate linguistic development (Tomasello, 2003; Lieven and Tomasello, 2008; Ambridge and Lieven, 2011). In such an approach, children develop lexical and grammatical knowledge from using specific utterances in specific contexts, which then build up as the child has more of these usage-based experiences. These experiences lead to representations of linguistic knowledge, and as more of these usage-based experiences with language arise, the child is increasingly able to extract some form of abstract representation (such as a grammar of his or her language) from a critical mass of representations. This usage-based approach is in contrast to the traditional, generative UG approach which argues that children have innate, abstract grammatical knowledge which constrains the way in which they might use and experience language and shapes the way they develop phrase structure grammar—the child's grammatical knowledge of his or her own specific language(s). There are a number of differences between a usage-based approach and the traditional generativist conceptualization of language acquisition. Perhaps most important to the present discussion is the role and/or power of the environment. In a traditionalist, generative view, the environment is important as a trigger. Without linguistic input, children do not experience language and they cannot develop their grammar. In a generative framework, the input triggers internal (innate) abstract knowledge and computational mechanisms to lead children to develop grammatical structure. In other words, the traditional view is an 'inside–out' approach where internal mechanisms are the driving force behind linguistic development (Hirsh-Pasek and Golfinkoff, 1996). In a usage-based approach, the environment is a much more powerful force than a mere trigger. The child's interaction with the environment, or context, interacts with general cognitive systems (such as memory, attention, and perceptual systems) to enable the child to build up grammatical constructions, shaped by his or her specific usage-based experiences. These constructions are initially 'low-scope' (Lieven and Tomasello, 2008, p. 168), in that they may be constructed around simple words or morphemes, but then become increasingly complex as the child has more experience and develops more complex constructions. As the environment is so powerful in a usage-based, or constructivist approach, factors which vary in the environment have been shown to have a powerful influence on the child's developing grammatical knowledge. These factors include such constructs as frequency, where both type (the frequency of a pattern) and token (the frequency of actual items belonging to a pattern) have a powerful effect on children's grammatical knowledge (Bybee, 2007, 2010). Consistency is another important variable in a usage-based or constructivist approach. Consistency relates to the extent to which form–function mappings are consistent and reliable. For example, how consistently the pattern 'verb + -ed' is used to indicate past tense. Where form–function mappings are less consistent, the child might have a harder time in developing knowledge of these forms (Lieven and Tomasello, 2008). Factors like frequency and consistency (and others) vary depending on the linguistic feature being acquired, and also with respect to the actual experience the child has with the language. As a result, these factors are argued to be powerful predictors of linguistic development. This usage-based approach can be considered a more 'outside–in' theory of language acquisition (Hirsh-Pasek and Golinkoff, 1996), as the environment, interacting with cognitive systems, is the driving force behind ultimate linguistic attainment.

Just as other theories developed to account for first language acquisition have been extended and applied to second language acquisition (SLA) contexts (see White, 1989), so too has the usage-based approach been extended to help explain L2 learning (Goldberg and Casenhiser, 2008; Bybee, 2008; Ellis, 2008; Ellis, O'Donnell, and Römer, 2013). As in the context of L1 research, usage-based approaches to L2 development attempt to account for how L2 learners converge on the same L2 systems, despite the individual nature of our respective linguistic experiences (Ellis et al., 2013). Factors such as frequency, saliency, and consistency are equally relevant in the L2 domain; yet at the same time, L2 learning is not always identical to L1, in that L2 learning is influenced in many ways by the previously established L1 grammar (see Ellis, 2008 for an extended discussion).

The contexts described in this volume vary with respect to the nature of the input—notably in terms of amount and type of exposure. If usage-based theories in the domain of L2 learning help explain L2 development, then presumably these theoretical approaches might help explain differing L2 outcomes as a function of context. It is important to reiterate, however, that the purpose of this volume is not to establish or evaluate the extent to which the usage-based approach, nor indeed the CPH, can account for L2 learning. Rather, these different approaches may help us to understand some of the theoretical principles that might underpin the findings discussed in this volume.

Educational implications

This volume is focused on the learner and learning and on identifying some of the different outcomes of L2 learning in different contexts. It is not focused specifically on pedagogy nor on evaluating the most appropriate and effective teaching methods in a given context. However, most of the contexts (in Chapters 3–6) are firmly rooted in formal primary education provision. Therefore the review of these findings will necessarily have some application in terms of educational policy and practice. Consequently, pedagogy will be a point of discussion where relevant (in Chapter 5 in the context of pedagogy in immersion settings and in Chapter 6 in the context of FL provision), but does not serve as the main focus of discussion throughout the book. Nonetheless, the educational implications of the findings discussed in the chapters are highlighted through a specific sub-section in Chapters 2–6, focusing on the extent to which the research reviewed in each context can inform educational practice or policy.

Conclusions

Being able to understand and use more than one language is an increasingly important skill in the modern world. Bilingualism is important for a range of reasons, with known socioeconomic, cultural, and cognitive benefits afforded to bilingual speakers. The research discussed in this volume highlights the extraordinary accomplishment of so many of our children. It also highlights where we can do a better job in helping them achieve it. This volume, I hope, underscores the importance of developing a more comprehensive understanding of the interaction between the environment and the child in developing appropriate L2 outcomes in the early school years.

Notes

1 Note I refer here to oral language proficiency and comprehension, not literacy.
2 http://www.netmums.com/activities/fun-at-home/learning-languages-for-children3
3 See White, (1989) for a discussion of theories and evidence concerning the extent to which UG mediates L2 acquisition in adults.
4 I use the term 'primary' in this volume to refer to the first stage of a child's formal education. This term excludes preschool or early childhood education, a context in which children are increasingly exposed to another language. In North American contexts, the term 'elementary' is used in lieu of primary, but as I live and work in England, and 'primary' is a term used internationally to signify a child's initial phase of formal education, I am going to use my local term—'primary'.
5 Sometimes, however, with the help of complementary community-sponsored educational programmes, minority language learners receive support and formal instruction focusing on development of their heritage L1.

2

Bilingual development in young children

Introduction

This chapter focuses on themes and issues emerging from the field of research into how children develop knowledge of two languages in early childhood. Bilingualism, as an area of research, encompasses a vast range of issues which include many fascinating and important areas of investigation such as bilingual memory (see Heredia, 2008 and de Groot, 2013 for brief introductions), bilingual speech processing (Green, 1986; de Bot, 1992), language disorders in bilingual populations (Paradis, 2010a; Armon-Lotem, 2012), and investigations into the nature of the bilingual brain (Paradis, 1990), to name but a few. These areas, while inherently interesting and obviously related to the content of this chapter, will not be included here because this chapter, and indeed this volume overall, is focused on typical language learning and development in young children, in particular in children who are developing knowledge of more than one language at the same time. The chapter begins with an examination of definitions—what does 'bilingual' mean exactly and what constitutes bilingual language development? Key findings within the areas of bilingual speech processing are presented, followed by a discussion of what empirical research reveals about whether and to what extent bilingual language development is similar to or different from monolingual development. This area of discussion leads to the question of whether young bilingual children represent knowledge of their two languages in one mental system or two, which in turn raises the issue of code-mixing and cross-linguistic influence in young bilinguals, and what interconnections between languages reveal about how young bilingual children represent their developing linguistic systems. The chapter then focuses on whether young bilinguals manifest any advantages or disadvantages as a result of developing knowledge of two linguistic systems, and concludes with the question of age in multilingual development in young children together with a discussion of relevant educational implications.

Defining bilingualism

Romaine (1995) describes six different contexts in which child bilingualism can proceed. These are characterized in Table 2.1 below.

Context of child bilingualism	Features
1 One parent, one language	• The child has parents who each speak a different native language to the child. • The language of the community is usually the language of one of the parents.
2 Non-dominant home language/one language-one environment	• The parents have different native languages, one of which is the language of the wider community. • Both parents speak the non-dominant language to the child in the home. • The child learns the dominant language outside the home.
3 Non-dominant home language without community support	• The parents speak the same native language and speak it to their child. • The parents speak the non-dominant language of the wider society.
4 Double non-dominant home language without community support	• The parents have different native languages and each speaks their own language to the child. • Neither of these two languages is used outside the home.
5 Non-native parents	• The parents share the same language. • It is also the language of the community. • At least one of the parents uses a non-native language with the child in the home.
6 Mixed languages	• The parents are bilingual. • The wider community may also be bilingual. • The parents use multiple languages and code switch with the child in the home.

Table 2.1 Romaine's (1995) six contexts of child bilingualism

A key issue to emerge from these categories is that the home environment is critical in developing bilingualism in young children. Furthermore, the six categories differ in the extent to which language use outside of the home also supports the development of one of the child's home languages. For example, in contexts 1, 5, and 6, community language use supports home language use, whereas in the remaining situations, what happens linguistically outside the home is quite different (and non-overlapping) from language use within the home. Other chapters in this volume describe in some detail how factors outside the home contribute to the development of bi- or multilingual proficiency in young children (see Chapters 3 and 4). It is clear, then, that the recipe for bilingual development is not the same in all children.

Of course, a child can be raised in one of the environments described above and fail to become bilingual—depending on how bilingualism is defined. Most people in the world have some knowledge of another language, even if it is only a handful of words. Does this constitute bilingualism? Or rather, to be considered bilingual does the child have to manifest native-like proficiency in both languages? Opinions vary—Bloomfield (1933) argued that to be considered bilingual an individual had to have full mastery of both languages, whereas Grosjean (1989) asserts that if the individual can communicate effectively enough for their own pragmatic needs, then they can be considered bilingual, or if the bilingual regularly uses both languages, then they are bilingual (Grosjean, 2008). Li Wei (2000) underscores the complexity of defining bilinguals by illustrating the wide variety (37) of different terms that have been used to describe types of bilinguals and notes that many individuals throughout the world can be considered bilingual and have varying degrees of proficiency across different language skills in two or more languages. This issue of *degree* of bilingual proficiency is tackled in Mackey (1962) where he suggests that proficiencies in comprehension and production in both oral and written expression will likely vary both across individuals and across the languages known by an individual. So for example, a bilingual might have strong speaking skills but comparatively weak writing skills in one language, but have excellent literacy skills with comparatively weaker oral skills in the other language. A bilingual's mastery of a specific skill (for example, phonology, syntax, lexis, etc.) is likely to vary within and across his or her known languages. Another distinction in classifying bilinguals, also related to the notion of degree, is between receptive and productive dimensions, where a bilingual may have differing receptive (comprehension) and productive skills within and across both languages (Döpke, 1992).

One issue that is not immediately obvious in Romaine's (1995) categories above is the difference between simultaneous and sequential bilingualism. Simultaneous bilingualism proceeds when both languages are present in the child's input from birth whereas in sequential or successive bilingualism the child has exposure to Language A from birth and then after a period of time is introduced to a new language (Language B) while also continuing to develop in Language A. Associated with this notion is the question of when the introduction of the second language exemplifies a case of young L2 acquisition vs. bilingualism? For example, L2 acquisition is typically characterized as the introduction of a second language after a first has been developed. If the child has not fully developed their L1 and another language is introduced, is this a case of L2 acquisition or a case of sequential bilingualism? De Houwer (1995b) argued the cut off between simultaneous and sequential bilingualism was as early as one month whereas McLaughlin (1978) identified aged three as the cut off (below age three it is a case of bilingualism, above age three it is a case of L2). Yip (2013) highlights that this cut off, while being arbitrary is also probably too broad as there is likely to be a continuum between simultaneous to successive bilingual development. Given these problems of definition, some scholars have opted for the term 'Bilingual First Language Acquisition' (BFLA), which is defined as 'the development of language in young children who hear two languages spoken to them from birth' (De Houwer, 2009, p. 2), whereas other researchers have suggested that a child who is exposed to two languages within the first year of life can be considered to be developing two first languages (Deuchar and Quay, 2000). De Houwer's (2009) definition of BFLA is both inclusive and restrictive. It is inclusive in that it does not require that the child speak either of these two languages or have particular levels of proficiency in either. It is restrictive, however, in that it does not resolve the problem of how to describe the linguistic context of the child who is exposed to another language at age two years along with the language heard at birth (Yip, 2013). In effect, very early sequential bilingual exposure falls somewhere in between simultaneous exposure since birth and sequential exposure in the older child. It may be useful, therefore, to view the distinction between simultaneous and sequential bilingualism as a continuum rather than a dichotomy. This problem (i.e. whether a child's linguistic experience is a case of BFLA, or sequential bilingual development) cannot be resolved here. It is important, however, to note the significant range of contexts in which a child can develop multiple L2 competencies and recognize that there may be differences in terms of development and outcome for children who develop simultaneously or sequentially (De Houwer, 1995a; 1995b). It would be unwise, therefore, to generalize research findings from one context (BFLA) to another (sequential). Much of the research discussed in this chapter is taken from contexts where the child is clearly learning two languages simultaneously and therefore constitutes a case of BFLA.

Bilingual speech processing

Infant speech processing is an area of research focused on identifying how infants process linguistic code. It is a fascinating field of study and many important and compelling findings have emerged from this domain of research that illuminate fundamental questions in language acquisition (Jusczyk, 1997; Gervain and Werker, 2008). From birth, infants can distinguish between different languages when they are prosodically distant (Mehler, Jusczyk, Lambertz, Halsted, Bertoncini, and Amiel-Tison, 1988). However, infants seem to lose this ability by as early as two months, as if their brains come to realize that languages that are prosodically distant from the maternal language are irrelevant. These findings suggest that by as young as two months old, babies have already extracted and represented key prosodic contours of their native language, which is argued to be an important step in 'cracking the code' leading to a child's ultimate language development. Researchers have devised rather ingenious methods of investigating discrimination abilities in infants. The two most common are the preferential looking paradigm (PLP) and the non-nutritive sucking technique (NNST). The logic underlying both is similar. When sounds are introduced in the environment, infants then orient (look) towards the source of sound in the PLP, or increase their sucking rate while listening to the sound in the NNST. In measuring whether infants can discriminate between sounds, researchers conduct a habituation followed by a test phase. In the habituation phase the infant gets used to hearing a given sound determined by a decrease in the amount of time the infant spends looking towards the source of the sound in the PLP and by a decrease in sucking rate in the NNST. In other words, the sound loses its novelty value to the child who then spends increasingly less time looking towards the source of the sound, or sucking while listening to the sound. Once the child has habituated, the researcher introduces a novel sound (test phase), at which point the infant will do one of two things. If the infant does not notice the new sound (i.e. they do not discriminate between the sound to which they habituated and the sound introduced in the test phase) the infant will stay bored and will not look up at the source of the new sound. There will be no increase in the amount of time spent looking towards the source of the new sound in the test phase (and no increased sucking rate in the NNST). However, if the infant does discriminate between the habituation sound and the test sound, the infant will 'dishabituate' and will notice the new sound and will start spending more time looking towards the source of the new sound, or increase the sucking rate when the novel sound is introduced. The NNST is particularly useful when testing neonates—infants just days old who are not physically capable of turning their heads towards different stimuli.

Until relatively recently, comparatively little work had been available investigating speech processing in bilingual infants, that is, infants exposed to two linguistic codes since birth. There have, however, been a few notable contributions. Bosch and Sebastián-Gallés (2001) investigated the perceptual skills of what they call 'bilingual-to-be' four-month-old infants exposed to two Romance languages since birth. Their focus was to identify whether the language differentiation processes described above could be observed in infants exposed to two different languages since birth. In their study, 28 Spanish–Catalan bilingual infants (mean age of 135 days) were tested on a preferential looking paradigm (PLP), where the dependent variable was whether the infant orients towards the source of an auditory stimulus. Recall that in the PLP, if the child switches attention when the auditory stimulus moves from one language to another, then the infant has heard something it perceives as being 'different' and can discriminate between the two sounds. Their findings indicated that even these very young babies (approximately four months old) could discriminate between Spanish and Catalan, despite the fact that they both share prosodic characteristics. One might predict that discriminating between two languages with similar prosodic contours would be exceedingly difficult for a four-month-old, yet this is precisely what they do. This discrimination ability is argued to reflect a key component of the skills used by bilingual (and monolingual) infants to segment speech and begin the task of extracting patterns from the input (Bosch and Sebastián-Gallés, 2001).

In a series of studies, Byers-Heinlein, Burns, and Werker (2010) measured both preference and discrimination between English and Tagalog (languages with different rhythmic contours) in bilingual-to-be newborns, using the non-nutritive sucking technique. Their studies illustrated clearly that prenatal bilingual exposure affected newborns' preferences, since infants who were only exposed to English during pregnancy were not 'interested' in Tagalog in their experiments. These findings are similar to the results of studies with monolingual neonates (Mehler et al., 1988). In a second study, Chinese (Mandarin and/or Cantonese)–English bilingual newborns were tested. Chinese is similar to Tagalog in that both languages are considered 'syllable-timed' but also different in that both have different rhythmic contours. Chinese is also a lexically tonal language, whereas Tagalog is not. Byers-Heinlein et al. (2010) predicted that these infants would fall somewhere between English monolingual infants and English–Tagalog infants in their preferences and indeed this is precisely the outcome of their study. The Chinese–English neonates did not show an outright preference for either English or Tagalog, though they were more interested in Tagalog than English monolingual infants were, arguably due to the shared prosodic features of Tagalog and Chinese. However, they were not as interested in Tagalog as Tagalog–English bilingual infants (due to the prosodic differences between Tagalog and Chinese). These data suggest that:

1 language acquisition begins at, or most likely even before, birth
2 that the same perceptual skills applied by monolinguals to their L1 are applied by the bilingual-to-be infant to their two languages.

Monolingual infants have 'universal' perceptual abilities for vowel and consonant contrasts before about six months, and then between six and 12 months there is a shift so that they can only discriminate contrasts present in their ambient language. For bilingual-to-be infants, the issue is whether they also undergo this shift to contrasts from two languages, and within the same time frame. As indicated in Bosch and Sebastián-Gallés (2001) these broad-based perceptual skills are rapidly fine-tuned towards the specific languages to which the bilingual-to-be infant is exposed. These issues are further examined in Bosch and Sebastián-Gallés (2003) where four-month-old Spanish–Catalan bilingual infants' skills in vowel perception were compared against Spanish and Catalan monolingual infants respectively. Spanish has five vowels while Catalan has seven. Bosch and Sebastián-Gallés (2003) examined whether infants could discriminate particular vowel contrasts used in Catalan but not Spanish. Monolingual Catalan infants can discriminate these vowel contrasts at four, eight, and twelve months respectively. Monolingual Spanish infants however, are only able to discriminate the Catalan vowel contrast at four months. They rapidly lose this skill as the Catalan vowel contrast is not relevant to them since, as monolingual infants, they are only exposed to Spanish. The bilingual infants, however, were able to discriminate this Catalan vowel contrast at four and twelve months, but surprisingly not at eight months. Bosch and Sebastián-Gallés (2003) attempt to explain this interesting finding by discussing the unique features of this particular Catalan vowel contrast and the frequency with which it appears in the input. However, the main point of these studies is that they clearly illustrate that from birth and beyond, bilingual-to-be infants have perceptual skills that enable them to contrast and 'recognize' different languages that are relevant in their linguistic environments, and while both monolingual and bilingual-to-be infants can, from birth, distinguish phonological contrasts, they steadily lose this ability if the contrast is not relevant to the language(s) they are learning (as, for example, the Spanish monolingual infants in Bosch and Sebastián-Gallés, 2003).

Another study investigating similar issues is found in Burns, Werker, and McVie (2003) using the preferential looking paradigm. The participants in Burns et al.'s (2003) study were French–English infants and the task was to identify whether they could discriminate specific contrasts between the French /ba/ and English /pʰa/ and an intermediate /pa/ sound which shares acoustic properties between the French and English phonemes. Crucially, the /pa/ stimulus is ambiguous in that how it is perceived depends on the language an individual speaks: French adult monolinguals perceive the /pa/ as /pa/, whereas English adult monolinguals perceive it as /ba/. In the habituation stage, children heard the ambiguous /pa/ sound until a 50 per cent decrease in looking time was reached (i.e. the infant habituates). At this point a novel stimulus is introduced (the test phase); either the English /pʰa/ or the French /ba/. If the infant notices a difference between the ambiguous /pa/ to which the infant has habituated and the novel stimulus, then they will dishabituate and start looking longer towards the source of the sound. If the infant does not notice a change in the stimulus, then they will not dishabituate and not show any change in their looking behaviour to the source of the novel sound. The question then is what the English–French infants would do with respect to discriminating across these different phonetic categories. Burns et al. (2003) tested infants of differing ages (6, 8, 10, 12, 14, and 17 months) using this paradigm. At six and eight months English monolingual and French–English bilingual infants showed the same pattern—they did not show effects of lan-guage-specific categorizations. In other words, they did not dishabituate—they habituated to the ambiguous /pa/ and did not change their looking behaviour when either the French /ba/ or English /pa/ was introduced following habitu-ation. By 10 to 12 months the pattern had changed: monolingual English infants discriminated between the English /pʰa/ and French /ba/. However, 10–12-month-old bilingual infants did not discriminate across these two categories (they did not dishabituate at the test phase). Burns et al. suggested this might be because bilingual infants at this age are still organizing their phonetic representations and hence their discrimination might be slightly delayed relative to monolinguals. At 14 and 17 months, the monolingual babies were only able to discriminate their own language's contrast, whereas the bilingual infants showed two different patterns. Four of the bilingual infants behaved like English monolingual infants and dishabituated to the English /pʰa/ but not the French /ba/, one infant showed the same pattern as French monolingual infants (dishabituated to the French /ba/ but not the English /pʰa/), and the remaining four infants discriminated between both. In other words, after having habituated to the ambiguous /pa/ sound they looked longer at both the French /ba/ and the English /pʰa/. Burns et al. (2003) argue that by 10–12 months bilingual phonetic representations are distinct from monolinguals' and beyond this age bilinguals either categorize stimuli as monolinguals do or maintain contrasts relevant to both languages.

These studies constitute just a few examples of a range of different investigations that have examined the nature of speech processing in bilingual infants—though it should also be noted that comparatively few studies have been carried out with BFLA infants relative to monolinguals. The bilingual environment the infant is in clearly has an impact on speech processing, showing that from the very earliest stages of bilingual development there are differences in the ways in which BFLA infants process and represent phonological characteristics of their linguistic input, with different developmental trajectories from monolingual infants. Whereas monolingual infants lose the ability to make specific phonetic contrasts, bilingual infants are able to maintain these contrasts for languages that are present in their environment. As suggested in Werker, Weikum, and Yoshida (2006), BFLA children have to be 'open' to developing knowledge of more than one language and therefore their perceptual skills might need to be flexible for longer periods of time before more entrenched and stable phonetic categories can be established.

Comparisons with monolingual development

An issue that has received focused attention in the developmental bilingualism literature is the extent to which bilingual children are comparable to monolinguals in terms of their linguistic development. Three major questions are specifically relevant here:

1 Do bilingual children reach the same basic linguistic milestones in their languages, and within the same time frame as monolinguals?
2 Do bilingual children manifest the same stages/patterns of development in their languages as monolinguals?
3 Do bilingual children develop their linguistic knowledge at the same rate as monolingual children?

A concern often expressed by parents who have the option of raising a child bilingually is that it might somehow slow down their child's linguistic progress if they have to learn two languages at the same time. It is therefore both important (practically) and interesting (theoretically) to compare the linguistic development in young monolingual and bilingual children. Such a research agenda is particularly theoretically important, as evidence from these studies allows for a determination between two competing hypotheses concerning the nature of the bilingual child's representational systems: the 'unitary language system hypothesis' relative to the 'dual language system hypothesis'.

The unitary language system hypothesis is a theoretical notion most closely associated with Volterra and Taeschener (1978) who argued that as bilingual children develop, their knowledge of both languages is initially represented within a single, unitary linguistic representational system. As children develop bilingual competence, they begin to differentiate between the two languages for lexis but not grammar, and then finally (argued to be around three years of age), they represent all knowledge of the two languages in separate, differentiated systems. This idea is contrasted with the dual language system hypothesis (Genesee, 1989), which proposes that from birth both languages are differentiated and, therefore, children never go through a developmental phase where they have one monolingual system containing linguistic code from more than one language. As Genesee (2006) remarks, the notion that BFLA children might go through a process of non-differentiation with their two languages exemplifies the concern above, that BFLA is in and of itself a process that puts undue strain on the child's developing linguistic system, possibly leading to delay in development or even 'deviant' forms (p. 47). Paradis, Genesee, and Crago (2011) articulate a number of different predictions that could be made if the unitary language system was valid. First, one might assume that the process of having to learn to differentiate the two languages might slow the child's linguistic progress down relative to a monolingual— hence one would expect to see particular linguistic milestones being reached at later ages for bilinguals relative to monolinguals. Secondly, one might predict frequent mixing of words and phrases from the child's two languages, independent of context or interlocutors if lexis from the two languages were combined into one system. In other words, it would be rather random as to which language the child might use to express a given idea and the child's linguistic utterances might seem confused. The same would be true of syntax where one would expect to see a mixing or blending of grammatical rules because it is not until a later stage of development (at around three years) that the bilingual child would differentiate their grammatical knowledge across the two languages. Finally, Paradis et al. (2011) suggest that bilingual children's language overall might be qualitatively different from a monolingual's if they were combining knowledge of two languages within the same mental system. These predictions afford a systematic evaluation of the relevant empirical evidence in relation to addressing each of the three major questions articulated at the beginning of this section.

Do children developing two first languages simultaneously reach their linguistic milestones in each language and do they do so within a similar time frame as monolingual children? The evidence suggests that they do indeed reach the same milestones and within a similar time frame. There is, in fact, little to no evidence suggesting that bilingual children achieve key linguistic milestones later than their monolingual counterparts. To illustrate, canonical babbling was investigated in Oller, Eilers, Urbano, and Cobo-Lewis (1997) who recruited a large sample of Spanish–English bilingual infants ($n = 73$), investigated longitudinally between 0;4 and 1;6. Their study examined the canonical babbling patterns in these bilingual infants relative to monolinguals (with monolingual infants matched on socioeconomic status). There was no evidence in Oller et al.'s (1997) study that onset of canonical babbling and the manner in which babbling developed in bilinguals was any different to that of monolinguals. Indeed, Oller et al. (1997) remark on the 'striking degree of similarity between monolingual and bilingual groups…' (p. 423). Both groups achieved the critical developmental milestone of babbling at roughly the same age, supporting the view that bilingual and monolingual children develop along similar linguistic trajectories.

Paradis and Genesee (1996) examined the language use of three[1] English–French bilingual children growing up in Montréal, Canada, who were being raised in the 'one parent, one language' environment described above. These children were filmed in their homes in a naturalistic play session lasting approximately one hour. There were three different sessions; one with the mother (who was English speaking), one with the father (who was French speaking) and one with both parents together. These sessions were recorded at the ages of approximately 2;0, 2;6 and 3;0. Among other features, the analyses focused on negation in French in English. French negation can be characterized into two broad stages:

1 The child puts the negative marker '*pas*' before the main verb '*Le bébé pas boire le lait* (the baby not drink the milk).
2 The negative marker is correctly placed after the main verb (which is inflected): '*Le bébé boit pas le lait*'. (Literally 'The baby drinks not the milk'—which is the correct French syntactic formulation). Monolingual French children typically make the transition from Stage 1 to Stage 2 at approximately 2 to 2;5 years of age. English negation, however, can be categorized into three stages:

1 The child places the negative marker in front of the sentence ('No me wearing mittens').
2 The child places the negative marker 'no' or 'not' sentence medially ('Me *no* want broccoli) and finally
3 The child places the negative marker correctly ('Martin *isn't* going to school').

Monolingual English children are typically older than age three when they manifest utterances from Stage 3 negation. In Paradis and Genesee (1996) the three English–French bilingual children's negative constructions were examined to identify what stage constructions were being produced at what age. Each child progressed from Stage 1 to Stage 2 in French negative construction before the age of three years. By the time the child was three, over 90 per cent of the negative sentences in French were target-like. This pattern is consistent with a French monolingual child. At age 2–2.5 years, the bilingual children's English negative constructions were for the most part in Stage 1 and shifted to Stage 2 at approximately 2.5–3 years of age. Again, the English negative constructions produced by these French–English bilingual children were following the same developmental trajectory as identified in monolingual counterparts. These data address questions 1 and 2 above, in that the bilingual children are reaching the same milestones in negation within the same time frame, and are also showing the same patterns/stages of development as monolingual children. Contrary to the unitary language system hypothesis, the bilingual child's development is neither delayed nor deviant.

Paradis and Genesee (1996) report a similar finding with respect to verb forms. Typical sentences in early child English drop the auxiliary and inflection (for example, 'The truck going over there' or 'The truck go in the box'). Children learning French also produce non target-like forms but they acquire the target system more rapidly than English children. The developmental patterns observed in the three English–French bilingual children in their study correspond to English and French monolingual developmental patterns respectively. The percentage correct in producing the target-like forms was consistently higher in the French utterances produced by these bilingual children than in their English utterances. Again, these children are reaching the same milestones at the same time as monolinguals, and showing very similar stages/patterns of development as monolinguals.

The pattern observed in Paradis and Genesee (1996) has been consistently found in the research literature. For example, Hulk and Müller (2000) examined linguistic constructions produced by two bilingual children. Data were collected for one of these children between the ages of 2;3 and 3;10 who was raised in Amsterdam with a French speaking mother and a Dutch father. The other child's language was recorded starting at age 1;8 and was raised in Germany by her Italian-speaking mother and German-speaking father. Both children were being raised in the 'one parent one language' context described above. The researchers examined a range of different constructions, including object drop (licensed in German and Dutch but not in French and Italian) and root infinitives. For both of these children, their development of the Germanic (Dutch–German) languages was happening autonomously to the development of the Romance (French–Italian) languages since both the cross-linguistic influence and developmental patterns were consistent with a separate (dual) systems perspective. Similar findings consistent with separate systems are reported in Yip and Matthews (2000), who examined a range of constructions (pre- and post-nominal relative clauses, null objects, *wh*-movement) in a Cantonese–English bilingual child. Thus, numerous studies have demonstrated that bilingual children's development of each of their languages is consistent with that of monolinguals in terms of reaching linguistic milestones within the same time frame and in terms of the overall stages/patterns of development.

The evidence does not seem to suggest that bilingual language development is somehow qualitatively different from monolinguals (it is certainly not deviant), as a number of studies have confirmed the findings described above: bilingual children reach the same linguistic milestones at the same time as monolinguals across a range of different linguistic features. However, the evidence is not as unambiguous with respect to investigating the *rate* of bilingual language development relative to monolinguals, where there are some differences across the two populations.

One finding that has emerged from research that suggests bilingual children might be different from their monolingual peers is in respect of vocabulary size. Pre-school bilingual children have been shown to have lower vocabulary scores in each of their two languages in comparison to monolingual children (Pearson, Fernández, and Oller, 1993). In Pearson et al. (1993) 25 English–Spanish children and 35 monolingual (English and Spanish) were compared longitudinally between the ages of 8–30 months on the MacArthur Communicative Development Inventory (CDI) (1989), an instrument the parent completes, identifying words the child produces spontaneously, comprehends, and both produces and comprehends. Their study illustrated that there is no difference between bilingual and monolingual children with respect to either rate of vocabulary growth, or range in vocabulary size. However, the vocabulary size measure for bilingual children was as much as half that of the monolingual child (the English–Spanish child's English vocabulary size score was statistically lower than that of the English monolingual child). When vocabulary size scores for both languages known by the bilingual child are taken together (English and Spanish) this composite score is not different from the monolingual child's score. The child's vocabulary score is positively correlated with the degree of input and nature of the interaction the child experiences, so that the more interaction the child experiences in a given language, the higher the vocabulary score in that language (Pearson, Fernández, Lewedag, and Oller, 1997). Other evidence has indicated that these findings might be mitigated somewhat by the many factors which impact on linguistic development (such as the nature and amount of interaction in the language), since adult bilinguals have been shown to score as high as adult monolingual counterparts on vocabulary tests in both languages (Eilers, Pearson, and Cobo-Lewis, 2006).

A good example of mitigating factors in determining vocabulary size is found in Thordardottir (2011) who measured vocabulary development in French–English bilingual children growing up in Montréal. In her study, she was able to control for a range of variables known to influence children's performance on vocabulary, such as age, socioeconomic status, and cognitive skills, and therefore more carefully examine the relationship between exposure (as identified from the detailed parent questionnaires) to a given language, and subsequent performance on vocabulary measures. All of the bilingual children in Thordardottir's study had had significant exposure to both languages since birth (so they were simultaneous bilinguals). However, the amount of exposure they had received in each language varied somewhat with some receiving more French than English (*n* = 20) and others receiving more English than French (*n* = 16); the remaining 13 children received roughly equal amounts of both. Standardized (norm-referenced) measures of both receptive and expressive vocabulary were administered in both languages. Thordardottir's results indicate a clear and strong relationship between the amount of exposure children receive in a given language and their subsequent vocabulary scores. As the amount of exposure to the language increases, so too does the vocabulary score—an effect found in both English and French in her study. Interestingly, the relationship between exposure and vocabulary performance is effectively linear for expressive vocabulary measures, but less so for receptive vocabulary, where the children reach a kind of asymptote, a point beyond which increased exposure does not correlate with increased receptive vocabulary scores. Thordardottir suggests this may be due to a ceiling effect on the test, though the same effect was found for both English and French receptive tests and the children were not at ceiling on both versions. It is more likely that this difference in the pattern of results might stem from a qualitative difference between the nature of receptive vs. expressive vocabulary in relation to the type of exposure and opportunities for use children receive. For the purpose of the discussion in this chapter, Thordardottir's (2011) study clearly demonstrates that vocabulary size is strongly associated with the amount of input the child receives in the language[2]. As the original studies of Pearson et al. (1993) demonstrating that bilinguals have smaller vocabulary sizes within each language were not able to control as carefully for mitigating factors as Thordardottir's study, we can assume that those differences reported in earlier studies may also be associated with differences in exposure. Thus, it may be that some young bilingual children have less vocabulary knowledge in a given language, but that with appropriate exposure, they are likely to develop comparable vocabulary knowledge in adulthood relative to monolinguals.

Notable differences between monolinguals and bilinguals have been demonstrated in other linguistic features as well. Hoff, Core, Place, Rumiche, Señor, and Parra (2012) investigated a group of Spanish–English bilingual children in the USA and compared them against English monolingual children (matched on SES) to identify whether and to what extent the bilingual children were similar to the monolinguals with respect to their vocabulary, basic grammar (words in sentences), and mean length of utterance (MLU)—a measure often used to reflect the complexity of a young child's linguistic productions where a higher MLU is argued to indicate more complex language. Hoff et al. demonstrated that bilingual children, while falling in the normal range in at least one of their two languages, tend to be at the lower bound of that range when compared to monolingual English-speaking children. Furthermore, they were shown to be developing English at a slower rate than the monolingual children (see also Paradis, Genesee, and Crago, 2011). Hoff et al. (2012) are careful to point out that their results do not contradict the findings described above (that bilingual children acquire each language '...within the normal range of variation for monolingual children') (p. 20). Rather, they argue that their data suggests that bilingual children can develop their linguistic knowledge more slowly than monolinguals. The lag observed between the bilinguals and monolinguals was less than three months when the children were tested at the earliest (grammatical) stages in their development. Furthermore, when the monolingual children were compared against only the English-dominant Spanish–English bilinguals there was no lag at all. Thus, Hoff et al.'s research corresponds with Thordardottir's (2011) study in illustrating that exposure to the language (leading to balanced or unbalanced bilingual development) influences rate of linguistic development. These findings are further supported by Paradis, Nicoladis, Genesee, and Crago (2011) who showed that in terms of accuracy with morphosyntactic constructions like verb paradigms, French–English bilingual children tend to lag behind monolinguals, but again, the extent of the lag depends on language dominance, exposure (as in Hoff et al., 2012 and Thordardottir, 2011), and other language-level factors (see also Paradis, 2010b).

In summary then, and referring back to the three major questions articulated at the beginning of this section, there is little evidence to suggest that bilingual development proceeds along a different trajectory than it does for monolinguals, since bilingual children achieve the same linguistic milestones roughly within the same time-frame as monolingual children. Furthermore, they also show similar patterns/stages of development. There is evidence, however, that bilinguals can be somewhat delayed with respect to their rate of development, lagging behind monolingual children on some measures (such as vocabulary, MLU, and morphosyntax (verbal morphology). This lag, however, has been directly attributed to the environment and specifically to the amount of exposure the bilingual child has to a given language,[3] as well as other factors relating to specific aspects of the linguistic feature being studied and/or task complexity. However, there is an important point to remember here—there is still a significant amount of research yet to be carried out in this area in that only a handful of linguistic features within a restricted number of languages have been investigated in the BFLA research literature. The evidence thus far, however, gives no cause for concern that bilingual development is somehow qualitatively different or deviant relative to monolinguals. This evidence therefore would appear to favour the dual language systems hypothesis (c.f. Genesee, 1989).

Differentiation of the two linguistic systems

The unitary language system hypothesis would predict that the bilingual child would go through a period of producing mixed language utterances, in effect, randomly picking elements of either language within utterances suggesting that:

1 The child's brain has not distinguished between the two languages.
2 The child is confused and unaware of learning more than one language.

Evidence for this view can be found in some of the earliest studies on childhood bilingualism. Leopold (1949) suggested that bilingual children pass through a stage where the two languages formed part of the same linguistic system (the unitary language system hypothesis). Leopold's diary studies of his German–English daughter indicated that she produced many mixed-language utterances, which is consistent with the notion that both languages were mixed together in the same mental system.

It is already evident from the discussion on bilingual speech processing that the child's brain can discriminate between more than one language. However, is there any evidence that the child is confused with respect to how to use the languages? Genesee, Nicoladis, and Paradis (1995) present compelling evidence that they are not. In their study, five children from French–English bilingual families (in Montréal, Canada) ranging in age from 1;10 to 2;2 were recruited to participate in the study. Three of the children were being raised in the 'one parent, one language' context while the parents of the other two reported that they mixed the languages regularly. Each child was visited by a bilingual researcher on three separate occasions within a three-week period; once with their mother, once with their father, and once with the mother and father together. During these visits the child and parents were encouraged to interact naturally in a free play situation. One of the analyses carried out by Genesee et al. (1995) was on identifying how much of the parent's language (produced by the child) was directed towards that parent. So for example, if a child had an English mother and a French father, would that child use English more with the mother and French more with the father? The results indicated this is precisely what four out of the five children in their study did—they consistently spoke more of the parent's language to the parent. Even when the children were interacting with both parents together, the children still differentiated their language use and spoke more of the mother's language (English) when addressing the mother and spoke the father's (French) when addressing the father. It is important here to recall the ages of the children—they were barely two years old (on average) in this study. Two-year-olds have trouble doing basic tasks such as eating without spilling their food everywhere, and/or getting dressed. Yet linguistically by this age, they are advanced, because they clearly are not confusing their two languages and are using the appropriate language with the appropriate interlocutor. An additional issue raised in this study relates to language dominance (see below). Some of the children were stronger in one language than the other—they did not each have an equal balance of proficiency across English and French. However, even children who had more limited skills in their non-dominant language were able to use their non-dominant language appropriately with the parent who spoke their non-dominant language. The one child who was not observed to follow this pattern had parents who code-switched frequently and thus it is possible that he did not differentiate his two languages in speaking to his parents, as a result of his inability to distinguish between his mother's and his father's language. Alternatively, he may simply have been following the pattern modelled for him in the input (that frequent code-switching is acceptable). Overall, this evidence suggests these very young bilingual children were not confused about which language to use with an interlocutor, is consistent with the dual language system hypothesis (Genesee, 1989), and speaks to the marvel that is language development in children. Not only are these children learning two languages at the same time but they use them appropriately with interlocutors—all by the age of two.

Another study which addressed similar issues is Genesee, Boivin, and Nicoladis (1996). They recruited four female children in their study who were being raised in an English–French environment (also in Montréal, Canada). As with the other study, the four children were observed interacting with their parents in the home—however, as well as interactions with each parent alone, Genesee et al. (1996) also observed interactions with a stranger—someone whose language preferences could not possibly be known to the child. For two of the children the stranger was a monolingual English speaker, while for the other two children the stranger was a monolingual French speaker. For three of the four children, the stranger's language was their non-dominant language which meant that to accommodate the stranger's language the children had to use more of their non-dominant, less proficient language and less of their more proficient, dominant language. The results indicated firstly that the children differentiated their language use in precisely the same ways as described in Genesee et al. (1995) (where the children spoke more of their mother's language to the mother and more of their father's language to their fathers). This is important because replication studies in child bilingualism research are few and far between, yet here is an excellent example of a previous finding being replicated, thus consolidating our confidence in this evidence. Secondly, the analysis of the children's language revealed that three out of the four children did accommodate the stranger and were able to adjust their language use directed towards the stranger (though there was some variability in the extent to which each of the four children did this). Nonetheless, the results were clear—the children were not confused about which language to use with whom, even towards someone they did not know. Genesee et al. (1995) and (1996) provide compelling evidence that very young bilingual children differentiate their two language systems and cannot be considered confused about their language use.

These results are not isolated examples. There are many illustrations within the BFLA literature on the language use of bilingual children indicating that children are able to produce more of the parent's language with them than would be predicted by chance. The same skills in differentiating to interlocutors has been shown in the cases of an Estonian–English bilingual child in Vihman (1985); a Portuguese–English child in Nicoladis (1998) and Nicoladis and Secco (2000); a Spanish–English child in Quay (1995), and a Norwegian–English bilingual child in Lanza (1992) and Johnson and Lancaster (1998). Despite the fact that in each of these studies the sample size is either four or fewer (often a case study of only one child) all the studies present the same picture—children are able to direct their two languages appropriately. Indeed, this finding is not that surprising when considered in the light of the bilingual speech processing studies described above. As early as only a few days old bilingual-to-be babies' brains are able to discriminate between different languages, so it is not inconsistent that by the time children are one to two years old they are able to use their languages appropriately to different speakers. In light of the debate between the unitary vs. dual language systems hypotheses, these findings are unambiguously consistent with the dual language view.

Code-switching

Despite the clear evidence that very young bilingual children differentiate between their two languages, this does not mean that their linguistic behaviour is like that of a monolingual—they are not 'two monolinguals in one' (c.f. Grosjean, 1989). One of the most immediately obvious ways in which the young bilingual child differs from monolinguals is in their code-switching behaviour. Young bilingual children, especially toddlers, code-switch frequently. Volterra and Taescher (1978) and Leopold (1949) before them considered this code-switching behaviour as indicative of a single linguistic system, the child's lexical and grammatical knowledge up until the age of three being represented within a unitary system, thus leading to random code-switched utterances. Is the single system hypothesis the best explanation of code-switching behaviour in young bilingual children, however?

There are two basic types of code-switching: intra-utterance and inter-utterance. Intra-utterance code-switching are examples of two codes (languages) used within the same utterance '*Alguien se murió en ese cuarto that he sleeps in*' (Zentella, 1999) while inter-utterance mixing occurs across phrases/utterances '*Pa ¿me vas a comprar un jugo? It cos' 25 cents.*' (Zentella, 1999). Inter-utterance mixing seems to be more common in the literature relative to intra-utterance mixing but this pattern is necessarily contingent on the child's linguistic competence. Very young bilingual children who are in the one-word or early two-word stages do not produce very long utterances and therefore their code-switching behaviour tends to be across utterances, while more linguistically developed children, in producing longer utterances, have more opportunities to mix within utterances (Paradis et al. 2011). The features of language that can be mixed in a code-switched utterance can range from phonological features to whole chunks and phrases.

Of significant concern in studying code-switching in young bilingual children is whether and to what extent their utterances represent atypical development and whether this atypical development is symptomatic of some form of deviance (c.f. Paradis et al., 2011) or whether, rather, it results from cross-linguistic influence. One of the first ways to tackle this problem is to identify whether the code-switched utterances are grammatically well formed (disregarding the obvious fact that two languages are being used either within or across utterances). Two influential models attempting to articulate constraints on code-switching can be found in Poplack (1980) and Myers-Scotton (1997). Poplack (1980) outlines a number of morphological constraints that she argues can account for all instances of code-switching, one of which for illustrative purposes here, is the 'free morpheme constraint' where code-switches cannot occur between a bound morpheme and a lexical form without phonological integration in the language of the bound morpheme (Poplack, 1980, p. 585). In other words, it is not possible to code-switch as in the following: "*Estoy* eat-*iendo*" since the Spanish bound morpheme (*-iendo*) is attached to the English lexical stem 'eat'. Poplack (1980) argued that examples such as this have not been found in the literature. Myers-Scotton's (1997) 'Matrix Language Frame' model contrasts a 'Matrix Language' against an 'Embedded Language' where the two do not equally contribute—typically in code-switched utterances there is more of one language than the other—one language being the 'matrix' and the other being the 'embedded'. The main point of these models is that there is 'traffic control' with respect to code-switched utterances: these utterances are not a random 'pick and mix' of different bits of language, but rather, obey specific constraints (c.f. Myers-Scotton, 2006). In reviewing a range of empirical studies examining the nature of code-mixed utterances in young bilingual children, Genesee (2006) concludes that, '...all researchers have concluded that child bilingual code-mixing is grammatically constrained' (p. 52).

Code-switched utterances in young bilingual children are frequent, and well formed—or at least are not a random haphazard mix of bits of language. The evidence, therefore, does not support the single system idea where one might predict such random utterances. Code-switched utterances obey constraints and seem to be well formed, in terms of adhering to these constraints. Why do children code-switch, however? What purpose (if any) does it serve? Numerous possibilities have been put forward, a few of which will be considered here.

One proposal is the 'gap filling' hypothesis (Deuchar and Quay, 2000; Genesee, 2006) where if children do not know a word in language A, they use the equivalent word in language B. Similarly, they might for lack of knowledge use a particular syntactic construction from language A while attempting to speak language B. Children do tend to code-switch more when using their non-dominant language. For example, in Nicoladis and Secco (2000), 90 per cent of the code-switched utterances identified in the Portuguese–English speaking boy in their study could be explained by a lexical gap when using the non-dominant language. Children are likely to have lexical and syntactic gaps, because in the context of language development they are unlikely to repeat every experience in each language. Some more recent theories of language development place a central emphasis on the role of the environment and the interactive context in which the child is being exposed to the linguistic input (Tomasello, 2003). A child, for example, learns about the lexis and grammar relevant to 'bath time' while having (or being given) a bath. If the child's French-speaking father is the carer who more typically gives the young child a bath, and if the child is developing in the 'one parent, one language' context, it is not at all odd to imagine that it may take some time for the child to learn bath time-relevant words and sentences in the other language. This example illustrates that it is unlikely the child will experience different situations equally in both languages. Hence it is logical that the child might not have learned the translation equivalents (or particular grammatical structures) across each language at exactly the same time. Similarly, a translation equivalent may not actually exist across languages, prompting the child to code-switch. Genesee (2006) provides an example from Québec French, where the word *dodo* which means 'nap' does not translate directly into an English equivalent because *dodo* is the diminutive of the verb *dormir* (to sleep) and is used almost exclusively to and by children. The child might use *dodo* in speaking English in this context because there is no English equivalent. Genesee further notes that this communication strategy (code-switching) is perfectly appropriate, particularly in cases where the child is developing alongside other children within the same bilingual community.

Other explanations for young bilingual children's code-switching might be due to pragmatic effect. Genesee (2006) notes that often speakers will repeat their wording to emphasize a point (for example, 'I was terrified, scared to death!'). Children might code-switch for the same pragmatic effect. Paradis et al. (2011) present an example of a child trying unsuccessfully to get a toy in French, who then requests it in English: *Donne-moi le cheval; le cheval; the horse!* In this example the child was not achieving the goal using French so switched codes for potentially greater emphasis. Social norms are also very important in shaping code-mixing behaviour as described by Poplack (1980) in a study of the Puerto Rican Spanish community in New York City, where rapid, frequent, and fluent code-switching acts as an identity marker. Thus as children develop, they learn the communities' patterns of bilingual usage and use these to align with that community.

In summary, there have been many candidate explanations for why children code-switch that have little or nothing to do with confusion or lack of differentiation of the two languages. Code-switching, therefore, cannot justifiably be used as evidence for a single underlying system, nor evidence for lack of sensitivity to or awareness of the linguistic and interactive context. In fact, quite the opposite has been clearly and repeatedly shown in the literature—children code-switch as a direct result of their environment, either in that they have not yet acquired translation equivalents for lexis or syntax, or because of family, community, societal, or pragmatic influences.

Cross-linguistic influence

While the evidence is largely unequivocal on the question of whether bilingual children represent knowledge of their languages in a single or dual mental system, it is clear that the two systems do not develop autonomously from each other. Rather, there is considerable evidence that knowledge of two languages can influence each other in different ways, resulting in grammatical or ungrammatical utterances[4]. There are two basic categories of cross-linguistic influence: qualitative and quantitative. Qualitative cross-linguistic influence results in utterances that are ungrammatical (in the sense that a monolingual would not produce them) whereas quantitative cross-linguistic influence results in a higher than baseline rate of particular types of language error that is typical in monolingual development (Paradis et al., 2011). To illustrate, Yip and Matthews (2000) present some interesting data from a Cantonese dominant–English bilingual child in relative clause formation. In Cantonese, relative clauses are positioned prior to the noun they modify, whereas in English they occur after the noun. One of the examples from Yip and Matthews was the following: 'Where's the *Santa Claus give me* the gun'. Here is an example of Cantonese relative clause placement before the noun, incorrectly produced in an English utterance. This is an example of qualitative cross-linguistic error, because typically developing English monolingual children tend not to make errors of this type. Examples of quantitative cross-linguistic influence can be found in Döpke (1998) who demonstrated that German–English bilingual children produced more sentences in German following the English subject first word order than is typically identified in monolingual German children. Subject-first German sentences are not incorrect, but the object can also be first depending upon the focus of the sentence. The higher than expected number of subject-first German sentences is indicative of quantitative cross-linguistic influence in Döpke's (1998) study. Quantitative cross-linguistic influence tends to occur more frequently than qualitative (Paradis et al., 2011) which is consistent with the research described above, that monolingual and bilinguals develop in very similar ways to each other—in which case, the kinds of language error the bilingual child makes are equally comparable to the monolingual—there just might be more of them as the child develops linguistic competence in both languages.

Cross-linguistic influence can affect a range of different features of language from complex syntactic forms, such as relative clauses described in Yip and Matthews (2000), to no less complex but lower-level linguistic features such as phonetic and phonological processes. For example, Holm and Dodd (1999) describe a longitudinal study tracking the phonological development of two bilingual children learning English and Cantonese. Both children were from families who had immigrated to Australia from Hong Kong—so had Cantonese as their L1 and were exposed to English (as the dominant societal language) from very young ages (one child was six months old when her family moved to Australia, the other was 18 months old). In a careful study tracking these children's phonetic and phonological development it was clear that they both had two separate phonological systems—a finding which supports the dual systems view (Genesee, 1989) but that some of their phonological processes were atypical. As one example, final consonant backing is atypical in English but not Cantonese[5]—however both children backed consonants in both English and Cantonese (despite it not being appropriate in English). They were, therefore, applying phonological properties from one language to the other.

Paradis and Navarro (2003) report on a study examining cross-linguistic influence in a Spanish–English bilingual child focusing on the use of overt subjects. In Spanish, it is possible (and sometimes preferred) to drop the subject, since verb endings (inflectional morphemes) mark subject agreement. For example, instead of saying *Yo soy estudiante* (I am a student) with the overt subject realized in *yo*, speakers of Spanish will typically say *Soy estudiante*. This option of dropping the subject pronoun is not licensed in English. Hence in Paradis and Navarro, children's use of overt subjects was in focus to identify whether this bilingual child was more likely to use overt subjects than monolingual Spanish children. Naturalistic language samples of the child interacting with her parents were analysed. In their study, the bilingual child included overt subjects more frequently in naturalistic speech than the two monolingual Spanish children. Interestingly, while cross-linguistic influence (the fact that null subjects are not allowed in English) is considered as one explanation for this finding, Paradis and Navarro also examined the parental input closely and identified that the parents spoke a dialect of Spanish that included a higher than typical proportion of overt subjects, suggesting that one possible cause for this particular cross-linguistic influence was not just knowledge of and influence from English but possibly also the specific frequency of overt and null subjects in the particular model of Spanish to which this child was exposed. Other studies have also shown a close correlation between parental input patterns and bilingual children's language use (see De Houwer, 2007).

Other examples of cross-linguistic evidence in young bilinguals have been discussed in Hulk and Müller (2000), Müller and Hulk (2001), Nicoladis (2006) and Nicoladis (2012), and elsewhere. Understanding the underlying causes of cross-linguistic transfer is critical. As Paradis and Navarro (2003) point out, if cross-linguistic influence is ubiquitous and random, then there is no difference between the unitary and dual systems hypotheses discussed above in that, if the non-autonomous aspect of the 'two but non-autonomous' systems is so fluid, then to what extent are the systems separated? They identify that in order to truly support a dual but non-autonomous systems idea, it is also necessary to be able to identify and understand where and on which linguistic features cross-linguistic influence is likely to occur. It is beyond the scope of this chapter to explore the different explanations in detail. However, Hulk and Müller (2000) and Müller and Hulk (2001) argue that cross-linguistic transfer is more likely to occur when there is structural overlap between the bilingual's two languages and where there is more than one structure with roughly the same meaning—at the interface between pragmatics and syntax, where discourse–pragmatic features will determine the choice of syntactic structure. To illustrate from Paradis and Navarro (2003), transfer from English to Spanish is expected because Spanish allows structural overlap for *both* null and overt subjects. Transfer from Spanish to English, however, is unexpected because English does not allow null subjects (there can be no overlap). Paradis and Navarro (2003) suggest that their results are consistent with this structural overlap view but Nicoladis (2012) claims that this explanation cannot account for all examples of cross-linguistic influence, since it has been documented in cases where there is no overlap across languages. Nicoladis (2006 and 2012) favours an approach that considers cross-linguistic influence a kind of speech error. Bilingual children have more choices as to which construction to use given they have knowledge of more than one language, so when they need to produce an utterance, forms from both languages are likely to get activated within a speech production model, and sometimes they will make an incorrect choice from competing activated linguistic features. To illustrate, in Nicoladis (2006), French–English bilingual children's adjective placement was investigated (English requires adjectives to occur before the noun ('the red house') whereas in French, adjectives typically occur after the noun (*la maison rouge*) but can sometimes occur before the noun (*le grand arbre*). Nicoladis (2006) explains that in activating 'green' and 'apple' (for example) the French equivalents (*vert* and *pomme*) will also receive some (smaller) level of activation in the child's lexicon. As a result, the French syntactic frame for adjective placement will in turn receive some (small) activation. This small but competing activation could lead the child to say 'apple green' instead of the correct 'green apple'.

In summary, cross-linguistic influence is a normal part of young bilingual children's development and does not seem to be either rampant and/or random. Different proposals have been put forward in an attempt to better understand when and for what reasons cross-linguistic influence will occur and no doubt this will be an area receiving greater focused research attention in the coming years.

Dominance

An issue that has been referred to repeatedly in the discussion above, but that has not been directly discussed is the notion of language dominance in children who are developing bilingually. A number of researchers within the BFLA and child bilingualism literature more generally seem to concur that the child is unlikely to develop precisely the same knowledge and/or skills and/or profiles of language use across both languages. Indeed, Meisel (2007) notes that '... It is frequently asserted that "balanced" bilingualism is impossible to achieve, and that one language will always be the dominant one' (p. 498). He goes on to query why this must be so, suggesting there is no 'principled explanation' for why this might be case, in that all the evidence from the early child bilingualism literature indicates that human brains have the capacity to acquire two languages from birth and there should be no *a priori* theoretical (nor indeed biological) reason why a bilingual child could not develop in a perfectly 'balanced' manner. It is undoubtedly true that one of a child's two languages might not be used as frequently, might be less preferred, and/or even possibly be less advanced linguistically relative to the other. However, as Meisel (2007) maintains, candidate explanations for dominance can all be attributed to the settings in which the child is developing. In other words, the context in which the child is learning the language may itself exert a considerable pressure to shape the child's linguistic development unevenly. A dominant language for a bilingual child might be associated with that language's stronger presence in the environment. Indeed, such a strong presence in the environment has been repeatedly identified as one of the reasons why minority language learners (whose home language is not the same language as that of the wider society) often end up not achieving full bilingual proficiency in both languages. In these contexts, when children move into formal education environments, there is often little support for the home language and they may at best end up with an unbalanced bilingual profile and, at worst, lose the home language altogether (see De Houwer, 2007 and Chapters 3 and 4 of this volume for a more detailed discussion).

In considering what constitutes and/or contributes to dominance, Meisel (2007) argues that three issues need to be disentangled:

1 the communicative and learning environment
2 the use that bilinguals make of their two languages
3 the development of the linguistic knowledge of the individual.

He also distinguishes between the construct of 'dominance', which he argues is the 'predominant of the ambient languages in a given setting' (p. 498), and 'preference' which refers to an individual bilingual's inclination to use one language over the other. Dominance and preference are very closely interrelated because if the child is living in an environment where a given language is dominant (the majority language in minority language learners' contexts), the child may have increased exposure to this language, which might consequently lead to the child developing a preference for using that language. In other words, dominance and preference are two separate but closely related constructs that are difficult to tease apart. An additional complexity is that the notion of dominance is not static. The balance between the two languages within a bilingual can change over time, depending on the bilingual's circumstances, environment, and communicative needs (Nicoladis and Genesee, 1996). These factors contribute to making it a difficult construct to define.

Measuring (identifying) dominance can be equally challenging and researchers have conceptualized dominance in different ways. In a number of studies described above (Genesee et al., 1996; Paradis and Genesee, 1996; Paradis et al., 2000) dominance was measured by vocabulary size and MLU, defined as the relative proficiency a bilingual child has in both languages. This constitutes a child-internal focus. The amount of exposure the child receives in each of the two languages is also another construal of dominance, which is child-external. The criteria for measuring dominance can include a range of measures such as fluency, language preference, mixing from other languages, word types, and the like (Bernardini and Schlyter, 2004). The problems inherent in measuring dominance are the target of Bedore, Peña, Summers, Boerger, Resendiz, Greene, Bohman, and Gillam's (2012) large-scale study. In their research they distinguish between experience-based measures (those which document for example, a bilingual child's language history with age of exposure, language use, etc.) against performance-based measures (those assessments which directly measure an aspect of the child's linguistic competence). Bedore et al. (2012) analysed data from 1029 pre-Kindergarten and Kindergarten Spanish–English bilingual children in the USA. It is important to note that these children were minority language learners (see Chapters 3 and 4) where the child spoke Spanish in the home/ local community but were living in the USA where English is the dominant language. A range of measures were administered in Bedore et al. (2012), including experience-based measures such as interviews and a comprehensive questionnaire carried out with and completed by parents, identifying the children's patterns of language use, the level of input from both English and Spanish, as well as the output (how many hours of each day were spent interacting in English and/or Spanish and with whom). Additionally they administered the BESOS test (Bilingual English Spanish Oral Language Screening) which assessed aspects of English and Spanish morphosyntax and semantics. Their analyses focused on the relationships between experience, proficiency, and dominance. The analyses of both the input and output measures identified the children as falling into one of five distinct groupings:

1 functional monolingual English (80–100 per cent of their language was English)
2 bilingual English dominant (60–80 per cent use of English and 20–40 per cent of Spanish)
3 balanced bilingual (between 40–60 per cent use of both English and Spanish)
4 bilingual Spanish dominant (60–80 per cent use of Spanish and 20–40 per cent of English)
5 functional monolingual Spanish (80–100 per cent of Spanish).

One outcome of their complex analyses indicated that the measures used to classify a child's linguistic proficiency made a difference to the classification itself (performance vs. experience-based) and relate to the notion of the dynamic nature of dominance, where language dominance and proficiency were found to vary as a function of the time point at which they were assessed as well as the way in which the child's language experience was measured. 'Current language use' was a factor that emerged as reliably predicting both language proficiency and dominance: the children tended to perform better (they had higher scores on the BESOS) in the language they had the most experience using.

The effect of the dominance patterns in bilingual children can have considerable impact on their linguistic knowledge and use. For example, in some of the studies discussed thus far in this chapter, dominance has been linked to a range of factors such as the likelihood of code-switching to fill lexical or syntactic gaps, where children were identified as code-switching more frequently to gap-fill in their non-dominant than dominant language (Nicoladis and Secco, 2000), as well as leading to particular types of cross-linguistic influence as identified in Yip and Matthews (2000). Similarly, the non-dominant language has also been identified as being more prone to attrition (Bolonyai, 2007; Francis, 2011).

Some researchers have also argued that a child's 'weaker language' is in some ways more similar to instances of L2 acquisition rather than bilingual L1 development (Schlyter, 1990; Bernardini and Schlyter, 2004). If it were true that a non-dominant language in a bilingual child was more like an L2 in its structural qualities, this would have important theoretical implications and would help identify the limits of multilingualism and what factors might lead to a failure in bilingual language acquisition. However, this proposal that the weaker (non-dominant) language can be more similar to a L2 has been criticized as not being consistent with the evidence. For example, Meisel (2007) argues that the 'weaker language hypothesis' does not provide a principled explanation for which features of language are more likely to be vulnerable (i.e. more like a L2). He notes there is an '...absence of predicted empirical evidence of this phenomenon' (p. 509). Furthermore, Bonnesen (2009) re-examines some of the data reported in Schlyter (1990) and demonstrates that the weaker language (French) in the two French–German BFLA children in Schlyter (1990) had French characteristics that were consistent with children developing L1 competence in French. Thus, there is currently evidence both in support of and contradictory to the idea that the weaker non-dominant language in some contexts can represent a failure of bilingual acquisition. As Francis (2011) notes, developing a better empirical and theoretical understanding of the imbalance of bilinguals will lead to a more refined development of underlying theoretical frameworks.

In summary, dominance can be considered in terms of the bilingual child's relative proficiency in each language, in terms of the status the language has in society (dominant/majority vs. non-dominant/minority) and in terms of the exposure and experience the child has with the language. While each of these construals of dominance has been supported by empirical evidence, a growing number of studies have indicated that unbalanced development between the two languages is closely tied to this third more input-based characterization of dominance (Bedore et al., 2012, Gathercole and Thomas, 2009) The power of the input in shaping the balance of linguistic development across the two languages is also further supported by some of the research on code-switching discussed above, where a child's code-switching behaviour can be directly attributable to the code-switching patterns present in the child's ambient environment.

Cognitive effects of bilingualism

Language is the jewel in the crown of human cognition, and indeed is arguably the most complex cognitive undertaking in which humans engage. Consequently, learning multiple languages might conceivably have an effect on other aspects of cognitive behaviour and processing. One of the first studies to explore the relationship between bilingual language development and other aspects of cognition is found in Peal and Lambert (1962). In their study, 89 10-year-old bilinguals and 75 monolinguals in Montréal were given a battery of tasks including:

1 measures of non-verbal and verbal intelligence
2 attitude measures given to both children and parents, aimed at identifying their attitudes towards learning French, being bilingual and French Canadians
3 teacher ratings of the children's academic and language achievement together with their actual grades in their French skills in dictation, speaking, and writing.

Their results indicated (among other things) that the bilingual children performed better on both the verbal and non-verbal IQ measures. Peal and Lambert (1962) suggest that being raised bilingually and having to regularly switch between two linguistic codes enables bilingual children to develop more mental 'flexibility' together with more diversified mental skills. Not only did the bilinguals achieve higher scores on the IQ measures than monolinguals but they also had higher scores overall in their academic achievement. Peal and Lambert (1962) expressed surprise at these findings because prior to their work, there had been a prevailing assumption that developing bilingually might have negative consequences on a child's cognitive and scholastic achievements. Not only did their results refute that assumption but other research is consistent with Peal and Lambert's (1962) interpretation and has illustrated a general advantage for bilinguals in a range of cognitive skills such as concept formation, classification, creativity, and analogical reasoning skills (Ben-Zeev, 1977; Diaz, 1983; Hakuta, Ferdman, and Diaz, 1987). Peal and Lambert (1962) noted a methodological flaw in their study in that they could not attribute the higher scores on the intelligence measures directly to being bilingual since more intelligent children might be more likely to become bilingual. However, other studies have indicated a strong positive relationship between degree of bilingualism and performance on these cognitive tasks which lends support to the idea that it is the bilingualism leading to the advantages on these aspects of cognition (Hakuta and Diaz, 1985).

Greater mental flexibility in the bilingual child can impact children's vocabulary learning. Marinova-Todd (2012) argued that bilingual children might be more efficient vocabulary learners, stemming from their ability to approach vocabulary learning tasks more flexibly than monolinguals. In her study, bilingual and monolingual Grade 3 children (between eight and nine years old) were compared on a word-learning task where they had to deduce the meanings of novel words that varied with respect to how abstract the sentential context was (for example, 'A *corplum* is used for support' is an abstract sentential context whereas 'A painter uses a *corplum* to mix his paints' is less abstract). Marinova-Todd's (2012) results indicated that as predicted, the bilingual children were more successful at deducing the word meanings of these novel words than monolingual children—despite the fact that the bilingual children in her sample had smaller vocabulary sizes relative to the monolinguals. One of the candidate explanations explored by Marinova-Todd for her results is the fact that bilingual children have been shown to be more cognitively flexible when processing language structures.

One particular advantage of being bilingual that has received considerable attention within the research literature is metalinguistic knowledge. Metalinguistic knowledge refers to the ability to go beyond the meaning of a language and focus on its underlying structure (Bialystok and Barac, 2013). Children who have metalinguistic knowledge and skill can analyse their language as a system, identify that there is such a thing as a language in the first place, and that words are arbitrary labels for concepts and referents, and the like. Vygotsky (1962) was one of the first scholars to posit that bilingual children would have increased metalinguistic skill since they had more experience with language and would be more able to see the arbitrariness between words and their labels. Since his proposition, many researchers have gone on to identify just that—that bilingual children have enhanced metalinguistic skill in a number of areas including syntax and phonology (Galambos and Goldin-Meadow, 1990; Campbell and Sais, 1995). Bialystok and her colleagues have carried out a number of studies investigating the extent to which bilingual children have a metalinguistic advantage over monolingual children (Bialystok, 1986, 1991; 2001). In a now classic grammaticality judgement (GJ) paradigm, Bialystok (1986) asked children to distinguish between sentences that were grammatically incorrect from those that were semantically anomalous. For example, Chomsky's well-known sentence, 'Colourless green ideas sleep furiously' is grammatically correct yet semantically anomalous. In asking bilingual and monolingual children to judge sentences of this type (for example, 'Apples grow on noses'), bilingual children were more likely to focus only on the structural features of the sentences and ignore the semantic anomaly. In other words, they were more likely to identify sentences such as 'Apples grow on noses' as grammatically correct than the monolingual children. This finding suggests then that the bilingual children are more able to use their selective attention skills and focus only on the structural features in a GJ task. Bialystok (1991; 2001) notes that these metalinguistic advantages are not found across all task types, however, and that bilingualism alone is not a guarantee for a metalinguistic advantage. She argues that there is a complex interaction between bilingualism, task demands, and other variables that will determine whether or not bilingualism will facilitate the development of metalinguistic ability. An advantage in metalinguistic skill is particularly interesting because many studies have highlighted a close and facilitative relationship between metalinguistic ability and literacy skill (see Bialystok 2001).

Another potential cognitive advantage for young bilingual children is in the development of Theory of Mind. Theory of Mind is a milestone in cognitive development that emerges sometime in the fourth or fifth year of a child's life. It is characterized by the child's ability to interpret other people's behaviours in terms of their mental states, such as what they might believe or predict. A classic test of Theory of Mind is the false belief task. In this task, children are asked to predict the thoughts or beliefs of an individual who may hold a false belief. In the so-called 'Sally–Anne' task, children are told a story about Sally who places a marble in a box and then leaves the room. While Sally is absent, another character 'Anne' moves the marble out of the box to a different location. Sally then returns, and the children are asked where Sally will think the marble is. If the children have Theory of Mind, they will say that Sally will think the marble is in the box, since that is where Sally last saw it and is unaware of the fact that Anne had removed it. If the children do not have Theory of Mind, they will assume Sally thinks what the child thinks—it is wherever Anne put it. In other words, without Theory of Mind, children are not capable of thinking about the mental states of others, and they cannot put themselves in the mind of another individual. Geotz (2003) examined the relationship between Theory of Mind and bilingualism in children. In her study, 104 three- and four-year-old children (32 monolingual English; 32 monolingual Mandarin; and 40 bilingual English–Mandarin) were given a range of tasks, including an appearance–reality task, perspective-taking tasks, and false belief tasks—all of which tap into aspects of Theory of Mind. Geotz' results overall indicate a bilingual advantage on the Theory of Mind tasks—they performed better than the monolinguals. Geotz discusses three possible explanations for this advantage:

1 more well-developed metalinguistic skills, which in turn lead to more fine-tuned representational skills allowing the child to have greater control over conflicting representations
2 more advanced skills at selective attention (c.f. Bialystok, 1991), so that they are not distracted by conflicting representations
3 difference in the child's sociolinguistic awareness—of the need to match their language to their interlocutor.

We have seen above that very young bilingual children are sensitive to the linguistic preferences of their interlocutors so this may be another possible reason why bilingual children outperform monolingual children on Theory of Mind tasks. Geotz' (2003) results were confirmed in a later study by Kovács (2009) with Romanian–Hungarian bilinguals. Like Geotz, Kovács argues that the advantage manifested by bilinguals over monolinguals on Theory of Mind tasks is due to more advanced executive function skills.

Executive function skills is the general term used to describe cognitive abilities that are at the core of all human cognition, including attention, selection, and inhibition processes. The claim that young bilingual children have superior selective attention skills (one example of executive function skills) was made by Bialystok (1991 and elsewhere). However, since the year 2000 (c.f. Bialystok and Barac, 2013) more research has been focused on trying to identify the extent to which bilinguals have superior executive control (see also Green, 2011 for a brief review). Bialystok, Barac, Blaye, and Poulin-Dubois (2010) carried out a study investigating these executive function skills in English and French (from Canada and France respectively) monolingual and bilingual children (from Canada) who were bilingual in English and one of 18 different home languages. They ranged in age from 2;5 to 5;0. The children were given a range of tasks including a measure of receptive vocabulary (in English or French) and a range of executive function tasks; the mutual exclusivity task which assesses how children assign novel labels onto novel objects, Luria's tapping task (a reverse imitation task) where the child has to perform the opposite of an action modelled by the experimenter, the opposite worlds task which requires the child to use an opposite label to name pictures, the attentional networks task which taps into the child's skills at inhibitory control, and finally a reverse categorization task where the child carries out a classification based on one rule which then switches. Bialystok et al. (2010) found a bilingual advantage in some (the tapping task, opposite worlds task, and reverse categorization) but not all of the executive function tasks. In contrast, the monolinguals performed similarly to each other even though they were developing knowledge of different L1s and were growing up in two different environments (Canada and France). They argue that these data reveal that even in children as young as 2;5 years old there is clear evidence of a bilingual advantage on some aspects of executive function.

Other studies have shown slightly different patterns to Bialystok et al. (2010). For example, Gathercole, Thomas, Jones, Guasch, Young, and Hughes (2010) compared bilingual and monolingual children on a range of tasks, like Bialystok et al. (2010). Gathercole et al.'s (2010) sample were recruited from Wales where the bilinguals spoke both Welsh and English and were compared to a group of monolingual English children. The children ranged in age from 6;4 to 8;11. They also included a group of older secondary school students aged between 12;4 and 16;0. Children were given a tapping task that was slightly different from Bialystok et al.'s (2010), in that the children either had to match the tapping pattern produced by the researcher, or reverse or switch the pattern. The bilingual children outperformed the monolingual children, and within the bilingual group, it was the children who came from either only Welsh-speaking or English-speaking homes (i.e. where their home environment was *not* bilingual, even though they were) who outperformed the bilingual children who came from Welsh/English homes. A second study where a Stroop task was presented showed more mixed findings for a bilingual advantage. Not all bilinguals showed an advantage nor across all conditions of the Stroop task. The home language environment (whether it was only Welsh-speaking, only English-speaking, or bilingual) as well as socioeconomic factors were also implicated in the findings. Gathercole et al. (2010) argue that there is a range of factors at play in identifying whether bilinguals have superior executive control skills. Furthermore, Namazi and Thordardottir (2010) argued that it is not bilingualism per se that leads to an advantage. In their study of English–French bilingual children in Montréal, they found that working memory skills were a more powerful explanatory variable on their visual controlled attention tasks. Therefore, while there is definitely support for the idea that bilingual children show advanced or superior executive control skills, more work needs to be done in order to identify more precisely the range of factors that contribute to this advantage.

In summary, there is a range of evidence to suggest that bilingual children have some cognitive advantages over monolingual children in the domains of metalinguistic awareness, Theory of Mind, and executive function skills.

The age issue

Research unequivocally shows that very young children can develop knowledge of more than one language, simultaneously, without any significant or notable consequences to their overall linguistic development. Even as early as a few days old, the bilingual-to-be child's brain has accommodated the presence of more than one language in the ambient environment. Similarly, they reach the same stages (canonical babbling, one and two word stages, etc.) at comparable ages of development as monolingually developing children. The only caveat here is from studies examining the rate of development of bilingual relative to monolingual children. Some studies have suggested that bilingual children can lag (by a few months) behind monolingual children in their rate of development. However, this potential problem has been shown to be resolved in adulthood (for example, in vocabulary size differences). In fact, not only are there no significant negative consequences to developing knowledge of two languages simultaneously, there are manifest advantages, such as in heightened metalinguistic skills, advanced Theory of Mind, and advantages in some executive function skills, not to mention the perhaps more obvious intercultural sensitivity/awareness and socioeconomic benefits.

It is important to illustrate, however, that even in the BFLA context where children are exposed to two languages from birth—and for whom the Critical Period Hypothesis should predict a free pass with respect to language development—the environment plays a powerful role. A number of the studies described above were carried out in 'one parent, one language' homes where there is a relatively even distribution of two languages spoken by each parent and many of these studies were carried out in sociopolitical contexts where the same two languages enjoy a comparable status (such as Montréal in Canada). In studies where this comparatively equal distribution of languages in the environment is not so common, differences emerge—in some cases a failure or delay in the development of one of the child's languages

(Schlyter, 1990; De Houwer, 2007; Bernardini and Schlyter, 2004; Meisel, 2007; Bedore et al., 2012). Similarly, the precise role of the input cannot be over-stressed here: the level of input (how much) and the kind of output opportunities the child has with both languages contribute substantially to their BFLA outcomes. For example, Paradis and Navarro (2003) and De Houwer (2007) among others have shown a direct link to the parents' language use and the child's language use. Similarly, in Genesee et al. (1996) the one child who did not differentiate the languages in the same manner had parents who were reported to code-switch extensively, thus making it challenging for this young child to identify language preference in his parents, whose environment modelled frequent code-switching. Similarly, the degree and kind of cross-linguistic influence identifiable in young children's language production is also in part determined by their immediate context. Finally, dominance is directly attributable to setting (Meisel, 2007). Therefore, while all of the children represented in the research described above had been exposed to and had been learning their two languages since birth, we do not see the same level of development, progression, or use—variability that is directly attributable to differences in the linguistic and social contexts in which these children were becoming bilingual. Therefore, context matters, even in very young children developing knowledge of two languages simultaneously. Age, therefore, is not the only, nor even the most explanatory variable that predicts bilingual proficiency in this context.

Educational implications

The focus of this chapter was on very young children growing up in bilingual first language acquisition contexts, a context which precedes formal schooling. As a result, none of the issues and/or research described above was carried out within educational contexts or on children who were school-aged (with a very few exceptions where the children were at pre-school or Kindergarten). Consequently, there are comparatively few educational implications to be drawn here. However, in the discussions above it was clear how even within BFLA contexts, the role of the input and the support for both languages have a considerable impact on linguistic development. Therefore, to the extent that both languages are supported in nursery settings, pre-school, and Kindergarten environments for BFLA children, their two languages will develop accordingly (more support for *both* languages + more opportunities to use *both* languages across a range of different social circumstances = more developed linguistic proficiency). Unfortunately this is not always possible to achieve, particularly in minority language environments (see Chapters 3 and 4).

Conclusions

This chapter has selectively reviewed some of the evidence emerging from the field of research investigating principles and processes of how very young children develop knowledge of two languages simultaneously. This field has unequivocally shown that with appropriate environmental support (i.e. plenty of exposure and output opportunities) children can develop bilingually with no negative cost but rather, with a range of possible cognitive and sociocultural advantages. However, even within this field, the context in which the child is developing will play an important role in determining the extent to which the child develops comparable knowledge and use across both languages.

Notes

1 It is worth commenting here that many such studies on BFLA recruit small numbers of children which is problematic from a methodological point of view. However, it is often neither pragmatically (i.e. difficult to recruit) nor methodologically (e.g., difficult to carry out too many transcriptions) possible to recruit larger sample sizes.

2 See also Thordardottir, Rothenberg, Rivard, and Naves (2006) for further discussion about bilingual children scoring lower than monolinguals on vocabulary measures and the relationship to input and exposure.

3 See also the section on 'Dominance' below.

4 Whether the utterances are grammatical or ungrammatical has not yet been adequately resolved in the literature. For more detailed discussions, see Hulk and Müller, 2000 and Yip and Matthews, 2007.

5 Phonological backing refers to a process of making a non-velar or non-glottal consonant velar or glottal (for example, *bun* is articulated as *gun*—the front sound /b/ is articulated with a back sound /g/).

3

Heritage language learners

Introduction

This chapter focuses on a population of language learners known as 'heritage language' (HL) learners. Broadly defined, HL learners are those who have a minority language in the home or community that is different from the language of the wider, majority community and usually different from the language of formal education (typically the majority language). The heritage language is the language of the home and is often the language of immigrant, refugee, or indigenous groups within the respective broader social context.

Defining who heritage language learners are is a complex business and indeed many scholars suggest that one single definition is not able to encapsulate all of the features and characteristics of HL learners across different contexts (Carreira, 2004). For example, many adult HL learners are in essence L2 learners if they do not have any proficiency in the HL and come to the classroom with only a cultural connection to the L2. School-aged children may be learning the HL as an L1 in the home or might also be taught formal characteristics of their HL at school (as if it were an L2). The HL in this case could be an L1 (if they learn the HL as one of their first languages) but it might also be similar to a taught L2 if they participate in taught HL classes either in formal or complementary educational programmes. HL learners are a very diverse group—HL learners are not always HL speakers (in the case of adults), and are not all actually learning the HL (in the case of many children). For a considerable number of HL learners, the language to which they are first exposed is the heritage language and as such, they learn the HL as an L1, with all appropriate context-supported linguistic input in place and very much as a typical native speaker of any language (from birth, at the optimal time within the critical period). However, as indicated below, many HL learners do not achieve full and native-like mastery of their HL. There are many candidate reasons for this, as will be discussed in this chapter, and it is particularly interesting to examine these learners because all the putative necessary ingredients for complete mastery of a language are initially in place for many HL learners—significant and authentic exposure from birth, with many opportunities for meaningful context-supported interaction with interlocutors of the language. However, HL learners often experience a language shift, where their L1 (the HL) becomes their L2, while their initial L2 (the majority language) becomes their dominant and more proficient language. Consequently, many young HL learners do not achieve full native-like competence in their HL, and as they develop, their HL looks like an undeveloped L1. Therefore, a focus on their HL learning raises interesting questions regarding the role of context for successful L2 language learning in childhood (see Montrul, 2013a for further discussion of this shift).

This chapter begins with a more detailed discussion of the problems of defining heritage language learners. Many different populations are subsumed under the overarching term of 'heritage language learner' and it is worth presenting the sociopolitical issues surrounding the ways in which researchers and educators have categorized and considered these learners. Some of the main educational policy dimensions surrounding HL education are also discussed, as this is a critical issue and one of the main factors identified as being responsible for the fact that HL learners often fail to achieve native-like mastery of their home language—due either to a switch to education solely through the medium of the majority language, or a complete lack of opportunity for formal education through the medium of the home language, or both. Educational policy decisions around the world and their impact on HL development are presented, followed by a discussion directly focused on HL development and competence. In contexts such as the USA, where the most frequently identified HL is Spanish (see Carreira and Kagan, 2011), learners can receive instruction in Spanish as either an L2 or even a Foreign Language (FL) in school, despite the fact of their initial exposure to Spanish as either an L1 or one of their L1s at birth[1]. A number of researchers have examined and compared these learners' HL competence against both native (monolingual) speakers of the HL and L2 learners of the HL to identify whether and to what extent HL learners are similar to or different from these comparison groups. In other words, is HL acquisition more like L1, or L2 learning?

HL speakers can vary considerably in the age at which they are first exposed to the majority language. Some children can be exposed to the majority language at birth, if they are living in a simultaneous bilingual context, where one parent speaks the majority language and the other speaks a minority language. However, HL children can also be more like sequential bilinguals if they are exposed to only the HL in the home and then have contact with the majority L2 once the child is older and the HL is more established (Rothman, 2009). HL speakers who are simultaneous bilinguals typically tend to have adult-like HL grammars that are less developed than those HL speakers who were sequential bilinguals, which may be due to the prolonged exposure to the HL before the majority L2 language becomes an influence (Montrul, 2008). As indicated above, many HL children shift to the majority language, owing to pressures of assimilation and identity (they may wish to identify themselves more with the majority L2 culture than their home culture) and in these cases, exposure to and interaction with the home HL can become so reduced as to have a significant negative consequence on the child's linguistic competence in the HL (Rothman, 2009). Rothman comments that 'Without adequate academic support of the heritage language during the school years, heritage speakers often miss the chance to acquire literacy skills in the language' (Rothman, 2009, p. 157). Unfortunately this is the reality for a great many HL speakers around the world, and as a result, they end up resembling L2 learners more than native speakers of the HL. HL learners have been shown to differ from monolinguals in a few key areas of their linguistic competence, many of which centre around morphosyntax. This could in part be due to the specific focus researchers have chosen to examine. For example, HL learners differ from monolingual speakers in terms of inflectional morphology, verbal morphology, and null subject pronouns. At the same time, however, they have been shown to be similar to native (monolingual) speakers in other areas such as case marked clitics (Montrul, 2004).

Some researchers (Montrul, 2008, for example,) argue that HL children's acquisition of their home language is 'incomplete', in the sense that it does not reach age-appropriate levels of morphosyntactic development and lies somewhere in between that of a native-speaker and an L2 learner of the same language. Many of the relevant studies examining this question do not actually investigate young children's L1/L2 knowledge per se or use the more appropriate longitudinal designs. Rather, a common research design in this paradigm is to compare adult HLLs against adult L2 learners and adult native (monolingual) speakers to identify whether the HLLs are more like adult NSs or L2 learners. It may seem at odds with the overall focus of this volume on child L2 learning to discuss research on adult learners. Nonetheless, the outcome of heritage language acquisition in young adults, which has been the focus of many HL studies, is deeply shaped by what happens in childhood. These adult studies present some interesting findings and have important implications for how we conceptualize HL learning in children and the role of the HL in formal education. A study of the process in childhood itself is the missing link in this population. Finally, the chapter culminates with a discussion of how studying language learning in this context contributes to the over-arching discussion of age and context in successful L2 learning in childhood.

Who are 'heritage language learners'? The problem of definition

There is a wide range of terms used to describe the population in focus when discussing issues of relevance for heritage language learners. The term 'Heritage Language' was fashioned in Canada in 1977 as part of the Ontario

Heritage Languages Program (see Cummins, 2005), aimed at supporting Heritage Language instruction in Ontario School board schools in response to a request from communities who had students/families interested in learning and studying an identified 'heritage' language. Duff (2008) notes that 'heritage' in this Canadian case refers to any language of relevance to a Native Peoples' community that is not one of the two official languages in Canada (English or French). The term Heritage Language began to be used more widely in the USA and around the world since the 1990s. HL learners can include individuals who speak an ethnolinguistically minority language (such as speakers of Cree in Canada (whose HL is Cree but who also speak/learn/are educated in English or French) but also those who speak a home language that is not ethnolinguistically a minority language (such as Spanish speakers in the USA who are learning and being educated in English). Spanish is not a minority language in an ethnolinguistic sense and indeed is the most studied foreign language in the world (after English), as well as being a majority (and oppressing) language in Spain and Latin America. However, Spanish can be viewed as a minority (and oppressed) language in the sense of being a non-dominant language in the wider sociopolitical context of the USA (Montrul, 2010b, Montrul 2013b). The term Heritage Language learner essentially, therefore, refers to a very diverse population with different linguistic, historical, and cultural backgrounds, who may have different motivations and attitudes towards learning the HL (Comanaru and Noels, 2009). Within the context of this volume specifically, and applied linguistics research more widely, HL learners are typically considered to be individuals who have/had achieved some competence in an L1 as a function of typical language socialization patterns in the home, but who did not achieve native-like mastery over this language—most likely due to the 'language shift' between learning a minority L1 in the home, to learning the majority L2 through formal education (Kondo-Brown, 2010). This conceptualization is often referred to as a 'proficiency definition' since to be considered an HL learner, some degree of linguistic competence in the L1 (HL) has to be have been developed. However, the term 'heritage language' can also refer to an ancestral connection to another language. Individuals with such a connection may or may not have a desire to (re)connect with the HL, and might possibly never have had any exposure to or experience with the HL itself (He, 2010). An example here would be native English speakers of Chinese ancestral descent growing up in Canada—but who did not learn Chinese in childhood. The proficiency-based categorization is adopted here because an HL learner who has an ancestral connection, but who did not actually learn the HL in childhood, is ultimately an (adult) L2 learner with a strong personal motivation to learn the L2. This volume is concerned with processes and outcomes of L2 learning in childhood. The HL learner who developed competence in the HL in childhood as one of their L1(s) presents interesting cognitive, linguistic, and socio-educational questions.

In reviewing work on HL learners, one is immediately struck by the problem of definition. Most research articles and books in this area begin with a discussion of how to identify/describe/define the construct of the HL learner, because this issue is by no means straightforward. A good and fairly representative discussion of these issues can be found in Bale (2010), who describes at some length the difficulties associated with categorizing the HL learner. In his discussion of international comparative educational approaches to HL education, he notes the added complexity of the inherent problems of defining HL learners, even when considered only within the context of a research perspective. For example, terms that have been used synonymously with 'heritage' include: *aboriginal, ancestral, autochthonous, (ex-)colonial, community, critical, diasporic, endoglossic, ethnic, foreign, geopolitical, home, immigrant, indigenous, language other than English, local, migrant, minority, mother tongue, refugee, regional,* and *strategic* (Bale, 2010, p. 43). One of the biggest criticisms of the term 'heritage' language is that it romanticizes *past* language use instead of focusing on actual and future language use (p. 43). This is a problem first raised in García (2005), who introduces her discussion of heritage languages in the USA with a quote from a 17-year-old Dominican recently arrived in New York City, who identifies 'heritage language' as something old, belonging to her great-grandmother. As García notes, the term 'heritage language' is certainly 'rear-viewing' and not something that can be 'projected into the future' (García, 2005, p. 601). García also comments on the tension between the idea that the term 'heritage language' signals a loss of ground for language minorities achieved in the civil rights era of the 1960s when the lack of support for a non-English speaking child in school began to be viewed as a human rights issue. At the same time its use has allowed educators, pupils, and parents to recognize that much of the educational policy in countries like the USA is based on a purely monolingual norm, one that is not relevant to a significant proportion of the pupil population. Bale (2010) discusses the dichotomy between a proficiency-based definition of the heritage language learner and a categorization based on the individual's affiliation with a specific ethnolinguistic group. He argues that the proficiency-based categorization has more direct pedagogical implications and notes that a significant amount of research in HL learning and education adopts a proficiency-based explanation (as noted above). However, such an approach will also necessarily exclude individuals who identify themselves with a particular ethnolinguistic community (without any HL proficiency), an idea echoed in Hornberger (2005) who argues that it is the individual who decides whether they belong to a heritage language community or not, regardless of the extent to which they can actually speak the HL.

As mentioned above, the term 'heritage language' was coined in Canada—ostensibly to differentiate the languages spoken in Canada that are not either of the official two languages (Duff, 2008). Other countries use different terms to identify the same type of situation, such as *community language* used more frequently in Europe and Australia, with 'Australian indigenous languages' or 'Australian languages' being the preferred choice of Aboriginal speakers in Australia (Bale, 2010). De Bot and Gorter (2005) distinguish between *regional minority* (RM) languages and *immigrant minority* (IM) languages, noting that IM languages have received some measure of support in various educational programmes in the Netherlands and other European countries. With RM languages, the concern is more focused on either revitalization or maintenance of the RM language with *The European Charter for Regional or Minority Language* (1992) and the *Framework Convention for the Protection of National Minorities* (1995) being important tools that help identify and maintain indigenous or heritage languages in Europe. Other researchers argue that the term 'heritage language' is not one that can be applied universally, a problem that becomes particularly clear when examining contexts outside of North America. For example, Brutt-Griffler and Makoni (2005) demonstrate that the proficiency-based definition becomes seriously problematic in the African context, since differentiating between linguistic varieties in the many highly multilingual contexts throughout Africa is difficult at best. They note that the conceptualization of 'heritage language' is based on cultures which are inherently monolingual, yet, in contexts like Africa which are very linguistically diverse, the notion of identifying a (single) heritage language is at best challenging, and likely to be problematic. This situation mirrors that in Australia, where the indigenous aboriginal languages are both numerous and highly diverse (Simpson and Wigglesworth, 2008). Brutt-Griffler and Makoni (2005) provide an example of the linguistic diversity in Ghana, where the largest ethnic minority speak the language Ga. As a result instruction is provided in Ga. However, with increased migration there are many students with different linguistic backgrounds, such as Hausa, who might still be allocated to a Ga mother tongue (heritage language) classroom. They also note there are many examples in the African context when children might use a language which is neither the ancestral language, nor the official language of formal education (such as English). If the educational system is to provide instructional support for one of these languages, which is it to be? The ancestral language or the language the child uses in social situations with peers, but within which they may not be receiving any formal education?

It is readily apparent, therefore, that there are significant challenges when it comes to identifying an appropriate and importantly, accurate and representative term for those learners who are being educated (and often living) in a system with a majority language that is not the same language spoken in the home. For the purpose of this chapter (and this volume more generally) the term 'heritage language' will be used in its broadest sense, following from Bale (2010) who used the term to include individuals' ancestral ties to a language, individual agency in identifying as an HL speaker, and how the HL is situated within the wider sociopolitical context. Furthermore, the term 'heritage language' is widely used in the literature (despite the diverse meanings sometimes associated with it), as illustrated by the *Heritage Language Journal* established in 2002. The journal publishes research related to educational issues surrounding HL speakers. A very broad and generalized categorization of the *who* and *what* of HL learners is shown in Table 3.1.

Who are heritage language learners?	
Proficiency-based	Ancestral-based
• They learned an HL in childhood, but are likely to have non-native-like competence in the HL in adulthood due to language shift.	• They have an ancestral connection to the HL but are really L2 learners (i.e., they did not learn the HL in childhood and have no linguistic competence in the HL).
What are heritage languages?	
• Languages that are in the minority in relation to the majority language in society, • even if may not even be ethnolinguistically minority languages. • Example: Spanish in USA, not ethnolinguistically a minority language since it is an important and widely spoken and learned world language, but in the USA is an HL in relation to English; as is Mandarin in Australia, Turkish in the Netherlands, and Urdu in the UK.	• Languages that are indigenous to the geographical region but are not spoken by the wider majority in the society and are not the languages of power, governance, or formal education. • Example: Cree in Canada, Māori in New Zealand (ethnolinguistically a minority language and also minority in relation to a dominant language spoken more widely in the society).

Table 3.1   The who and what of heritage language learners

Sociopolitical context, educational policy, and identity

There are difficulties in identifying the most appropriate terminology to describe the heritage language context. One of the reasons for this difficulty is that whatever term is used, it will be very closely tied with the identity of the HL learners themselves, and be an index of how the wider (majority) community situates the HL community. This notion in turn will dictate educational policy about whether and to what extent HL learners should/will receive any kind of formal education in their HL. In this section, I present a brief snapshot of some of the different types of provision available to HL learners globally, though note this will be neither an exhaustive nor a systematic review, but will provide a description of some of the different policy approaches to HL education found internationally.

In addition to providing an excellent discussion of some of the definitional problems in categorizing HL learners, Bale (2010) provides a good review of different educational policies associated with HL education around the world including Africa, Southeast Asia, India, North America, Oceania, Republic of Ireland, and the UK.

In Africa, Bale (2010) makes reference to the work of Djité (2008), who provides a comprehensive review of African educational policies related to language and HL issues. Language-in-Education schemes have been implemented in many countries in Africa in response to the 1953 UNESCO statement promoting education through an African language at primary level (often Grades 1–3), at which point children are transitioned to English as a medium of instruction, while the African language in question becomes taught as a subject. These policies are similar to the transitional bilingual programmes discussed in Chapter 4. As with other transitional programmes, these policy decisions go a long way to signalling to the child that their home/ ancestral language is not as important as English. The fact that English is used throughout many parts of Africa for official purposes can have a negative impact on the implementation of indigenous language education. Three factors have contributed to problems in this respect:

1 lack of planning between local and national educational authorities
2 shortage of teachers available to teach the languages themselves
3 problems with assessment and achievement (Adegbija, 2004).

Points 2 and 3 are particularly problematic, because even with the best will in the world, education of HL speakers is only going to go as far as the teachers who educate HL children. If there are no appropriately qualified teachers then policy is useless. Further problems associated with implementing indigenous language education policy in Africa relate to tensions from parents. Iyamu and Aduwa Ogiegbaen (2007) report on a study where a large sample of parents and primary school teachers were surveyed on their attitudes towards HL educational policy. Both parents and teachers reported that while they appreciated the value of HL education and understood the HL education policy, they were nonetheless concerned that HL instruction could hamper learning, an idea echoed in Tembe and Norton (2008, c.f. Bale, 2010), who report that parents wanted children to learn English as quickly as possible. In this way, the parents themselves may not fully appreciate the value of HL education and act as competing forces against promoting HL education for their children. Bale (2010) further notes how the definitional issues he discusses at the beginning of his review have a direct impact on educational policy in contexts such as Africa. He cites the example of a Non-Governmental Organization (NGO) which worked towards changing the status of Tonga from 'minority' to 'indigenous' language, which then enabled Tonga to become a medium of instruction rather than 'only' a taught language. Clearly, closer examination of the relationship between policy decisions and language, literacy, and educational outcomes in children needs to be carried out in highly diverse linguistic contexts such as Africa. Bale's (2010) discussion of the African context highlights competing tensions between governments, communities, parents, and teachers in implementing policies on HL instruction. Furthermore, while the transition from the HL to English as the medium of instruction might be viewed as socially and politically necessary, it also signals to the child that their home language is not as important as English and can have significant (negative) consequences on the child's sense of identity and academic outcomes in both the HL and English.

These issues are further described by Chimbutane (2011) who argues that the high rates of academic failure in specific areas of Africa can be linked back to the educational policies requiring children learn through a foreign language and/or be transitioned away from mother tongue education too early. He describes three types of African bilingual education:

1 improved previously existing bilingual programmes without changing the extent of use of African languages as media of instruction (as in Northern Nigeria)
2 extended use of African languages as media of instruction from age two or three to all of primary education (for example, the six-year primary project in Nigeria)
3 use of African languages (for the first time) as media of instruction (in projects in Cameroon and Mozambique).

Despite the fact that many of these programmes have been successful, they have not been extended to wider areas, mostly due to a lack of funding, ideologically-based misconceptions about education in African languages, or lack of political will (Chimbutane, 2011). To underscore this last point, Chimbutane argues that '…language policy decisions in Africa are not guided by research findings but mainly by political pragmatism' (p. 21).

A more recent discussion about the issues surrounding language in education policy and practice in Africa can also be found in McIlwraith (2013)—a collection of papers in which many of the issues described above are discussed in detail. The overall conclusions from this volume reaffirm the points above, that the HL learners of the different regions in Africa need to be supported and maintained through appropriate educational programmes that enable children to receive education in their home language, facilitating the development of academic language and literacy skills.

English is used as a medium of instruction in a number of contexts in parts of Southeast Asia such as Malaysia (in Science and Maths at all levels) and in Singapore—which is officially a 'bilingual' country, but where English is used alongside three official mother tongues (Malay, Mandarin, and Tamil). Malay is a mother tongue for the majority of pupils in Singapore (Bale, 2010). In Hong Kong, a policy was introduced in 1998 (which coincided with the handover of power to the Chinese from the British, when Hong Kong became a Special Administrative Region of China). Schools previously using English as a medium of instruction had to switch to Cantonese. Interestingly, however, this switch from English to Cantonese was not mandatory if 85 per cent of the student population were academically in the top quintile, if the teachers had sufficient proficiency in English, and if the schools had sufficient support for students who might struggle with English. Again, this policy signals to pupils, parents, and the wider community that English is the language for the most academically able, the elite. Bale (2010) reviews a few studies that examined the consequences of the change in policy from English to Cantonese as a medium of instruction. He notes that overall this policy change has not had a significant impact on the attitudes towards English, in that the demand for English education is as strong as it was before the handover. This situation is not unlike that in Africa, where educational policies have been developed to promote education in the home language (Cantonese in Hong Kong and mother tongue in Africa) but where parents, pupils, and members of the society at large are nonetheless very keen on formal education through English. Again, there are significant and problematic tensions between educational policy and the demands and needs of pupils and families in these contexts.

India can be considered to have a 'three languages formula' which requires a regional mother tongue as the medium of instruction for the first five years of schooling, Hindi (in non-Hindi states) or another Indian language (in Hindi states) to be taught as a subject in lower-secondary school, and then English as a third language to be introduced from Year 3 (Bale, 2010). The situation is complicated even further in areas of India where a regional minority language is spoken by at least 10 per cent of the population. In those regions, communities can choose this minority language as a medium of instruction in the early primary years. As with Africa, we see a similar type of transitional bilingual education, in which a home or regionally important language is taught in the early primary years, with a transition to other languages (one of which is English) in the later years. Perhaps the most frustrating aspect of these policy decisions for scholars is that there is no theoretical or empirical rationale for setting up HL education for children in the early years of formal education and then withdrawing it later on. There *is* a theoretical rationale for setting up HL educational programmes but not for withdrawing them. This transitional approach goes against what we know about language development—that young children are more than capable of learning and becoming literate in more than one language (see Chapter 2). This transition from mother tongue to majority language medium of instruction further creates problems for language maintenance and increases the chance of language attrition in childhood. If formal education in the HL is withdrawn, then it is much more likely (and indeed practically inevitable) that children will not be able to develop and maintain their HL to high proficiency levels.

In each of the contexts above (Africa, Asia, and India), there is an evident competition between English and the other respective languages in the country. English could be viewed as a 'predator' language (c.f. Hornberger, 1997) in these contexts—in the worst case actually endangering these other languages, particularly in contexts such as Africa and India that have a significant diversity of regional languages which might not receive any formal educational support; and in any case, signalling to speakers of regional or indigenous languages that their languages are not as important or valued as English.

One of the most widely studied contexts in terms of HL education policy has been North America. However, despite the fact that the term 'Heritage Language' was conceived in Canada, comparatively little research on HL education policy has been carried out in Canada itself, partly as a consequence of a lack of funding (c.f. Duff, 2008). Duff and Li (2009) describe the context of indigenous language education and research in Canada and specifically highlight the unique challenges for francophone minority learners in an Anglo-dominant context. They note that as of 2008, there were more than one million people identifying themselves as 'Aboriginal' or Indigenous Persons in Canada, yet fewer than 30 per cent of these reported being able to actually speak an Indigenous language. This issue relates to the definitional problems mentioned above—on a proficiency-based categorization only, these individuals would not be considered HL learners at all. While programmes have been developed and implemented that are aimed to help (re)learn or reconnect with indigenous languages (such as the one described in Sarkar and Metallic (2009) which promotes Mi'gmaq), each new census in Canada shows fewer and fewer speakers of the significant majority of indigenous languages in Canada, with the exception of Inuktitut, Cree, and Ojibwe. The remaining indigenous languages are not expected to survive into the next century.

The need to support young Indigenous children's language development in Canada is discussed in Ball (2009), who demonstrates that fewer children within the Canadian context are learning their native (Indigenous) language despite the fact that nearly 4 per cent of the population of Canada comes from an Indigenous context and the birth rate in the Indigenous peoples is double that of the non-Indigenous people of Canada. International research has also consistently shown the importance of:

1 early language development on academic achievement
2 language and culture on identity issues and outcomes
3 understanding the problem of equity within the wider society.

These are three important issues that are highly relevant to the context of HL education in Canada. A lack of funding, a lack of relevant infrastructure support to monitor the development of young indigenous people appropriately, together with culturally inappropriate education are all candidate explanations for the lack of research in this area. Specialist services and assessment procedures are reported to have frequent negative consequences for Indigenous children, examples being either over- or under-recognition of children with developmental problems, including higher than expected levels of language delays, school failure, and drop-out rates. Ball concludes her report by calling for greater investment in the design, delivery, and evaluation of language development programmes that are both culturally and linguistically relevant for the Native Peoples of Canada. In many ways, reports such as these make grim reading and present a sad irony that within Canada, the inventors of 'heritage language education' as a construct—we should see such stark statistics on lack of appropriate support for Indigenous language education.

The picture, however, is not entirely negative, as indicated in Guèvremont and Kohen (2012), who review the statistics from the 2001 Canadian Aboriginal Peoples survey identifying factors affecting whether children were learning to speak an Aboriginal language, and how speaking an Aboriginal language relates to school outcomes. In this analysis, after controlling for child and family factors such as age, sex, health status, household income, and other such demographic variables, speaking an Aboriginal language was associated with positive school outcomes for children aged 6–14 if they learned the language at school. The importance that parents placed on learning the language was consistently related to the child's knowledge of the Aboriginal language, since parental support in the home is a key variable here. Unfortunately, the positive relationship between speaking an Aboriginal language and school outcomes was found only in the child cohort of this large-scale analysis. Adults who spoke an Aboriginal language were *less* likely to have completed high school than those who did not. Guèvremont and Kohen (2012) speculate that there could be a shift in moving from primary to secondary school that could impact on self-esteem—speakers of an Aboriginal language might feel less engaged with the formal educational system at the secondary level and thus less acclimated to the majority language system (English or French in Canada, depending on region). Clearly more focused attention needs to be paid to this shift, and appropriate policies need to be implemented to ensure that speakers of Aboriginal languages are able to maintain positive academic outcomes throughout their time in formal education. These findings echo the negative impact of transitional bilingual programmes. If the educational provision at secondary (high) school does not value the Aboriginal (heritage) language, this can have adverse effects on academic outcomes. One explanation for these problems could be a lack of appropriate written materials to teach advanced academic content across several disciplines in these indigenous languages. Since they are not considered 'standard' languages, materials developers may not feel it worth the effort to develop them. Shortage of materials in indigenous languages also affects Latin America. In other parts of the world, where governments have been willing to spend money promoting a standard use of languages there are more relevant and appropriate materials (as in the Basque Country in Spain).

Recent interest in HL educational policy in the USA can be attributed to the 9/11 tragedy and linked to issues of national security. Heritage language policy research in the USA is almost exclusively focused on a resource-based approach—HL speakers are seen as a resource for national security, enabling the intelligence community to recruit more heritage speakers from languages such as Arabic and Farsi (Bale, 2010). In addition to this national security focus, however, HL educational policy is also seen as a resource for meeting social and educational needs, in the sense that HL speakers are considered more effective language teachers (as 'native speakers' of the HL) and HL communities are identified as 'ideal venues' for teacher education (p. 54). Overall, therefore, HL educational policy in the USA is considered important in promoting an awareness of language and culture, of promoting L2 skills and in some more rare cases, of promoting advanced language specialists (Bale, 2010).

Related to HL educational policy is the wide range of bilingual education programmes that have been developed in the USA to help young children from different heritage language communities best develop and adjust to formal education. Some of these programmes are discussed in some detail in Chapter 4 in connection with minority language learners, since all of these are aimed at promoting the majority language of these HL learners. It is worth noting here, however, that the extent to which these programmes aim to support and *develop* the HL is an important indicator to HL learners of the perceived status of HL learners' culture.

Formal educational policy of course, is not the only way children in the USA and elsewhere become multilingual. A recent volume by García, Zakharia, and Otcu (2013) presents an interesting collection of papers describing the wide variety of bilingual education in New York City. They illustrate how different ethnic communities have attempted to help develop bilingual and multiple ethnolinguistic identities in America. García et al. (2013) also describe different programmes developed by parents and/or educators, based in community, religious, and ethnically-oriented schools to promote multilingualism in a wide range of linguistic communities (Arabic, French, Greek, Hebrew, Japanese, Mandarin, Turkish, and Yiddish). This is particularly interesting because it illustrates that *despite* more formal educational policy (that does not typically foster or support these HLs), children's multilingual identities nonetheless are being developed and maintained through their own communities, who see the value of ensuring their children learn their heritage language.

Heritage language educational policy in Australia and New Zealand has also been widely discussed. For example, there have been many attempts to promote and revitalize Māori in New Zealand. However, despite such initiatives (for example, the immersion programme described in Harrison, 1998), there are few recent analyses of the effectiveness of these programmes (Bale, 2010). There are three major issues to consider with regard to Māori education in New Zealand:

1 educational programmes aimed at supporting and maintaining Māori cannot mitigate against negative practices and attitudes towards indigenous peoples in the wider society—hence the need to look beyond the classroom to support Indigenous language and culture
2 one of the benefits of Māori medium of instruction education is that it allows the Māori community to take control of their own cultural and linguistic future
3 there is a paradox in the tensions between state-funded language revitalization programmes, and increasing state control over community-oriented language programmes (Bale, 2010).

This latter point in particular is relevant to most of the contexts of HL education discussed so far. Government funding for language revitalization and maintenance programmes allows the government to exert more control over the development of key aspects of these Indigenous communities. Without it, however, the programmes would not exist in the first place.

In Australia, three major levels of HL educational policy aim to support HL development as:

1 a taught subject in formal education contexts
2 as Saturday (complementary) school programmes
3 as after-school programmes to supplement the normal curriculum.

Worryingly, and again, like some of the contexts above (notably Canada), research being carried out in Australia on HL educational policy is also under-funded, and the amount of support for community based language programmes is declining (Bale, 2010). There is a tension between support for Indigenous languages and support for immigrant, notably Asian (Chinese, Filipino, Japanese, and Vietnamese) languages, since these are seen as being more economically useful. A range of variables complicate the effective implementation of HL educational policy in Australia; these factors include teachers' often insufficient level of HL proficiency, the level of training offered specifically to primary school teachers, and the perceived status afforded to the HL itself.

Throughout Europe, a number of programmes have been established to revitalize indigenous languages such as Irish, Welsh, and Scottish Gaelic in the UK. 'Medium of instruction' programmes, in which children are taught through the medium of the HL have been developed in attempt to revitalize and maintain these indigenous HLs (see below under 'Educational implications'). Despite an increase in such programmes, there are problems of significant variability in the HL proficiencies of participating pupils that create challenges for teachers. For example, Irish is often offered as a taught second language in schools in Northern Ireland, but there is a concern that teacher education for teaching Irish has been limited. It is not always easy to evaluate the effectiveness of these policy decisions. There are positives here, however, in that there have been moves to develop an Irish medium of instruction that offers students more 'everyday' and useful language than just academic or school language. Furthermore, the majority of students in the Republic of Ireland study Irish at some level—either as a taught subject or learned through Irish education (see Irish immersion below). This situation highlights the importance of getting HL educational policy right, not just in Ireland but also in all of the geopolitical contexts discussed throughout this chapter. The educational context is an incredibly powerful force in the development (or lack thereof) of HL speakers. If there is a sociopolitical move to support these languages, the educational decisions and provision must be up to the task.

Throughout Europe there is an increase in HL educational policy that supports what de Bot and Gorter (2005) refer to as Immigrant Languages (IM) and Regional Languages (RM). For example, in the Netherlands and other regions (such as the Basque country and Catalonia in Spain), IMs are taught for as much as 2.5 hours a week. With Catalan and Basque, as with Welsh mentioned above, there are medium of instruction programmes for developing linguistic competence, and teaching the HL effectively through school (see Montrul, 2013b for a more detailed discussion of Basque and Catalan, and Chapter 5).

Despite the inherent variety and complexity with respect to the nature of provision of support for an HL, some consistent patterns can be identified. A major problem in many of the contexts described above is one of funding and finding space to support HL education in already crowded primary curricula. Governments have to be motivated to support the HL if they are to allocate sufficient funds to developing appropriate educational programmes to maintain or revitalize an HL. The international HL picture is consistently bleak with respect to funding, both in the amount and the extent to which it is available. There are also problems of implementation—sometimes in relation to how HL learners are categorized (notably in Africa) and sometimes in relation to teacher education (as in Northern Ireland). Perhaps most consistently, we see the impact and importance of the home and local community on how HL education develops. For example, in the African context, we saw that parents might be reluctant to develop the HL through education for fear their children might be delayed in their English learning, which could have negative consequences on developing the HL. It is also clear in contexts such as the USA that the home and local community can exert a powerful positive force on HL education and support, which can have a positive impact on HL learning and development.

Finally, a very important consequence of these HL educational policy decisions is the message they send regarding the perceived importance and/or status of the HL itself and, by extension, to speakers of the HL. The majority language, being the language of power, governance, and formal education, with strong literate traditions, can oppress the minority language (a speaker of the minority language with few linguistic skills in the majority language is unlikely to be able to 'get ahead' in the wider society). There will be fewer available job opportunities and less scope for professional and economic development without fluency in the majority language. If the languages and culture themselves are not seen as important in the wider community, the effectiveness of HL educational policy will at best be diminished and at worst, fail. The large-scale survey of Guèvremont and Kohen (2012) is one of many studies that present a worrying pattern in older learners' language and academic achievements after having been transitioned out of HL medium of instruction. Society, including teachers themselves can convey and reinforce the idea that the heritage language is less important for economic development. Learning the HL therefore, is often not seen as an asset, rather as a liability. These ideas are described in detail in the work of Cummins (1996, 2000).[2] The well documented more generalized advantages of being bilingual are perhaps less familiar to policy makers and families—or indeed individuals outside the academic community. It is clear from much of the research on simultaneous bilingualism (described in Chapter 2), that children are cognitively capable of learning and using more than one language without negative consequences on either language development or academic attainment. Furthermore, being an active bilingual brings with it a host of other cognitive advantages (Bialystok, Craik, Klein, and Viswanathan, 2004). This being the case, educational policy should be doing everything it can to promote bilingualism. This does not often happen, however, since there are comparatively few initiatives at Government level to promote bilingualism—in some cases funding to support multilingual learners in schools is being withdrawn. For instance, the UK government has significantly reduced funding to support the education of minority language pupils.

In considering the relationship between HL learning, education, and identity, Cummins (1996, 2000) has consistently argued for the notion of social justice through education and has passionately and convincingly articulated the damaging effect of particular educational policies on HL learners' identity and ultimate academic outcomes. Linguistic and psychological research does not and cannot address the issue of why certain culturally diverse groups consistently under-achieve in relation to their majority language-speaking peers. Cummins argues that these issues need to be considered within a wider sociological and sociopolitical context: to the extent that specific cultural groups are marginalized in society, one can expect to observe the implementation of educational policy that does not value their cultural heritage and erodes self-esteem and ethnic identity. He highlights (in 2000 and elsewhere) the importance of educational programmes that support and develop *additive* bilingualism—where students *add* a second language to their cognitive repertoire while at the same time developing their L1. If children's educational experiences do not help them to develop adequate literacy skills in L1 *and* L2, then their ability to understand ever-increasingly complex instruction in the L2 will be significantly diminished, hence proficiency in *both* L1 (the HL) and L2 are required (Cummins, 1976, 1981).

Cummins (2000 and elsewhere) proposes two specific principles that should be considered in light of the issues described above. The *interdependence principle*, originally described in Cummins (1981) states that provided there is adequate support, exposure, and motivation to learn *both* languages, the two languages can mutually support each other with respect to developing bilingual proficiency. In other words, proficiency in one language does not have to be developed at the cost of proficiency in another. Hence for HL learners, if educational support were in place to promote *additive* bilingualism, HL learners would be able to develop fluent linguistic and academic skills in both languages. Another important principle formulated by Cummins is the *Common Underlying Proficiency* (CUP) framework which argues that promoting proficiency in the HL (L1) can itself promote proficiency in the (majority) L2. In other words, there are no costs to the development of the (majority) L2 proficiency and academic skills as a function of focusing on developing (minority) HL proficiency. These two principles together, taken in consideration of the discussion above, leads one to question why in so many countries around the world, greater care is not taken to develop full proficiency, including academic language skills, in both their HL and their L2. Cummins (1996, 2000) also argues that international patterns of school success and failure indicate that power and status relations are at work in contributing to the relative academic failure of subordinated groups. This point is echoed in Bale's (2010) discussion of Māori revitalization and maintenance programmes—these are successful to the extent that the Māori language and culture is considered valuable to everyone.

One solution to these difficulties is in developing bilingual education programmes that promote additive bilingualism. These programmes are readily feasible in parts of the world where there is a large homogeneous L1 group all learning the same L2—such as Spanish-speaking students in the USA, or Cantonese-speaking children in Hong Kong. However, the reality for many countries and educators is one of 'super diversity' (Martin-Jones, Blackledge and Creese, 2012) within a school population. In the UK for example, over 360 different L1s are represented in the million plus primary school children who are being educated within the majority L2 (NALDIC, 2012). In any given classroom, teachers may have minority language learners from many different HL backgrounds. In these situations, developing bilingual programmes which support both the L1 and L2 is significantly more challenging, as it is not obvious what the L1 would be in these linguistically diverse situations (the same is true of Africa, as described earlier). Cummins (2005) notes, however, that there are still a variety of pedagogical practices that can be implemented to empower HL students. By attending to cognate relationships between the L1 and L2, providing opportunities for students to use their L1s in some aspects of classroom work, through student-authored dual language books, for example, and by promoting student collaboration within multiple languages, Cummins argues that cross-language transfer can be fostered and monolingual instructional assumptions can be challenged. These types of bilingual instruction strategies are examined and developed more widely in Issa and Hatt (2013), who present a detailed discussion of different pedagogical practices in relation to linguistically diverse pupils.

In summary, international educational policy with respect to HL education varies in the extent to which the HL is developed through formal or informal educational programmes. There is no evidence to suggest that helping to promote strong linguistic and academic language skills within two languages through formal education has negative consequences on developing proficiency of the majority L2 or on academic outcomes. Indeed, Cummins' Linguistic Interdependence and Common Underlying Proficiency Framework models indicate the reverse, that supporting proficiency in Language X can mutually support developing proficiency in Language Y, given appropriate support and motivation. Similarly, developing fluency, literacy, and academic language skills in the HL can have positive influences on the development of the L2. Whatever approach different countries take with respect to the education of their young HL citizens, the consequences of implementing different policies are wide-reaching, not just in relation to the promotion of linguistic proficiency in specific languages, but also in terms of the extent to which they develop empowered bilingual students with feelings of self-worth. Where the implementation of additive bilingual programmes is not feasible, teachers can still nonetheless validate HL learners' home language and culture through specific pedagogical strategies.

Incomplete acquisition?

The discussion in this chapter has so far focused on who HL learners are, what their educational experiences may be around the world, and how different educational policy decisions can impact on both HL proficiency and academic achievement. What has not been discussed is the actual HL linguistic competence of HL learners. As noted above, researchers tend to adopt a proficiency-based categorization of HL learners, hence the HL learners under investigation in most studies will typically have had some level of linguistic competence, at least if only early on in their lives. Actual linguistic competence of HL learners has not been as widely documented as educational policy, partly as a result of the considerable linguistic diversity represented in HL speakers around the world. It is very difficult indeed to adequately track the linguistic HL development of learners when they represent linguistically a highly diverse population. It is nonetheless an important endeavour from many perspectives. Rothman (2009), for example, identifies key areas that need further attention, such as which aspects of HL learners' grammars are likely to be different from monolinguals, and what relative contribution of internal (cognitive) and external (environmental) factors influence the extent of this difference.

Montrul, (2008, 2009, and elsewhere) argues that HL acquisition can be viewed as a case of 'incomplete' acquisition—neither like that of a monolingual who develops full competence in the HL nor of a L2 learner for whom the HL is more akin to a foreign language. She considers incomplete acquisition and L1 attrition as different examples of language loss where incomplete acquisition is characteristic of the mature (adult) linguistic state. This mature linguistic state is incomplete, due to the fact that specific linguistic features (for example, aspects of morphosyntax) do not have the chance to fully develop to age-appropriate standards, as is the case with typical native-speakers of the language who go on to develop full native-like competence. The main difference between L1 attrition and incomplete acquisition is that in the case of L1 attrition, there was some linguistic competence to lose in the first place—learners acquired a particular linguistic property in childhood and then lost it later in life, whereas in the case of incomplete acquisition (which she argues more readily encapsulates the situation for many HL speakers), they never fully learned those features in the first place, since they had limited input and opportunities for use; in this way they are not examples of attrition per se (Montrul, 2008). The problem is not one of capacity—the HL child is more than capable of learning the HL—but given the limitations in the environment they fail to develop complete grammars in their HL. Montrul (2008) presents numerous examples of research which leads to this conclusion from a range of different contexts, examining language attrition in children and adults, as well as L2 learning and bilingualism in children and adults at different stages of development.

One such example is found in Montrul (2009) in investigating knowledge of tense, aspect, and mood in HL speakers of Spanish. In her studies, she recruited native speakers of Spanish and compared them against HL speakers of Spanish on a range of tasks, including proficiency measures, elicited oral production tasks, written morphology recognition tasks, and a sentence conjunction judgement task. Her overall findings revealed group differences on these tasks between the native and HL speakers of Spanish. In particular the latter make more errors than native speakers with grammatical aspect and mood, where mood is more vulnerable than grammatical aspect. Monolingual Spanish-speaking children acquire mood later (by approximately age 13) relative to tense and aspect. Since HL learners receive less input than monolingual speakers, they do not end up developing the entire, complete mood system. Tense and aspect, being acquired earlier, are features that are better developed in the HL learners' grammatical system. Montrul frames her discussion of these results within the 'interfaces theory' described in Tsimpli and Sorace (2006) and Sorace (2011)—the notion that there are grammatical interfaces that act as 'bridges' between different levels of linguistic knowledge (such as morphology, syntax, phonology, etc.). Interfaces where, for example, phonology meets phonetics, or syntax meets morphology, seem to be the most vulnerable and susceptible to erosion, attrition, or 'incomplete' acquisition (c.f. Tsimpli and Sorace, 2006; Sorace and Filiaci, 2006; Sorace, 2011).

In a more recent example, Montrul (2010) compared adult L2 learners of Spanish against adult HL speakers of Spanish on features of Spanish clitics and word order. The specific focus was to investigate whether HL speakers (with low-intermediate proficiency in Spanish) were more competent than L2 learners of Spanish in phonology over morphosyntax, as has been claimed in the literature. Twenty-four adult L2 learners and adult HL speakers of Spanish completed a range of tasks, including oral production, written grammaticality judgement, and speeded comprehension. In these tasks, the HL speakers of Spanish were more native-like than the adult L2 participants, where HL speakers have advantages over adult L2 learners in pronunciation and phonology, as well as some aspects of morphosyntax, which Montrul argues may be attributable to the fact that HL learners first develop knowledge of these features when they are young. However, what is not currently known is whether HL speakers know *more* than their adult L2 counterparts, or whether their knowledge is somehow *different,* for example, possibly represented more implicitly than in adult L2 learners, leading to more native-like performance. Montrul echoes the point made by Rothman (2009) on the importance of identifying the specific features of linguistic knowledge that

HL speakers retain and those that remain incomplete, in order for vulnerable features to be targeted in classrooms.

The general pattern of results from studies like those described above seems quite similar, in that across a range of different studies and HLs, HL competence seems to be most affected at the morphosyntactic interface. Studies investigating HL speakers of Russian (Polinsky, 2008) and Arabic (Benmamoun, Albirini, de Houwer, and Montrul, 2008, see Montrul, 2010b) have each shown specific problems in relation to inflectional morphology, supporting the 'interfaces hypothesis'. As mentioned above, Montrul (2008) has also demonstrated that HL speakers who are simultaneous bilinguals suffer a greater sense of 'incompleteness' in the adult HL grammars than sequential bilinguals, which she argues is likely due to the fact that sequential bilinguals perhaps experience more prolonged exposure to the HL before the majority L2 becomes such a significant influence on the child's developing grammatical competence. Heritage language acquisition, then, seems to fall somewhere between L1 and L2, in that children with an HL are exposed to the language at birth or very early on in their lives through authentic input richly supported by context. As a result, when tested on the HL in adulthood, they tend to perform better on oral tasks, which tap into their phonological processes and competence, and tasks which rely less on metalinguistic or morphosyntactic competence. Interestingly, L2 learners tend to outperform HL speakers on tasks which draw more heavily on metalinguistic and/or morphological knowledge (c.f. Montrul, 2010a).

Pires and Rothman (2009) argue for a refinement of the notion of incomplete acquisition to distinguish between incomplete acquisition of linguistic features present in the linguistic input and available to HL speakers in their childhood, but which were never fully acquired, and 'missing-input competence divergence,' which they argue is the situation in which HL speakers do not acquire certain linguistic features due to a lack of exposure to a particular (often standard) dialect usually present for monolinguals through formal education. In other words, they argue that HL acquisition can be incomplete for (at least) two reasons: either because linguistic features did not fully develop, or because they could never have developed fully, due to a lack of input to the standard dialect. They view HL acquisition as being a context through which research can examine key questions in relation to diachronic linguistic change (the study of how languages change over time). If certain HL speakers are only exposed to the colloquial dialect, and certain features are not present in the colloquial dialect, then incomplete acquisition of those features is directly attributable to the fact they were only ever exposed to that dialect. This argument may appear somewhat obvious—clearly children learn the dialects to which they are exposed. The point here, however, is that the differences between HL and native (monolingual) speakers is attributed to dialectal differences, not due to incomplete acquisition. Pires and Rothman (2009) cite research where Brazilian Portuguese speakers of colloquial dialects do not include inflected infinitives, even though Brazilian Portuguese monolinguals do, argued to be a direct result of the fact that Brazilian Portuguese HL speakers were only ever exposed to a dialect that did not include inflected infinitives (c.f. Rothman, 2007).

Pires and Rothman (2009) elaborated on this idea by comparing HL speakers of European Portuguese with HL speakers of Brazilian Portuguese. This comparison is relevant because all dialects of European Portuguese include inflected infinitives. They argue that if HL speakers of European Portuguese (like monolinguals of European Portuguese, and unlike HL speakers of Brazilian Portuguese) demonstrate full mastery of inflected infinitives, then these group differences could be attributed to exposure to different dialects. This exposure to the input then becomes a more critical variable than just being an HL speaker. To examine this assumption, Pires and Rothman (2009) recruited HL speakers of European Portuguese, born and living in the USA and exposed to European Portuguese from birth to a minimum of age six. Participants were asked to complete a grammaticality judgement task and an interpretation-matching task designed to identify participants' knowledge of inflected infinitives. The results on these measures indicated no significant differences between the HL speakers of European Portuguese in relation to native, monolingual speakers of European Portuguese. Given that previous research had shown that HL speakers of Brazilian Portuguese are different from monolingual speakers of Brazilian Portuguese, Pires and Rothman conclude that this constitutes good evidence for the role of exposure to specific dialects. The HL speakers of European Portuguese were exposed to a dialect that manifests inflected infinitives in the same way as the standard dialect does, whereas the HL speakers of Brazilian Portuguese were exposed to a colloquial dialect (not having received any formal education through the medium of Brazilian Portuguese) and hence did not develop knowledge of these linguistic features. Pires and Rothman (2009) conclude by suggesting that the notion of 'incomplete' acquisition needs to be elaborated to include a greater emphasis on the role of the input to which speakers are exposed, and which could explain differences between HL speakers and monolinguals of the same language. They argue that incomplete acquisition of HL speakers can also be attributable to exposure to different dialects, and not just due to some qualitative distinction between HL and monolingual native grammars.

One of the difficulties with this research as it relates to understanding HL development is that many of the studies described above are focused on adults. Inferences are made about what the adults may or may not have lost, or may or may not have learned in their heritage language. More longitudinal studies are required to investigate HL children and, specifically, to track the development of HL knowledge in children. While we do not yet have anywhere near the number of studies needed, there are a few notable exceptions worth mentioning here. The first is Polinsky (2011), who investigated comprehension of subject and object relative clauses in both child and adult speakers of Russian. The focus of her study was on identifying whether performance on relative clauses in adult HL speakers might be due to either fossilization of their child language (relative clause knowledge in child HL Russian speakers failing to develop completely), or attrition (knowledge which had once developed being lost). In order to investigate this question, she recruited child and adult participants from both HL and monolingual populations. These participants took part in a picture-description task in which participants heard a sentence containing a relative clause and had to identify which picture from a set of pictures matched the sentence they heard (such as 'Where is the cat that is chasing the dog' or 'Where is the dog that the cat is chasing'). There were no differences between the child HL and mono-lingual groups; however, the adult heritage group differed from all the other groups in their comprehension scores and also had lower scores. Polinsky (2011) concludes that from these data there is no evidence for incomplete acquisition, since the child HL speakers were as accurate as the child mono-lingual Russian speakers. She argues that her results are more consistent with the idea that relative clause knowledge in Russian attrites as a result of a lack of consistent input in the HL. Polinsky also argues that these results should not be considered as an overall argument against the idea of incomplete acquisition. Rather, both incomplete acquisition of some features and attri-tion of other features, together with language transfer and other factors could all lead to lower performance in adult HL speakers relative to monolinguals.

Another study which directly investigated child HL speakers is found in Montrul and Sánchez-Walker (2013) who report on a study with child HL speakers, focusing on differential object marking (DOM) (which refers to the overt morphological marking of some direct objects as in *Juan vio a María* [Juan saw Maria] where *María* is preceded by the preposition *a*. DOM does not happen in English. Child and adult HL speakers were tested on two dif-ferent oral production tasks, story retelling and picture description, to determine whether child HL speakers are similar to adult HL speakers, who tend not to manifest DOM in their use of Spanish, relative to monolinguals. Importantly, Montrul and Sánchez-Walker (2013) also controlled for age and the onset of bilingualism, and compared simultaneous and sequential HL learners in an attempt to better determine whether any child–adult differences were due to incomplete acquisition or attrition. Their results indicated that both the child and adult HL speakers showed significant omission of DOM relative to the monolingual native speaker groups of adults and children. There was some slow but observable development in DOM in the bilingual children, suggesting that for this particular feature it does develop as the HL child matures. However, many of the HL children investigated in this study did not reach native-like levels of DOM by young adulthood, a finding more consistent with incomplete acquisition than attrition. These findings contrast with Polinsky (2011), who argued that HL speakers' knowledge of relative clauses attrites. Montrul and Sánchez-Walker (2013) argue that DOM is 'fuzzy', with unclear, semantic and pragmatic constraints, if any, in contrast to relative clauses which conform to less ambiguous linguistic rules. Further-more, DOM in Spanish is not particularly acoustically salient. Neither study, therefore, offers a definitive conclusion with respect to whether inaccuracies and inconsistencies in adult HL grammars are due to incomplete acquisition or attrition. Indeed, it could be a combination of both.

Clearly this is an area demanding further close investigation, and one which requires more longitudinal studies such as Merino's (1983) research, that tracked development of both Spanish and English in HL children in two studies. In her first study, children were investigated from Kindergarten to Grade 4, showing that by Grade 4 there were marked reductions in the children's Spanish skills. In Merino's second study, the same children were tested two years later and again there were significant reductions in the children's growth in Spanish contrasted with continued improvement in English. This study illustrates the importance of the environment in providing sufficient input and opportunities for use with the HL in order to sustain growth and maintain linguistic knowledge.

In general, research has clearly demonstrated that while HL speakers might have incomplete grammars (or grammars which have attrited), they can benefit from instruction, though as Montrul (2010b) argues, the extent to which HL speakers can take advantage of instruction and outperform L2 learners is not yet fully understood. It is therefore as of yet, unclear whether and to what extent instruction can mitigate against the incomplete grammatical competence described above.

If one adopts the proficiency-based definition of HL learners that assumes they had a degree of HL competence in their childhoods, then an important question to ask is what becomes of the HL learners' knowledge of the HL? The results above suggest that in some key aspects, their knowledge of the HL is superior to that of L2 learners, particularly in oral language tasks relying more on phonological knowledge. However, they also show evidence of incomplete grammars or attrition in certain areas, particularly those areas where different levels of linguistic knowledge (for example, morphosyntax) interact (Polinsky, 2011). All of the research reviewed so far has argued for a need for much closer identification of precisely which features of language are susceptible to attrition or not becoming 'complete'. Therefore, more research needs to be done on different HLs around the world. There is also a need for more longitudinal studies that track the development of the HL, to better identify when the developing grammatical competence of the HL learner begins to falter.

The age issue

As we saw earlier, HL learners present an interesting domain from a variety of perspectives, not least of which is in consideration of the critical period hypothesis (CPH). If the CPH is a valid construct, then HL learners should be at a real advantage over older, L2 learners since they are exposed to the HL within the Critical Period. Indeed, the evidence described above would seem to support the CPH at one level, since HL speakers do tend to show superior performance on phonological and oral tasks relative to L2 learners. As indicated in the discussion of the CPH in Chapter 1, despite numerous disagreements in the literature about exactly when the onset and offset of the CPH might be, many researchers concur that if there is such a thing as the CPH, it will be relevant for phonological knowledge. The context of the HL learner seems to support this idea. However, what is also clear from the HL context is that it is not sufficient to be exposed to a language within the critical period and to experience sustained authentic input—for this is what HL learners initially experience, yet, as Montrul (2008) has demonstrated, HL speakers' knowledge of the HL often ends up being incomplete in certain respects.

There are many possible factors responsible for the fact that despite early and sustained exposure in childhood, HL learners fail to acquire complete grammatical competence. The factors in focus in this chapter are the educational policy decisions of the country in which the HL learner is being educated, and identity. In many of the geopolitical regions described above, children either experience no instruction in the HL at all, leading to lack of complete grammatical development, or they experience a transition from education through the medium of the HL to education within the majority L2. Both situations significantly contribute to the fact that HL learners are not given the opportunities to continue developing their language and expanding their linguistic repertoire through academic instruction. In the HL situation, being young when learning the HL is not sufficient.

Educational implications

It is clear from the work of Cummins (2000) and others that one of the best ways of mitigating against the problems described above is through bilingual or indeed multilingual, education, where HL children experience instruction through the HL *and* through the majority language throughout their educational experience. Children who receive formal educational support for their home language can expect to have more positive outcomes on their majority L2 development (c.f. Cummins' *Common Underlying Proficiency* and *Interdependence Framework*). The reality though is that these forms of bilingual education are not always feasible. Countries around the world have very linguistically diverse populations. In the African context, for example, decisions about which of the many possible languages will be either taught or be a medium of instruction are highly complex. Even in countries such as the UK, not always considered as linguistically diverse as Africa, one finds that with the vast number of HLs represented in the home languages of minority language children (currently over 360 different home languages), it would be difficult to choose which of these should be the medium of instruction alongside English if bilingual education were ever to be implemented in the UK. Furthermore, there is a real and concrete problem associated with both funding and professional development. Countries need to invest in bilingual education to develop effective programmes and this investment includes pre- and in-service teacher education and development. Nonetheless, Cummins (2005), Issa and Hatt (2013), and others illustrate how it is possible to promote particular pedagogical strategies that use the children's HL as a resource, not a liability, even in linguistically diverse contexts and classrooms. This enables children to feel that their home language is interesting, valued, and important even within the majority L2 classroom.

Another way in which the HLs of HL speakers throughout the world is supported is through immersion education. Chapter 5 of this volume discusses immersion education in the context of majority language learners (for example, French immersion in Canada). However, there are a number of contexts around the world where immersion education is offered to help children connect with, learn, and maintain their HL. Immersion education or 'medium of instruction' programmes are those in which a significant proportion of the child's school day is spent in the medium of the language to be learned. Academic content is taught through the medium of the target language, with the child receiving language arts education in the majority language as well. The precise ways in which the school day is divided between the target (minority) and majority languages, together with the number of years in which the child can engage in this immersion education varies from programme to programme. Overall, these programmes have been shown to be relatively successful, but as is typical, the success of the programme very much depends on level of support, how much input and how many opportunities for use of the target language the child has, together with the quality of the teaching and materials. Materials development is often a challenge in ethnolinguistically minority languages without strong literate traditions. Examples of these kinds of immersion programmes are found throughout the world. Programmes such as Māori in New Zealand, Hawaiian in Hawaii, Navajo in the USA, Mohawk in Canada, and Sámi language immersion programmes in Scandinavia are just a few examples (García, 2009; May, 2013). Similar programmes are found for regional minority languages such as Irish in Ireland (Harris, 2007; Ó Baoill, 2007; Parsons and Lyddy, 2009), Welsh in Wales (Siân Hodges, 2012) and a range of mother-tongue programmes in the most linguistically diverse country in the world: Papua New Guinea (Malone and Paraide, 2011). These are just a few examples of the indigenous immersion or mother-tongue bilingual education programmes that have been developed throughout the world in an attempt to revitalize and maintain minority languages. As Richards and Burnaby (2008) argue in their discussion of Aboriginal language immersion programmes in Canada, many of these programmes last only for the first few years of the child's education and consequently these children seldom achieve full functional proficiency in the target (heritage) language. Furthermore, as these programmes tend to be developed for members of the indigenous language community only—they are typically not shared by majority language speakers—such immersion programmes still do not adequately resolve the problem of demonstrating the value of these languages overall.

It is a very positive move that governments around the world are investing money in developing these immersion programmes for minority languages. However, it would be even better if more programmes continued throughout primary and on into secondary-level education and if they could be shared by majority language speakers (see discussion on dual immersion programmes in Chapter 5). Despite these challenges, however, indigenous immersion education is a very good start and certainly seems effective at revitalizing and maintaining regional minority languages, particularly when parents, policy makers, and funders all work together.

Conclusions

This chapter has focused on the context of heritage language learners, whose home language is different from the language of the majority community and of formal education. The focus in this chapter has been on the development of their home or heritage language. Categorizing HL learners is seriously problematic, as they are a highly diverse population, one which represents a growing proportion of primary school students in many countries. HL learners have particular profiles—they are learners with a strong familial or ancestral connection to a particular language and culture, one less represented and typically less dominant or prestigious relative to the majority language and culture in the society in which they are living. The ways in which different countries educate HL learners also varies considerably and can have very significant negative and positive consequences on their academic outcomes and identity. HL learners who are fortunate enough to be able to participate in bilingual education programmes which support the development of *both* their home and majority L2 tend to perform the best on academic outcomes and have the highest levels of bilingual proficiency (see Chapter 4). Unfortunately, this is not a reality for the considerable majority of HL learners internationally and as such, they represent populations of students at risk. As Cummins (2000) has argued, those cultures that are marginalized in society are likely to also be marginalized within the school system. A greater focus on the sociopolitical context for many HL learners is needed to rectify this situation.

From a theoretical perspective, heritage language learners are particularly interesting when we examine the 'younger is better' question. HL learners are young, usually exposed to the HL at birth, just as typically developing monolingual children. Yet as Montrul (2008) and others have shown, adult HL speakers tend to have grammars which are not fully developed relative to monolinguals. The HL context therefore, illustrates that younger may be better in certain areas (as evidenced by the fact that adult HL speakers often outperform L2 learners on phonological and oral language tasks), but that it is not sufficient to have been exposed to the language since birth. The extent to which the HL learner will become proficient in two languages is not solely determined by whether they have exposure to the HL within the critical period. Rather, the role of education and the perceived status and experience the HL learners have with the HL through their childhood will have a profound impact on the extent to which the HL learner develops full bilingual proficiency. Instruction can help in the form of bilingual education; but where that is not possible, pedagogical strategies that include the HL child's home language and culture can go some way to improving the situation.

Notes

1 Note that HL learners in the USA from other HL backgrounds (for example, Mandarin) are also able to participate in HL educational programmes, depending on what is available in their community.

2 Here is a personal anecdote to underscore that HL speakers are considered problems rather than assets within many formal education settings. I had the opportunity to sit as a parent governor on the Board of Governors of my son's primary school. Given my research interests, I asked the head teacher (principal) about the number of English as an Additional Language (EAL—minority language) children at the school. The head teacher's reply was that the school was 'very fortunate' in that there were only two children with EAL throughout the entire school (out of a total number of 175 students).

4

Minority language learners

Introduction

Chapter 3 reviewed research on the heritage language (HL/L1) learning of minority language learners. The focus of this chapter is on their majority language (L2) learning. The term 'minority language' learner is used in this chapter (as opposed to heritage language learner) to reflect the focus on their L2 development. Their home or heritage language is a minority language in relation to the majority L2 that is dominant in the society in which they live. As discussed in Chapter 3, minority language learners are usually educated within a linguistic context that does not mirror the linguistic environment in their home. Whereas children typically grow up speaking the same language in the home as that used at school, children from a minority language background can reach school age without having had any consistent or sustained exposure to the majority language (L2). All children have to adjust to the social and cultural challenges involved in starting formal education; minority language learners have to navigate through this monumental change in their lives through the medium of a language with which they might have minimal familiarity or oral proficiency. Even minority language learners with comparatively well developed oral L2 skills are likely not to have the same levels of L2 vocabulary knowledge as their native-speaking peers. Underdeveloped L2 oral proficiency and competence can have consequent problems for both language and literacy development in school and can certainly make adjusting to a new school environment even more of a challenge.

In 1990, the United Nations Department of Economic and Social Affairs (UNDESA) data indicated that there were approximately 156 million migrants worldwide. This number increased to 214 million in 2010 (Castles, 2013). With such unprecedented rates of global migration, the number of children from minority language backgrounds in majority language classrooms is increasing—in settings where they are educated in a language that is not their home language. For example, in the UK, the proportion of primary school children who have English as an Additional Language (EAL) has risen from

8.7 per cent in the year 2000 to 18.1 per cent (nearly a fifth of the primary population) (NALDIC, 2013). The question of how best to support minority language learners' majority (L2) and academic learning in school therefore has global importance. Typically, minority language learners are from families that have immigrated to the majority language culture. However, in relation to the distinction made by de Bot and Gorter (2005) between regional and immigrant minority languages, children from indigenous language backgrounds are also frequently educated through the medium of the dominant (majority) L2 (Simpson and Wigglesworth, 2008). While children from immigrant families characteristically have very positive attitudes towards education and schooling, outcomes from the Program for International Student (PISA) studies launched by the OECD (Organisation for Economic Co-Operation and Development) have illustrated that across many nations participating in PISA, second and first generation children tend to underperform relative to native-speaking peers on different aspects of the curriculum (notably reading and mathematics) (cf., OECD, 2003). To illustrate, Figures 4.1 and 4.2 taken from the 2003 OECD report illustrate the difference in overall performance between native-speaking children and 1st and 2nd generation children from immigrant families.

Findings such as these from the PISA (OECD, 2003) study illustrate the corresponding finding that children from immigrant families are over-represented in remedial support programmes in school (Paradis, Genesee, and Crago, 2011). An illustrative example of the gap between minority language learners and native-speaking children in the PISA studies is discussed in detail within the context of Germany in Marx and Stanat (2012) and Stanat and Christensen (2006). Children from immigrant families in Germany, constituting approximately 21.7 per cent of the students participating in the PISA studies, are at much greater risk of having difficulties in reading than native-speaking children (Marx and Stanat, 2012). This pattern is associated with lower socioeconomic status (SES); immigrants in Germany tend to be disadvantaged in both their social and educational backgrounds, both of which are predictive factors in reading skill (Lesaux, Koda, Siegel, and Shanahan, 2006). Marx and Stanat (2012) argue that it is therefore important to establish appropriate instructional interventions that target key aspects of minority language learners' developing L2 vocabulary and reading skill.

These patterns underscore the importance of understanding how best to support both linguistic and academic development in minority language children. An 'achievement gap' between minority language and majority language children has been well documented in the literature across a range of geopolitical contexts (Mancilla-Martinez and Lesaux, 2011; Genesee, Lindholm-Leary, Saunders, and Christian, 2006). In settings where there is a degree of homogeneity with respect to the L1 of the minority language learners (such as with Spanish-speaking English Language Learners (ELLs) in the USA), it is possible to develop bilingual education programmes to help support both the developing first language (in this case Spanish) and the L2 (English)

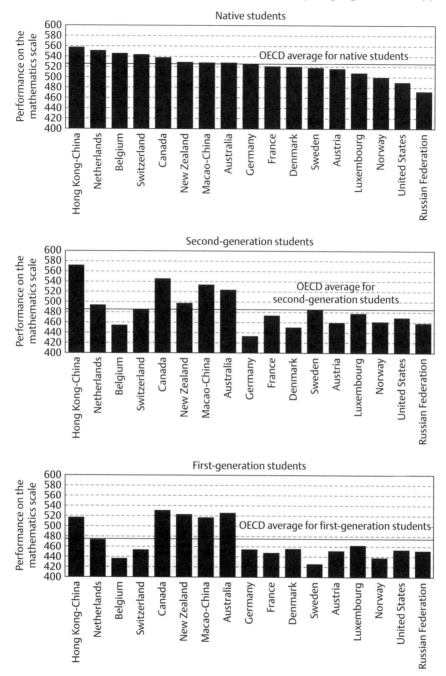

Figure 4.1 Performance on the PISA (2003) Mathematics Scale for native-speaking, 1st, and 2nd generation children from immigrant families

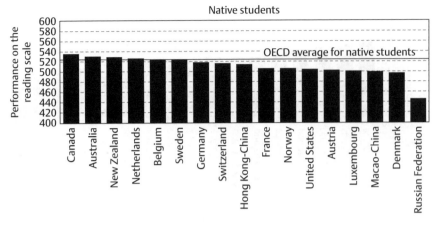

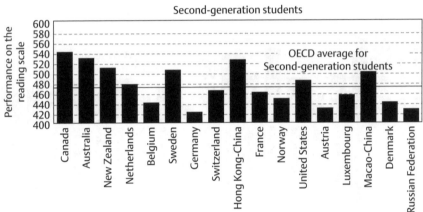

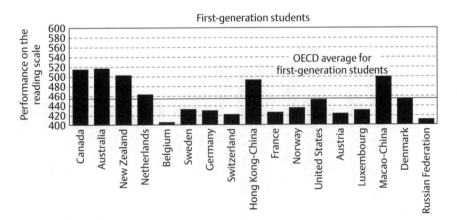

Figure 4.2 Performance on the PISA (2003) Reading Scale for native-speaking, 1st, and 2nd generation children from immigrant families.

(Genesee et al., 2006; Collier and Thomas, 2004; Thomas and Collier, 2002). These dual immersion programmes are discussed in Chapter 5 and will be examined in this chapter in terms of minority language learners' outcomes. Unfortunately, there are relatively few other comparable settings around the world with the same level of homogeneity in the first language community. In the UK, for example, over 360 languages are represented in the home languages of the minority language primary school population (NALDIC, 2011). This heterogeneity can pose significant educational and linguistic challenges to both the children themselves and also to the teachers who are educating them. For example, in highly linguistically diverse contexts such as the Indigenous language communities in Australia, a number of different languages and dialects can be spoken within a single family, making it even more challenging to provide education in a single mother-tongue (Wigglesworth and Billington, forthcoming; Simpson and Wigglesworth, 2008).

The educational needs of minority language children have been widely researched. However, most of the research has been carried out in a context where the majority language is English and where minority language learners are referred to as either ESL (English as a Second Language), ELL (English language learners), or EAL (English as an Additional Language) learners[1]. From a pedagogical point of view, there is a significant body of work (though more is needed) identifying the best ways of supporting the English language and content learning of minority language learners (Wigglesworth and Billington, forthcoming; Bartlett and García, 2011; Andrews, 2009, August and Shanahan, 2008; Genesee et al., 2006). Unfortunately, comparatively less research has been carried out to systematically track the L2 development of minority language learners. The majority of the work available has been carried out in North America (Kohnert, Bates, and Hernandez, 1999). More research focusing on the development of different linguistic features in the L2 across a range of geopolitical contexts is urgently needed. This lack of research is partly due to the relative shortage of international large-scale longitudinal studies tracking different aspects of L2 development in children learning the L2 throughout the school curriculum. Of the large-scale longitudinal studies that exist, the majority have been conducted within the North American context, resulting in a North American bias in the research literature, most of which has examined the oral language and literacy development of minority language learners. Within the oral language literature, the majority of the studies have examined vocabulary development. Consequently, this chapter will focus on the research that speaks to the development of oral language (vocabulary) and literacy skills[2]. Developing strong literacy skills is one of the major goals of primary education. Literacy development is a particular concern for minority language learners, since children begin primary school learning how to read, and need to complete their primary education with reading skills that enable them to 'read to learn' (Chall, 1983). As a result, all children need to have developed sufficiently advanced literacy skills to be able to access the curriculum. Minority language students tend to struggle with reading comprehension. Therefore, it is critical that we have a solid under-standing of the development of language and literacy skills in this population in order to be able to develop appropriate pedagogical support.

Vocabulary development in minority language learners

Oral language proficiency in the L2 is a critical skill needed to access the primary school curriculum, because oral language skills predict later reading comprehension (Roth, Speece, and Cooper, 2002; Cain, Oakhill, and Bryant, 2004). A range of studies conducted within the L1 context have demonstrated that children with weaker oral vocabulary knowledge tend to have reading comprehension problems (Nation, Cocksey, Taylor, and Bishop, 2010; Nation, Clarke, Marshall, and Durand, 2004). Given the importance of oral language to reading comprehension skill, it is vital to understand how oral language develops in children from minority language contexts. However, comparatively less of the available published research investigating language and literacy development in minority language children has been devoted to or even reports the oral language outcomes of these children. For example, Saunders and O'Brien (2006) note that only a small number of studies identi-fied in their systematic North American review focused on oral language development in the L2 (and only a quarter of the number of studies focused on literacy). In the UK the situation is similar—there is little longitudinal research focused on how L2 oral language skills develop in minority language pupils. Indeed, this lack of longitudinal research is a cause for concern in the UK (Andrews, 2009) and elsewhere.

The research that has been carried out on examining oral language skills in minority language learners has tended to focus on the development of vocabu-lary. Vocabulary development is particularly important for a number of reasons. Even in the absence of much grammatical knowledge it is possible to convey essential meaning with knowledge of basic words and extra-linguistic cues (gestures, facial expressions, intonation). Being able to quickly acquire a sufficient amount of vocabulary is therefore important for basic communica-tion. Vocabulary is also important because vocabulary knowledge itself can include a range of linguistic features—not just the obvious semantic referent. For example, knowing a word includes knowledge of phonological, ortho-graphic, morphological, syntactic, semantic, and pragmatic principles along with phrasal expressions and other associated words (collocations) in which the word appears (Nation, 2001). A rich lexical representation in a well developed lexicon includes a range of such variables and has numerous con-nections to other related words in the lexicon. A considerable amount of linguistic knowledge is therefore associated with knowing a word, apart from its meaning alone. In addition vocabulary is of course a critical variable for reading and developing reading comprehension skills.

One of the consistent findings emerging from the research on vocabulary knowledge is that children from minority language backgrounds tend to have lower scores on vocabulary measures than native-speaking peers. For example, Bialystok, Luk, Peets, and Yang (2010) present a meta-analysis of studies conducted by Bialystok and colleagues over a seven-year period using the *Peabody Picture Vocabulary Test* (PPVT; Dunn, 1965) as a receptive vocabulary measure. In the PPVT, children are shown a page with four pictures, and the tester reads out a word that corresponds to one of the four pictures. The child's task is to point to the picture that matches the word the tester has said. Versions of the PPVT (for example, the British Picture Vocabulary Scale (BPVS) in the UK) have been developed in different languages (for example, French, Mandarin, Spanish) for other linguistic and educational contexts around the world and is a widely used test internationally. In Bialystok et al.'s study, PPVT data from a large sample of bilingual children ($n = 966$) were analysed and compared to monolingual children ($n = 772$) across a range of ages (from 3–10 years). In all age groups, the monolinguals had significantly higher scores on the PPVT than the bilinguals. This finding, particularly the fact that even the oldest bilingual children at age 10 were still significantly lower on the PPVT, is a concern, given that it is around this age that children finish primary school and move into secondary school. While the work presented in Bialystok et al. (2010) was not a longitudinal study, it does raise the issue of whether and to what extent minority language children are able to close the gap between themselves and native-speaking children with respect to their receptive vocabulary knowledge.

Other evidence showing that minority language children tend to have lower oral language scores is found in Dockrell, Stuart, and King (2010). In their study, children aged 3–5 were recruited from inner city pre-schools from a borough in London, England. The sample comprised both monolingual, native-speaking English children and minority language learners from a range of different L1 backgrounds, including Amharic, Bengali, Sylheti, and Turkish. Children were tested on a range of English language skills prior to participating in one of two interventions being compared in this study—one which aimed to promote oral language skills, and another which focused more on story reading. The context from which these children were recruited was relatively socioeconomically under-privileged. Consequently, and perhaps not surprisingly, the native-speaking English language children had relatively low scores on the English language assessments (which included measures of verbal comprehension, naming vocabulary, and sentence repetition). However, the minority language children had even lower scores. The minority language learners, recruited from pre-schools did, however, make big improvements on these skills as a result of participating in the interventions being examined in this research; nonetheless, their scores were still lower than those of the native-speaking children (Dockrell et al., 2010).

The vocabulary gap between native and minority language learners can be seen in much older students, even after 10 years of formal education in English. Cameron (2002) compared native English-speaking and children with EAL (minority language learners in the UK) on two different vocabulary measures: Nation's vocabulary levels test (Nation, 1990) and Meara's *Yes/No* task (1992). The children with EAL had lower scores on the vocabulary assessments than the native-speaking children, even with some of the most frequent words on Nation's (1990) levels test. Other studies have demonstrated similar differences in vocabulary between native-speaking and minority language learners. In the USA, Nakamoto, Lindsey, and Manis (2007) carried out a longitudinal study of 261 native Spanish-speaking ELL children from Kindergarten to Grade 6. The children's Spanish and English language skills and their early reading skills were tracked to establish the developmental trajectory on these skills throughout the primary school years. On receptive vocabulary, the minority language students were performing below national percentiles; however they did show significant growth in vocabulary from Grade 1 to Grade 6. Proctor, Carlo, August, and Snow (2005) report a similar finding: their sample of Spanish-speaking Grade 4 ELL children in the USA performed below grade-level norms on a picture vocabulary task (similar to the PPVT). Indeed, research that has investigated oral language and vocabulary skills across a range of contexts (the Netherlands, North America, the UK) has consistently demonstrated that oral language skills in minority language learners lag behind their majority language peers (Aarts and Verhoeven, 1999; Carlisle, Beeman, Davis, and Spharim, 1999; Burgoyne, Whiteley, and Hutchinson, 2011; Hutchinson, Whiteley, Smith, and Connors, 2003; Droop and Verhoeven, 1998, 2003; García, 1991; Geva, 2000; Kieffer and Vukovic, 2013; Lesaux, Crosson, Kieffer, and Pierce, 2010; Mancilla-Martinez, and Lesaux, 2011; Manis, Lindsey, and Bailey, 2004; Nakamoto, Lindsey and, Manis, 2007; Páez, Tabors, and Lopez, 2007; Proctor, Carlo, August, and Snow, 2005; Swanson, Saez, and Gerber, 2006; Verhallen and Schoonen, 1993, 1998; Verhoeven and van Leeuwe, 2012).

These findings are consistent across much of the literature that has investigated vocabulary knowledge in children from minority language backgrounds, illustrating a trend that they tend to score below norm levels on vocabulary. On a more positive note, Proctor et al. (2005) demonstrate a significant degree of diversity in the range of vocabulary scores which, in their view, highlights the varying linguistic skills of these children, despite the fact they were recruited from relatively similar backgrounds. In other words, while it is the case that the overall pattern indicates children from minority language backgrounds have less vocabulary knowledge, it is not necessarily the case for all children. This heterogeneous nature of minority language learners is discussed at length in McKendry (2013) who argues that it is unwise to generalize across all minority language learners given the significant diversity of language skill within this population. Nonetheless, there is an abundance of research that consistently demonstrates weaker vocabulary skills in minority language children relative to their majority language peers.

A particular difficulty with expressive (productive) vocabulary has also been demonstrated in many studies. For example, expressive vocabulary alone seems to be a powerful predictor of reading comprehension (Hutchinson et al., 2003), leading some researchers to argue that '… it is expressive rather than recep-tive vocabulary that is the key to comprehension' (p. 30) for children with EAL in the early years of their primary school education. McKendry's (2013) research also identified a particular role for expressive vocabulary. In her study, 9–10-year-old children with EAL were compared with native-speaking peers matched on nonverbal IQ, on the basis of vocabulary assessments administered in her study, including the TOWK—Test of Word Knowledge (Wiig and Secord, 1992). The children with EAL consistently scored lower than the age and IQ-matched native-speaking children on the expressive subtest of the TOWK. This finding again confirms that vocabu-lary, particularly expressive vocabulary, is a relative weakness in minority language learners.

Academic vocabulary is another important aspect of lexis in this context. Academic vocabulary includes the types of words required for making argu-ments, defending propositions, and synthesizing information (Snow, 2010). The vocabulary in academic language is usually the more infrequent vocabu-lary used in complex grammatical structures (such as the passive voice) and in discourse conventions that are not typical of everyday conversational language. Examples of academic vocabulary items include words such as *amend, boundary, compromise, inference, sustain*. A pedagogical focus on academic vocabulary can prove to be beneficial to all students. Carlo, August, McLaughlin, Snow, Dressler, Lippman, Lively, and White (2004) carried out an intervention study where both ELLs and native-speaking Grade 5 children participated in a 15-week instructional intervention where 12 target words (including academic vocabulary) were taught each week. Pre- and post-intervention assessments were given to the students, measuring differ-ent aspects of their vocabulary and reading comprehension skills. The results of the intervention illustrated that all children benefitted from the intervention—vocabulary and word analysis skills were improved, and gains were made in reading comprehension outcomes. This study demonstrates the benefit of targeted vocabulary instruction, with a particular focus on academic vocabulary. Importantly, there were favourable outcomes on reading comprehension scores, despite the fact that the intervention did not include activities focused on reading comprehension skills per se. This study indicates the importance of the role of vocabulary knowledge in general, but academic vocabulary in particular for reading comprehension (see also Kieffer and DiFelice Box, 2013).

One of the limitations of studies like those described above is that they typi-cally use relatively narrow assessments of vocabulary. For example, they tend to measure either receptive or expressive vocabulary knowledge using stand-ardized, norm-referenced tests, such as the PPVT or the TOWK. There is much more, however, to vocabulary knowledge than can be reflected in a standardized score from an assessment of vocabulary breadth such as the PPVT or TOWK. More research, therefore, is needed to tackle the rich com-plexity that is vocabulary knowledge. Some researchers have begun to examine such aspects of vocabulary knowledge with a view to obtaining a more comprehensive view of the differences and similarities between native- and non-native speaking children. Schwartz and Katzir (2012) for example, report on a longitudinal study in Israel, examining both breadth and depth of vocabulary knowledge in a population of Russian–Hebrew speaking minority language learners (with L1 Russian). Breadth of vocabulary knowledge was assessed by administering the Hebrew version of the PPVT. Depth of knowledge was also assessed, using word description tasks where children were given one of five high-frequency concrete nouns and asked to articulate as many different meanings as possible through a series of prompt questions (*Tell me everything you know about the watermelon*). Both paradigmatic and syntagmatic aspects were analysed in the children's descriptions, as well as antonym knowledge. The children manifested different patterns of performance as a function of the tasks administered. Furthermore, the longitudinal element of the study indicated that while the gap between minority and majority language speakers narrowed over time on expressive vocabulary, gaps remained in measures of depth of vocabulary knowledge (Schwartz and Katzir, 2012). Results such as these underscore the importance of measuring many different aspects of word knowledge and tracking the development of lexical knowledge longitudinally to gain a more comprehensive understanding of lexical development in minority language learners.

Morphological awareness, as an aspect of vocabulary knowledge, has also been investigated in the context of minority language learners. Morphological awareness is knowledge of the morphological structure of words—an understanding that different morphemes play different roles in relation to the overall meaning of the word (for example understanding that adding the derivational morpheme [-er] onto a verb turns a verb into a noun (*teach* (V) + [-er] = *teacher* (N)). A considerable body of research has indicated that morphological awareness is important in developing literacy skills (Kuo and Anderson, 2006). However, until relatively recently, comparatively less research had investigated morphological awareness in minority language learners' developing lexical and literacy skills in the majority L2. Lam, Chen, Geva, Luo, and Li (2012), for example, showed that knowledge of morphological structure predicts variability in both vocabulary and reading assessments. In their study, children of Chinese descent who were growing up in Canada were examined on a range of tasks, including derivational awareness (for example, 'Farm. My uncle is a _____', where the child has to supply the correct derivation from the root word *farm* (*farmer*); and compound awareness (for example, 'Early in the morning, we can see the sun rising. This is called a *sunrise*. At night, we might also see the moon rising. What could we call this?', where the child who has compound awareness would say 'moonrise'). The results of Lam et al. (2012) indicated that even when the children were in Grade 1 (6 years old) their developing knowledge of morphological awareness contributes to both vocabulary and reading. To illustrate, derivational awareness predicted over 27 per cent of unique variance in receptive vocabulary (using the PPVT). Similar patterns of results have been shown in other studies, such as Kieffer and Lesaux (2012), who illustrated the predictive power of morphological awareness in reading skill in three different groups of minority language learners (from Filipino, Spanish, and Vietnamese backgrounds) (see also Kieffer and DiFelice Box, 2013). Additionally, morphological awareness in one language has been shown to influence morphological awareness in the other language in bilingual children, even in typologically distinct language groups (Hayashi and Murphy, 2013).

Other aspects of vocabulary that are just beginning to be researched in the context of minority language learners focus on figurative language such as idioms and collocations. McKendry (2013) investigated idiom comprehension in children with English as an Additional Language (EAL) in the UK, with a view to identifying whether profiles of performance on this measure were similar to those of native-speaking children. McKendry's analysis indicated that while children with EAL use the surrounding context to understand idioms in a similar way to native speakers, they were more affected by whether the idiom was a real idiom or not in the comprehension task used in her study. Furthermore, expressive vocabulary made a stronger contribution to performance on idiom comprehension for children with EAL than for native-speakers. Finally, performance on the idiom comprehension task was a significant predictor of variability on a measure of reading comprehension (McKendry, 2013). Similar findings were documented in Smith's (2013) study investigating multi-word vocabulary knowledge in children with EAL. Multi-word expressions such as 'by the way' can present particular problems for minority language speakers because each of the individual lexical items within the phrase are high frequency, potentially leading the learner to assume they understand the phrase overall. Indeed, previous research with adult L2 learners has shown that L2 learners' reading comprehension performance is affected by the extent of idiomaticity in the text, where the number of multi-word expressions is negatively correlated with scores on reading comprehension (Martinez and Murphy, 2011). Smith identified differential patterns of growth in multi-word expressions across Grades 3, 4, and 5 between minority and majority language learners in the UK. As in McKendry's study, she also found that performance on a multi-word vocabulary task significantly predicted variance on a measure of reading comprehension. These studies illustrate that vocabulary knowledge is a highly complex construct, and this complexity is not currently well represented in the literature on vocabulary development in minority language learners.

As indicated in the Nakamoto et al. (2007) study, there is usually significant growth in vocabulary knowledge in children from minority language backgrounds in the primary school years. Several studies (as those above) have reported strong positive correlations between L2 oral proficiency and L2 vocabulary knowledge. Even on more explicit aspects of vocabulary knowledge, such as the ability to provide definitions to target words, higher proficiency with the L2 is associated with higher scores on measures of vocabulary (Snow, Cancino, Gonzalez, and Sriberg, 1987; Carlisle, Beeman, Davis, and Spharim, 1999). However, while it is important to recognize growth overall, it is also important to consider the rate of development, particularly in relation to children from minority language backgrounds, as there is often an impression that children who come to school speaking little of the target L2 often quickly catch up. Cummins (1984; 2000; 2009) and others (Hakuta, Goto Butler, and Witt, 2000; Paradis, 2007) have indicated that it can take five to seven years for children from minority language backgrounds to gain anything like native-like control over these aspects of oral language vocabulary. Cummins (1984, 2000) draws attention to two very important components in any communicative situation: context and the cognitive demands placed on the interlocutor. He notes that communicative situations can vary depending on how well they are supported by the context, and how cognitively demanding the situation is. For example, a conversation in the school playground about what the child did at the weekend or about the child's favourite sport is considerably less cognitively demanding and more supported by context than having to present the results of a science experiment. Where the communication falls on these two continua will determine to some extent the ease and facility with which any speaker, and non native-speaking interlocutors in particular, can cope with conversational demands. Cummins (2000) notes that children from minority language backgrounds often make relatively rapid gains on those aspects of communication that are both well supported by the context and are relatively cognitively undemanding. Basic conversational skills are acquired by typically developing children by the time they are three or four years old—indeed children from minority language backgrounds can also develop these basic interpersonal communication skills (BICS) relatively quickly and thus appear fluent in the target L2 simply because they are fluent in these aspects. However, on aspects of discourse that are not well supported by context or that make greater cognitive demands (i.e. academic language proficiency) the L2 child can have significant difficulty and can take years to develop these skills and knowledge. It is possible, therefore, for children learning the L2 in these contexts to appear very fluent, but still lack the specific linguistic knowledge that would enable them to achieve their full potential at school. It is also possible for teachers to be unaware of this problem and assume that the child has a more general academic problem as opposed to a specific linguistic one, given their comparatively well developed conversational skills.

In terms of rate of oral language proficiency, the few studies that have adopted either a longitudinal or cross-sectional design have indicated that, as Cummins (2000) argued, it can take several years to develop native-like oral language English proficiency. It is important to consider this timescale seriously, since the notion that children can 'soak up language like a sponge' when they are young is pervasive and yet, developing even basic oral language skills can be a time-consuming endeavour. Other studies examining rate of development have shown that there is a considerable degree of variability within this population, indicating that not all L2 children learning the majority L2 in this context develop at the same rate. This variability seems to stabilize somewhat around Grade 5 at which point near-native-like skills being to emerge (cf. Saunders and O'Brien, 2006). Interestingly, the kind of educational programme in which the child is enrolled does not seem to be an important factor in determining rate of development of oral language skills (see 'Educational implications' below). All L2 children seem to make rapid progress as they begin to learn the L2 in school but make slower progress in achieving upper-proficiency levels in the L2 (Saunders and O'Brien, 2006).

Non-linguistic factors and vocabulary development

Many factors can influence how children from minority language back-grounds learn their L2, and identifying those factors and understanding precisely how they lead to successful or unsuccessful L2 development is an important area of research. Having a better understanding of those factors will enable both researchers and practitioners to provide the best environ-ment possible for these L2 students. Outside the school environment there are a number of different factors that have been identified as being related to L2 learning in minority language children.

Personality factors play a role in L2 oral language development in minority language learners. An early study on this issue by Strong (1984) investigated integrative motivation in Kindergarten students with Spanish as L1 learning English as L2 in the USA. Interestingly, Strong found that those learners of English who progressed the fastest did not show any marked difference in motivation relative to L2 learners who made slower progress. However, those learners who started Kindergarten with higher levels of the L2 (English) did show higher levels of integrative motivation—a greater desire to play with the native English-speaking children. From his study it seems that integrative motivation is a variable for students who arrive at school with an already high degree of L2 proficiency and that integrative motivation is more a result of successful L2 learning rather than its cause. Other work has suggested that children can initially be demotivated or reluctant to learn the L2, but fortu-nately this attitude tends not to persist (Wong-Fillmore, 1979).

Wong-Fillmore (1983) also noted that learner and situational characteris-tics can influence successful L2 development. Learner characteristics are those related to the child's social style—whether they are outgoing and talka-tive, and language learning style—whether they are analytic. Situational characteristics relate more to the classroom environment—whether it is group-oriented or teacher-centred for example. In her study of young L2 learners in California, she reported that approximately 38 per cent could be classified as 'good language learners' and there were two general types of learner: highly social, outgoing learners who sought out opportunities for L2 use and interaction and more quiet, shy, but analytic learners who were very attentive and able to cope academically with class demands. Importantly, in her study learner and situational characteristics interacted with each other. Teacher-centred classes tended to suit the quiet, analytic learners, and group-centred activities seemed more suited to the outgoing learners. The important conclusion to be drawn from work such as this is that there is no single 'one style fits all' formula of classroom and learner variables that leads to rapid success in the L2 for minority language learners.

Other factors that influence L2 development are cultural and social backgrounds. Children from minority language backgrounds can have cultural norms in the home that are absent or not well represented in the classroom. Different cultures might have different sets of expectations regarding appropriate language use or socialization patterns that can conflict with patterns expected in the classroom. These differences can lead children to withdraw and not initiate conversation, and make it difficult for them to engage in classroom activities (Jule, 2010). Family background factors such as socioeconomic status correlate with both linguistic and academic outcomes, not just in minority language pupils. Children from homes with lower SES consistently score lower than children from higher SES homes on a range of linguistic and literacy measures. Socioeconomic status is not the cause, but correlates with other issues, such as levels of maternal education, experience with books in the home, writing at home, getting help from parents or siblings (Walker, Greenwood, Hart, and Carta, 1994). Qualitative and quantitative differences have been observed in the words encountered by high and low SES children (Hart and Risley, 1995), and the research suggests that children who come from low-income backgrounds tend to have lower language abilities than their peers when they begin school (Hoff, 2003; Hoff and Naigles, 2002). Unfortunately, children from minority language backgrounds are typically over-represented in lower SES categories, which can influence their success at learning the L2.

Despite the very strong relationship observed between SES and linguistic performance across a range of studies, maternal education was not found to predict vocabulary development in Chinese- and Spanish-speaking children in a study by Chen, Ramirez, Luo, Geva, and Ku (2012). In their study, maternal education was considered as a proxy for SES, and yet it did not significantly predict vocabulary in either group of minority language learners. Chen et al. suggest this result could be due to the fact that maternal education is mediated by home language use, since in their study, both the Chinese and Hispanic parents used the L1 of the children 98 per cent and 92 per cent of the time in the home, respectively. There was no variation in home language use across the two groups, despite the variability in maternal education.

The importance of out-of-school factors in developing L2 vocabulary is highlighted in Uchikoshi (2006) who investigated vocabulary growth over one academic year for minority language learners who spoke Spanish in the home but were growing up in the USA and attending Kindergarten in English. In particular, she focused on home literacy practices and the effect of watching specific television programmes aimed at developing language and early literacy skills in pre-school children. Uchikoshi found that home literacy practices did indeed influence vocabulary growth, since viewing shows specifically aimed to help develop vocabulary was positively related to vocabulary growth. The number of books in the children's homes, mother's level of education, and SES all contributed to vocabulary development of the minority language learners in this study. Furthermore, Uchikoshi found some interesting effects of gender—the boys in her sample started with higher scores on vocabulary at the beginning of the Kindergarten year and maintained their higher scores over the academic year. Previous research on gender and early language learning is mixed with respect to gender (Uchikoshi, 2006), highlighting the need for more research evaluating the specific contribution of gender on early language and literacy skills.

Summary of vocabulary development

The above discussion has highlighted a number of points concerning the oral language development in children from minority language backgrounds. First, it is an area that requires further investigation, as there are comparatively few longitudinal studies that have charted the developmental trajectory of different linguistic features in this population, though this is slowly changing. The significant majority of studies have been carried out within a North American context, yet minority language learners are found throughout the world. There is a significant need, therefore, for more large-scale longitudinal studies from a range of different countries and languages, tracking the L2 oral language development of minority language learners. There are also pressing concerns regarding assessment. Many of the studies described in this chapter and in the literature more widely have used standardized assessments, typically standardized on a predominantly monolingual population where the reliability and validity statistics of using such measures with minority language learners is perhaps not as applicable. In other cases, studies may have used researcher-developed unstandardized measures. Neither situation is ideal for a confident understanding of children's developing vocabulary knowledge.

The problem of appropriate assessment is particularly challenging, as has been demonstrated in contexts with considerable linguistic diversity. For example, in Australia, the NAPLAN (National Assessment of Proficiency in Language and Numeracy) is a widely used test to assess the English language skills of children. On this multiple-choice test, an incorrect item intended as a distractor item was in fact a legitimate, correct item in the Kriol spoken by the Indigenous children taking the test (Wigglesworth, Simpson, and Loakes, 2011; Wigglesworth and Billington, forthcoming). In other words, the test was biased against indigenous children taking this test. This example illustrates the danger of using tests devised for monolingual populations with children from other linguistic contexts.

Literacy development in minority language learners

A considerable amount of research on the nature of L2 learning in language minority pupils has focused on their literacy development. This focus on literacy (reading specifically) is associated with the consistent findings identified in the PISA studies (cited earlier) that there is an overarching trend for children from minority language backgrounds to under-perform relative to their native-speaking peers on literacy measures[3]. Literacy is of course exceedingly important in education when children begin the primary school years *learning to read* but end the primary school years *reading to learn* (Chall, 1983). If children struggle with 'reading to learn' (i.e. comprehension) then they will have significant consequent difficulties in academic outcomes. The majority of research investigating minority language children's literacy skills has focused on their reading development. It is important to note, however, that there is a pressing need for research focusing on other aspects of children's literacy development, not just their reading and comprehension skills.

Gough and Tunmer (1986), in their 'simple view of reading' have argued that the ability to understand text derives from a combination of word decoding skills and language comprehension skills, including listening comprehension, a notion that has received considerable support in the research literature (Muter, Hulme, Snowling, and Stevenson, 2004; Hatcher and Hulme, 1999; Gough, Hoover, and Peterson, 1996). Nation and Snowling (2004) demonstrated that in addition to listening comprehension, expressive vocabulary knowledge and semantic fluency were identified in their study as being significant predictors of reading comprehension. Good reading accuracy skills are therefore important for developing reading comprehension; indeed research has suggested that this is the case for both monolingual children (Ehrlich, Kurtz-Costes, and Loridant, 1993) and children learning to read in an L2 (Sen and Blatchford, 2001).

If good reading comprehension skills are a reflection of good word decoding skills, vocabulary knowledge, and semantic fluency, the question is whether and to what extent children learning the majority language in a minority language context are able to develop these skills. Factors relevant to word decoding skills include phonological awareness, lexical access, working memory, and syntactic awareness (Jongejan, Verhoeven, and Siegel, 2007). Skilled readers need to be able to decode words rapidly (Bowers, 1993). Failure to develop these skills can result in slower and more effortful processing, with consequent difficulties in reading comprehension (Kame'enui and Simmons, 2001). A number of studies have compared L1 children to minority language learners on measures of word decoding, and these studies consistently demonstrate that the two groups perform equally well on such measures. For example, a meta-analysis of studies carried out in Canada, the Netherlands, the UK, and the USA on learners from a range of L1 backgrounds and educational contexts found no difference between the word reading and phonological skills of native-speaking and minority language children

(Lesaux, Geva, Koda, Siegel, and Shanahan, 2008), despite the fact that these two groups of children tend to differ on measures of oral language. A two-year longitudinal study carried out in the UK, comparing children with EAL against native-speaking English children matched on age, nonverbal IQ, and gender found no differences between these two groups on word reading skills (Hutchinson et al., 2003). Similar results have been found in Burgoyne et al. (2009; 2011). Age-appropriate decoding skills have been reported in Spanish L1 children from low SES backgrounds (Nakamoto et al., 2007) and in Dutch minority language learners (Verhoeven, 1990; 2000) as well as studies in Canada with both high- and low-SES and mixed L1s (Lesaux et al., 2006, 2007; Lipka and Siegel, 2007; Jean and Geva, 2009). There is clear and consistent evidence, therefore, that native speaking and minority language speakers have comparable word decoding skills across a range of settings, and despite typically demonstrating less vocabulary knowledge.

As for the impact on reading comprehension, the research shows an overall trend for minority language learners to have lower scores on reading comprehension measures than their native-speaking peers (Genesee et al., 2006; August and Shanahan, 2008). Several studies in both educational and linguistic contexts have reported significant differences between L1 and L2 children on reading comprehension measures (Burgoyne et al., 2009; 2011; Hutchinson et al., 2003; Nakamoto et al., 2007). In the Hutchinson study, the L2 children were performing on average one year behind the L1 children on the reading comprehension measure, a difference which persisted throughout the two-year course of the study. Nakamoto et al. (2007) followed the reading outcomes for 218 low SES Spanish L1 children from Grades 1–6 learning ESL in a bilingual programme in the USA. They report a decline in the L2 children's reading comprehension scores by around Grade 3 of primary school, and the group were in the bottom quartile for the normative English-speaking sample by Grade 6, even though their basic word reading skills were in the average range throughout the course of the six-year study. The same pattern of findings has been reported in the Netherlands (Verhoeven, 1990; Verhoeven and Vermeer, 2006). Thus, despite a very few exceptions (Lesaux et al., 2006, 2007, Lipka and Siegel, 2007[4]), the overall pattern across different educational and linguistic contexts is that children from minority language backgrounds have comprehension profiles that are more like those of native-speaking children with comprehension difficulties (Nation, 2005; Nation and Snowling, 2004) than typically developing English-speaking children.

Listening development in minority language learners

Listening comprehension skills have also been identified as contributing to reading comprehension skills (Gough and Tunmer, 1986). Children from minority language backgrounds tend to have difficulties with listening comprehension tasks relative to native-speaking children. For example, Hutchinson et al. (2003) reported that minority language learners performed two years below their L1 peers on an oral version of the reading comprehension passage measure (Neale Analysis of Reading Ability (NARA)). In the USA, Proctor et al. (2005) identified that the Grade 4 Spanish children in their study performed at near grade level on passage comprehension but closer to L1 second grade children on an equivalent test of listening comprehension. More recently, McKendry and Murphy (2011) administered a range of listening comprehension measures to children in Years 2, 3, and 4 and found that the L1 children had significantly higher scores on these measures than the L2 children. Similar differences between minority and majority language learners have been shown in Geva and Farnia (2012), who also demonstrate that while listening comprehension was a significant predictor of reading comprehension in the Grade 5 minority language learners in their study, it did not make a unique contribution to comprehension skill in the native-speakers (see also Mancilla-Martinez and Lesaux, 2011).

In summary, while children from minority language backgrounds seem to have comparable word decoding skills as native-speaking children, they tend to demonstrate less well developed listening comprehension skills, less vocabulary knowledge, and as a result have consistent difficulties on reading comprehension measures relative to their native-speaking peers. These findings suggest that minority language children may continue to have areas of difficulty in literacy, specifically related to vocabulary knowledge and comprehension, even after five years of schooling. It should be noted, however, that comparatively little research has investigated writing skills in minority language children and so it is difficult to say at this point the extent to which their writing profiles are different or similar to those of native-speaking children. An emphasis on teaching vocabulary—particularly abstract and academic words—may be helpful for those children identified as having poor comprehension (Carlo et al., 2004). However, further research is needed, particularly in contexts other than North America.

Bilingual education and minority language learners

An important variable not yet addressed in this chapter concerns the type of educational programme in which children from minority language backgrounds are educated. It is not possible within the scope of this discussion to explore all the different types of educational programme available throughout the world (see Baker, 2006; Garcia, 2008). It is worth examining, however, whether there are any significant differences to linguistic and academic outcomes in minority language students depending on educational programme. A number of different bilingual education programmes have been implemented by schools to help support the L2 learning of minority language children. The most researched of these are found in North America, where a number of different types of bilingual programme have been established in which minority language students can participate (Thomas and Collier, 2002; Genesee et al., 2006). These programmes vary in terms of the extent to which they use the students' home language and the majority language (English) for instruction.

Types of bilingual programme

Developmental bilingual programmes are those that aim for full bilingual proficiency and grade-appropriate standards in academic subjects. English (the majority L2) and the home language are used to teach both literacy and academic subjects throughout primary school and sometimes also secondary school (Collier, 1992; Garcia, 1991; Genesee et al., 2006). *Two-way immersion/dual immersion programmes* are those where half of the students in a classroom are native speakers of the majority language (for example, English) while the other half are native speakers of the minority language (for example, Spanish). These programmes aim for full bilingual proficiency in English and the minority language for both the majority and minority language speakers, and both languages are used for literacy and academic learning (Genesee et al., 2006). These are *additive* bilingual programmes in that the focus is to achieve proficiency in both languages, while at the same time achieving appropriate grade-level academic performance. These two-way programmes are discussed in detail in Chapter 5 in the context of immersion education for majority language learners. It is worth examining here the outcomes for minority language learners in two-way immersion education.

There have been numerous large-scale evaluation studies examining both minority and majority language learners' oral language proficiency and literacy development within two-way immersion programmes (Thomas and Collier, 2002; Collier and Thomas, 2004; Genesee et al., 2006; August and Shanahan, 2008). These evaluation studies have been remarkably consistent in demonstrating that minority language learners who participate in two-way immersion programmes achieve similar or higher levels of English relative to their peers who are in English-only education. Furthermore, these students achieve at or above-grade levels in their L1. These findings are consistent across a range of settings such as, for example, with children from low SES backgrounds, since SES Hispanic children participating in dual language immersion show the same patterns reported in the large-scale evaluation studies (Lindholm-Leary and Block, 2010).

Most of the research on minority language learners' L2 development has been carried out in the North American context, with a focus on vocabulary and literacy development. There are some examples, however, from other contexts, though not nearly enough. Duarte (2011) reports on the success of two-way language immersion programmes in Germany. She reports on the outcomes of implementing bilingual education programmes in German–Portuguese, German–Italian, German–Spanish and German–Turkish schools in Hamburg. The discussion earlier in this chapter on the achievement gap noted in Germany in the PISA studies was one of the main motivating factors leading to the development of these programmes, based on the success of the two-way immersion model in the USA. In this review, the findings regarding student outcomes are equally positive, illustrating that minority language learners in two-way immersion in Germany make similar gains in developing both L1 and L2 proficiency and literacy skills at no cost to academic achievement.

Transitional bilingual programmes are those where the L1 of the minority language students is used at the beginning of primary school only, where the idea is to use the L1 as a scaffold to help the child early on in their school experience. By the end of Year 3, the students are switched or *transitioned* to the majority language. The aim here is not for bilingual proficiency, but rather for the minority language students to develop proficiency in the majority language (English in the USA). There is evidence that participation in these transitional programmes can have positive outcomes at the beginning stages of primary school. Tong, Lara-Alecio, Irby, Mathes, and Kwok (2008) compared outcomes from transitional bilingual education with structured English immersion programmes for Kindergarten Spanish–English minority language students in a project which included over 500 children. Receptive vocabulary, listening comprehension, and an overall measure of language proficiency (Woodcock Language Proficiency Battery) were collected over a two-year period. All children (regardless of programme) made consistent gains in English during the two-year project. Importantly, those children who participated in the transitional bilingual programme, where the L1 was also used as a medium of instruction, had similar English language scores as those children who were in the structured English immersion programmes. In other words, using the L1 did not retard the development of English (the L2). However, the long-term goals of these transitional programmes are not additive, but subtractive—the focus is to provide support in the early years of primary school so that the child can transition into English-only education. This problem is highlighted in Menken and Kleyn (2010) who illustrate how minority language learners at secondary level who have received subtractive education still have under-developed English language and literacy skills. In other words, without additive forms of bilingual education, minority language learners are more likely to struggle with L2 language and literacy at secondary school.

A final type of educational environment available for children from minority language contexts is the *L2-only programme*. Structured English immersion programmes are included here as the goal is really simply to offer pedagogical support for English language to children from different L1 backgrounds. There is no provision for the children's home language. These types of programmes do not aim to promote bilingual proficiency, but rather aim to enable the child to develop proficiency in the majority language so as to be able to take full advantage of the academic curriculum. Both transitional and L2-only programmes are in essence a form of subtractive bilingual programme in that the aims of these programmes are not to promote bilingualism. Arguably, most children from minority language backgrounds around the world are in L2-only programmes, where there is no support for the development of the L1. In the UK for example, the language of instruction is English and children do not have a statutory right to be educated in any other language[5]. Children with EAL in the UK are mainstreamed and are not withdrawn from the classroom for any significant period of time to help them with their English development. Schools are often encouraged to draw from the L1 of the pupils where possible, but this process depends largely on teachers' knowledge and school resources. Often EAL coordinators and teachers are not sufficiently familiar with the L1s of the EAL children in their classrooms and there are often too many L1s represented in any one class for this to be feasible. Funding is allocated to support activities that promote the English development of ethnic minority pupils, where the amount of funding is determined in part by the proportion of children with EAL in the schools. In some schools with higher proportions of children with EAL, specific EAL coordinators are available, trained to offer targeted support to these children. However, even in these cases, the children with EAL receive only a small amount of English support outside their normal classroom environment and the L1 is rarely if ever considered as part of the curriculum.

The extent to which minority language learners might be offered the opportunity to receive education through both the L1 and L2 varies internationally. As mentioned earlier, dual language immersion programmes have been discussed in countries such as Germany (Duarte, 2011) and mixed education programmes in China (Tsung and Cruickshank, 2009; Wang, 2011; Ding and Yu, 2013). The language and literacy development of these children occurs within one of the educational contexts described above, so it is important to be aware of the role of the programme as a contributing factor.

One of the main ways in which these programmes differ is with respect to how much time is devoted to developing the L1. In two-way and developmental bilingual programmes, the L1 is used for a significant period of the child's primary school experience, whereas in transitional or L2-only programmes the L1 is either only used for the beginning stages or not at all. One might assume that focusing on the L1 takes time away from learning the L2. If it is easier for younger children to learn an L2 than older children, then one could also argue that it is better for the L2 child to be completely immersed in the L2 (as in L2-only programmes) or be 'weaned' off the L1 (as in transitional programmes). Interestingly, those studies which have systematically evaluated the effectiveness of these different programmes have identified that the L2 linguistic skills of children in developmental and two-way programmes is either the same or better than those of children in transitional or L2-only programmes (Thomas and Collier, 2002; Genesee, et al., 2006; August and Shanahan, 2008). For example, Saunders and O'Brien (2006) in their review of studies describing oral language development in minority language children, report that rates of L2 oral language development seem to be consistent regardless of measures used, samples recruited, type of bilingual programme, or the L1 of the participants. Therefore, bilingual educational programmes which focus on supporting and developing L1 skills not only fail to pose a risk to the developing L2 of minority language children but can facilitate their L2 development.

The age issue

Many issues described in this chapter reflect the 'younger is better' attitude towards L2 learning in children. These are most salient with respect to the comparative ease with which minority language learners tend to develop some aspects of oral language—those that are supported by context and are cognitively undemanding (Cummins, 2000). For these aspects of communication, it does indeed seem that language learning is easy for young learners. However, even though children from minority language contexts are exposed to the L2 within the so-called critical period, they develop knowledge of different aspects of the L2 at differential rates. Whereas it may take only a year or two to develop Cummins' 'basic interpersonal communicative skills' it can take up to seven years or more to develop appropriate academic language in young minority language learners. Additionally, the research described in this chapter illustrates how even with formal education in the L2, and living in a community where the L2 is the majority language, minority language learners still lag behind native-speaking children in some key areas of vocabulary. It is therefore simplistic to suggest that learning an L2 for primary school-aged children is either easy or rapid.

Educational implications

Educational provision for minority language learners reflects an interaction between the amount of exposure to the L2 and the age at which the child receives and experiences this exposure (Murphy, 2010). Traditional L2-only programmes exemplify the so-called ideal of 'younger is better' by opting for the minority language student to have complete instruction in the majority language, stemming from the belief that maximal exposure to the L2 from the moment formal education begins in Kindergarten, for example, yields the best outcomes. At the other end of the continuum is the 90/10 two-way immersion programme (see Chapter 5) where the minority language learner might spend as much as 90 per cent of the school day in the L1. The evidence is compelling in terms of favouring the two-way bilingual programmes over the transitional or L2-only models.

   In terms of educational programmes, one might have assumed that one which focuses exclusively on developing skills in the L2 and maximizes the amount of time in the L2 from the earliest ages would lead to the best L2 skills. This does not seem to be the case. Rather, additive bilingual programmes, in aiming for proficiency in both the L1 and the L2, seem to lead to superior L2 skills (Genesee et al., 2006). The message from this research is that support for the L1 and in particular for literacy skills in the L1 is advantageous to developing L2 skills. This finding raises interesting questions for the 'younger is better' argument since L2-only programmes feed the child with a steady L2 diet from the youngest ages, yet do not seem to be the most effective at L2 development.

However, bilingual education per se is not sufficient to guarantee successful biliteracy outcomes for minority language learners. Minority language learners need to have sufficient access to print in the L1 and L2, together with literacy engagement in the L1, as part of a bilingual and biliteracy programme (Cummins, 2012). Cummins argues that negative attitudes towards the immigrant minority groups in different contexts can reflect power relations in the wider society—where the L1 of putative 'low status' communities is not included in a meaningful or effective way in the classroom. He argues that teachers need to 'expand the pedagogical space' (p. 1987) to include the L1 as a resource to support communication. Even in contexts where there is significant linguistic diversity and no easily identifiable L1 with which to develop bilingual education (as in the UK) there many bilingual pedagogical practices that teachers can implement to illustrate to minority language students that their L1 is valued (Cummins, 1996; Issa and Hatt, 2013).

Conclusions

A number of notable major themes emerge from the issues discussed in this chapter:

1 First, minority language learners can appear to be quite fluent relatively rapidly. Conversational skills required for cognitively undemanding and context-embedded communication can develop quite quickly (Cummins, 2000). However, with some oral language skills it can take up to seven years for the minority language learner to appear native-like. Seven years is a long time in the life of a child and certainly underscores how L2 learning for children, even in this context with regular, significant, and sustained authentic input is definitely not 'easy'—they do not soak up language like a sponge.

2 Minority language students seem to make excellent progress at single word reading and phonological skills and can relatively quickly match or sometimes exceed the performance of their L1 peers. Despite this skill at single word reading, however, an overwhelming pattern of having less well developed listening and reading comprehension skills has emerged in research from North America and Europe. Indeed, the research has shown that even when the student has finished primary school and is moving to secondary school—a time when comprehension skills are even more critical for academic success—they are behind in both vocabulary and comprehension relative to their native-speaking peers. Very few studies have investigated this population through into the secondary school context, so it is difficult at this time to identify the point at which minority language learners can 'catch up' with the native-speaking moving target, or indeed if they ever do.

3 Another issue is language dominance. Given that minority language children are living in the majority language culture, as they grasp the L2, they typically switch their language dominance to the L2 (see the discussion on the 'language shift' in Chapter 3). In other words, whereas they start school dominant in their home language, during the course of their schooling and L2 development they are likely to become dominant in the L2, and unfortunately in many cases lose some of their L1 skills. Kohnert, Bates, and Hernandez (1999) examined the transitional phase between descending L1 skills and ascending L2 abilities in Spanish L1–English L2 children and adolescents of Mexican–American descent in California. Specifically, they examined the speed and accuracy with which children recognized and named words in both Spanish and English at different ages (5–16 years old). They found that productive word-processing skills were stronger in Spanish until they had had about 10 years' experience with English, when dominance shifted from Spanish to English. Ten years is quite a long time! This finding again underscores the fact that L2 learning takes time and effort, even in a context such as this, where the target L2 is literally all around.

Children from minority language backgrounds could be argued to be well supported in their L2 learning and indeed they make rapid gains and many go on to become dominant and fluent in the L2. Interestingly, many children from minority language backgrounds begin life as bilingual first language (simultaneous bilingual) children. As discussed in Chapter 2, there are well documented cognitive advantages to becoming bilingual in areas such as metalinguistic awareness and certain selective attention abilities in specific contexts (see Bialystok, 2001). Certainly compared to children learning an L2 in a foreign language (FL) context (see Chapter 6) minority language learners make significant progress and indeed in many aspects of their L2, even in primary school, they achieve native-like skills. They start L2 learning young (around five years old, depending on the country) and they live in communities where the majority language is ubiquitous. Furthermore, the L2 is the language of many of their peers with whom they may wish to identify socially. Not surprisingly they do indeed learn a lot of L2 relatively quickly and in some respects are indistinguishable from native-speaking children. However, on many other important measures such as vocabulary, reading, and listening comprehension, minority language children typically score below their age-matched peers, against whom their academic outcomes are compared at school.

A considerable body of research has been carried out across a range of contexts, investigating aspects of language and literacy development in minority language learners. However, there is an urgent need for much more, as the research discussed in this chapter focuses relatively narrowly on vocabulary, reading, and listening. Considerably less research has been carried out on other aspects of minority language learners' L2 development (for example morphosyntactic, grammatical, pragmatic areas). Furthermore, there is a marked distinction between the amount of research focused on minority language learners' reading skills relative to their writing skills. Additionally, while the work on vocabulary and reading is largely consistent within a range of countries (Canada, the Netherlands, UK, USA), these are just a handful of contexts in which minority language learners are educated. Research in China (Wang, 2011) and Australia (Wigglesworth and Billington, forthcoming) has illustrated some of the challenges of minority language programmes in different parts of the world. However, these are just a handful of studies and even they do not focus specifically on different aspects of the child's L1 or L2 and how linguistic features and literacy skills develop.

It is important to stress that despite the significant gains minority language learners make in their L2 learning, by the end of primary school they can still score below their native-speaking peers on measures of vocabulary and reading comprehension. The notion that L2 learning in childhood is 'easy' and 'rapid' is clearly not appropriate, because even in this context, where children have a considerable amount of authentic exposure to the L2, it takes years for them to develop their L2 knowledge. This pattern suggests that there are a number of ways in which we can help support their L2 development and indeed some studies (for example, Carlo et al., 2004) have illustrated how successful targeted pedagogical support can be.

Notes

1 ESL and/or ELL are the terms used mostly in North America while in the UK children from minority language contexts are referred to as EAL.
2 Note that there is detailed discussion of international educational policy regarding minority language (or heritage language) learners in Chapter 3. Hence this will not be addressed in this chapter.
3 It is worth pointing out here that while there is a good argument for not being overly concerned with how L2 learners compare with native speakers in particular research domains (Cook, 1991), it is important to make that comparison here, since minority language learners are educated alongside their native-speaking peers, and their academic performance is compared regardless of language status.
4 In these studies the reading comprehension measure that was used was different (Stanford Diagnostic Reading Test) from those used in other studies (for example, the Neale Analysis of Reading Ability) thus making comparison across studies problematic.
5 There are fee-paying independent schools where the child can be educated in another language, both in the UK and in other countries around the world.

5
Majority language learners: immersion education

Introduction

Majority language learners are in focus in this chapter. Specifically, the discussion here concentrates on immersion programmes that are available for majority language learners, the nature and prevalence of these programmes, outcomes that relate to the L2 learning that arises from participation in these programmes, and the academic achievement of these students. It is a very different context from that discussed in Chapters 3 and 4 where the focus was on minority language learners.

Unlike minority language learners, immersion education for majority language speakers is an additive form of bilingual education where both pupils' L1 and L2 language and literacy skills are developed. The bilingual education models discussed here include those developed exclusively either for majority language learners (one-way immersion programmes) or those that majority language learners participate in alongside minority language learners (such as dual-language or two-way immersion)[1]. A more detailed comparison of how majority language learners benefit from bilingual education relative to minority language learners is addressed in Chapter 7.

The idea of education through the medium of two different languages is not new. Indeed, over two thousand years ago as part of the Roman Empire's quest for world domination, bilingual education was extended to many different cultures. At that time upper-class families in Rome educated their children in Greek as well as Latin to ensure that their offspring would develop a well rounded, multilingual and multicultural education in order for them to maximize their potential and get ahead in the world (c.f. Coyle, Hood, and Marsh, 2010). How little we have changed over two thousand years! As civilizations developed and the different regions of the world became more interdependent, we now live in a global village where growing internationalization of business and commerce, migration of families, and advances in telecommunication have all made it even more relevant and indeed necessary to be bi- (or in many settings) multilingual (Genesee, 2008). Arguably it is important for all citizens of this global village to develop knowledge of more than one language, particularly in light of the cognitive advantages of becoming bilingual discussed in Chapter 2. In many geopolitical contexts around the world, children grow up in highly linguistically diverse environments (for example, in most countries in Africa, Asia, and many communities in Europe and elsewhere) and as a result they are likely to develop at least some knowledge (even if not literacy-based) of more than one language. However, despite the prevalence of multilingualism, evidenced in part by the increasing difficulty in finding true monolinguals with little to no experience of or exposure to another language, there are still contexts in which it is possible to be educated without having had sufficient targeted L2 exposure to enable children to develop into what Cook (1999) would refer to as 'L2 users' who are capable of using the L2 even if their proficiency in both languages is not balanced. In these contexts, bilingual education programmes through formal education have enormous potential to fill a gap in relatively linguistically homogenous societies, by educating children through the medium of another language and consequently helping them to develop knowledge of another language (i.e. to develop both implicit and explicit knowledge of the language). In contexts where one language is predominant, as in North America, schools have tremendous power to encourage and develop plurilingual citizens, since children spend a considerable amount of time in formal education (Baker, 2006). The focus of this chapter, then, is to provide a selective global snapshot of immersion education available to majority language speakers and to consider the extent to which participation in these programmes meets the goal of developing bilingual proficiency.

Given that majority language speakers living in less linguistically diverse contexts have a particular need for bilingual education, it is perhaps not surprising that in many significant ways, the birth of bilingual education took place in North America. Fortune and Tedick (2008) describe two so-called 'grass roots' efforts in language education that started what we consider bilingual education today. The first example they discuss is the development of French immersion in Québec, Canada (Lambert and Tucker, 1972). A common theme that has been emerging throughout this volume is the role of parents in developing bilingualism in their children—and the role of the parents was no different in the development of French immersion in Canada. English-speaking parents in French-speaking Canada became motivated to discover more effective methods of developing their English-speaking children's French and, importantly, biliteracy in French and English. This led to Lambert and Tucker's (1972) famous French immersion model developed in the mid-1960s as an alternative to the traditional 'core' French language programme English speaking children typically received up to that point. Early total French immersion offered all curricular content through the child's L2 (French) and French was also the language in which early literacy skills were developed. At Grades 3 or 4 (8–9 years of age), programmes began to introduce instruction in some academic content through English and by about Grades 5 and/or 6, children aged 10–11 years were experiencing approximately 50 per cent of the school day in English and the remaining half in French.

The second 'grass roots' programme described by Fortune and Tedick (2008) also originated in North America, but this time in Florida—the Miami-Dade County's (two-way) bilingual programme, bringing English-speaking Spanish learners and Spanish-speaking English learners together in the same classroom. As with French immersion, this programme was developed as a result of parental concern; in this case, the parents were Cuban exiles working in Florida who wanted to ensure their children developed the skills they needed in English (the majority language), yet at the same time to develop linguistic and literacy competence in Spanish. A major difference between these two revolutionary educational programmes is who the participating children were. The French immersion programme was developed for English-speaking children to develop knowledge of French and English, hence the French immersion class was homogenous in the linguistic background of the participating children. The Miami-Dade county programme, however, was the first of what has become known as a 'two-way' (or dual language) bilingual education programme meant to include *both* English and Spanish native-speaking children. As will become clear below, these two vanguard programmes became enormously successful and quite literally spread throughout the world.

One of the features of bilingual education programmes for majority language learners relates to the notion of *additive* vs. *subtractive* bilingualism. Additive bilingualism refers to the development of oral language proficiency and literacy in *both* of the student's languages through participation in bilingual education. Subtractive environments are those in which the programme does not aim to develop bilingual and biliteracy skills but, rather, to scaffold the child to become more proficient in the dominant, majority L2[2] (Baker, 2006). The programmes discussed in this chapter are additive, having been established with the aim of developing bilingual proficiency in at least two languages, together with good literacy skills in both, at no cost to academic achievement.

This chapter begins with a discussion of the key characteristics and major empirical findings relevant to the effectiveness of immersion and two-way (dual) bilingual education (immersion) programmes. Content and Language Integrated Learning (CLIL) programmes are then discussed, as they share many characteristics with immersion programmes and were developed, like immersion education, for majority language learners. A global snapshot of the way in which these programmes have been developed and extended internationally is then provided. Finally, the chapter ends with a discussion of what the immersion education context can reveal with respect to the issue of age and L2 learning by comparing the outcomes of early vs. late immersion programmes and providing a summary of educational implications.

Immersion programmes

The French immersion programme initially developed by Lambert and Tucker (1972) for English-speaking children in Québec, Canada, has been adapted and extended to a number of different contexts around the world. There are different reasons why different educational authorities might wish to develop and/or implement an immersion education programme. As Genesee (2004) points out, these include promotion of:

1   national policies on bilingualism (French immersion in Canada)
2   national languages in contexts where there is one official language, but citizens speak a range of other first languages (i.e. Estonian immersion for Russian-speaking students in Estonia)
3   important regional and/or world languages (for example, English immersion in Japan)
4   proficiency in heritage languages (as in Welsh immersion in Wales, UK)
5   indigenous languages at risk (for example, Cherokee immersion in North America)
6   foreign language learning (such as French immersion in the USA).

Key characteristics of immersion education, as developed in the original Lambert and Tucker (1972) model and in current instantiations are presented in Table 5.1.

Key characteristics of immersion education

- Immersion language (L2) is used as the medium of instruction for academic subjects for at least 50% of the school day, usually to Grades 5–6, sometimes up to secondary school.
- Additive bilingual and biliteracy development is promoted through sustained/enriched instruction in the two languages.
- Teachers fully proficient in both languages are employed for instruction.
- Teachers teach separately for each language for sustained periods of time.
- Immersion programmes are voluntary and are offered through the public school system.
- Curriculum is content-driven but language-attentive.
- Language, culture, and content are integrated.
- Students are cognitively and linguistically challenged through pedagogical tasks.
- The instructional approach reflects developmentally and linguistically appropriate support, with frequent use of the L2.

Table 5.1   Characteristics of immersion education

In classifying different types of immersion programmes, Genesee (2004, 2008) explains the difference between early, delayed, and late instantiations of immersion at primary level. Early immersion programmes typically begin either in Kindergarten or Grade 1, whereas delayed immersion introduces the L2 as the medium for academic instruction in the middle of the primary school years. Late immersion programmes are those that either introduce the L2 near the end

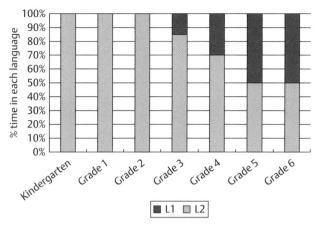

Figure 5.1 Early immersion programmes (from Paradis, Genesee, and Crago 2011)

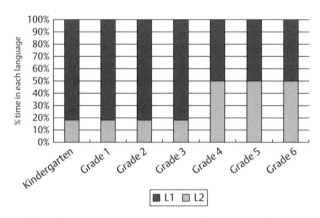

Figure 5.2 Delayed immersion programmes (from Paradis, Genesee, and Crago 2011)

of primary, or even in secondary education. Figures 5.1– 5.3 graphically represent the distribution of L1 and L2 in these different types of models.

The key features of immersion education described in Table 5.1 require that students achieve appropriate (standard) level academic outcomes together with linguistic competence and literacy skills in the L1 and L2, appropriate for the students' age and grade level. Genesee (1987 and elsewhere; see also Paradis, Genesee, and Crago, 2011 for a review) discusses the research evidence that addresses the English (L1) language and academic outcomes of pupils who have participated in French immersion programmes in Canada, together with the evidence describing their L2 French development.

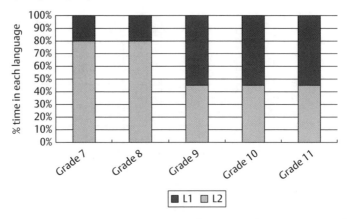

Figure 5.3 Late immersion programmes (from Paradis, Genesee, and Crago 2011)

Key questions addressed by research have been the effect on native language development of participating in immersion programmes and whether academic achievement suffers as a consequence of participation. Research has investigated these questions by comparing the performance of students in immersion programmes against those in traditional educational models and also by comparing immersion students' performance in standardized language and academic tests to that of test norms. For example, in French immersion programmes, students would be compared against English monolingual and French monolingual students with respect to their English and French language outcomes, respectively. In addition, studies have compared children participating in early immersion relative to later immersion programmes, to try and tease apart the relative effects of age and exposure on outcomes in immersion programmes.

Genesee (1987, 2004, 2008, and elsewhere) reports that children participating in immersion programmes achieve higher levels of functional L2 proficiency than children who receive traditional forms of L2 instruction. This overall conclusion is valid across a variety of educational settings and across the whole range of linguistic skills (speaking, listening, reading, and writing). At the same time, their L1 development is comparable to that of students who are not in immersion programmes—in other words, participating in immersion in no way retards the development of these children's oral language and literacy in their L1. The only caveat to these findings is that there can sometimes be a lag in the rate of development of some L1 literacy skills (for example, spelling) among students in early immersion programmes (see Figure 5.1) where the majority of their time at school is in the L2 until Grade 3. However, this lag is typically resolved by the end of Grade 3, when children receive instruction in English language arts (i.e. after one year's instruction in the L1). Therefore there is no evidence to suggest that education through immersion impedes the development of the child's L1 oral language or literacy skills. In terms of academic achievement in curricular subjects such as mathematics, science, and social studies, research again has shown that children in immersion programmes achieve the same grade-appropriate levels of achievement as pupils in traditional educational programmes (Genesee, 2004; 2008). The one proviso with these findings is that assessment of children in immersion education should ideally be carried out in the language of instruction. If children learn history in English but are tested about history in French, they are more likely to score lower than children not participating in immersion. If the language of instruction is matched with the language of assessment, however, children in immersion are likely to be on a par with the non-immersion children on these academic subjects. The overall success of the French immersion experiment in Canada is why it has become such an important and influential educational movement throughout the world, since research clearly shows advantages in L2 development and parity with traditional methods on L1 and academic outcomes (Genesee, 1987, 2004, 2008; Paradis, Genesee, and Crago, 2011; Genesee and Lindholm-Leary, 2013).

Pedagogical issues

Although there is some direct language instruction in immersion, it was its focus on the use of the target L2 for communicative (functional) purposes that distinguished it from other educational programmes. Nonetheless, there is a growing body of research pushing the boundary between L2 for communication only and instructed L2 within the immersion context. While the research described above unambiguously demonstrates that immersion students have higher levels of functional L2 proficiency than children in traditional L2 instructional programmes, it is also the case that researchers have noted a lack of grammatical accuracy on certain key features. For example, Harley and Swain (1984) were among the first researchers to note that English-speaking children participating in French immersion had problems with verb forms despite many years of participating in French immersion programmes. Other areas of difficulty are (lack of) lexical diversity and non-idiomatic usage. In a related vein, Lyster (1994) found that children in French immersion programmes benefited from pedagogy that drew the learners' attention to form and function in those aspects of the target language that they have difficulty acquiring (for example, the differential use of *tu* and *vous* in French). In other words, being taught academic content through French, in the absence of a systematic focus on the formal properties of French was not sufficient to ensure grammatical accuracy in the target language, at least with respect to certain linguistic features. Consequently, researchers began to identify ways in which pedagogy in immersion settings might be adapted to promote greater grammatical accuracy. Lyster reviews a number of studies which investigate the benefits of a focus-on-form approach in immersion pedagogy with a view to identifying effective instructional practices that maintain the advantage of a functional approach to language teaching, yet at the same time promote greater grammatical accuracy. The studies reviewed in Lyster (2004, 2007) focus on a range of French grammatical features, such as perfect and imperfect tenses, conditional mood, and second person pronouns. From his review, Lyster demonstrates that a focus on form in immersion settings can lead to short-term improvements, but can also lead to longer-term improvements in the mastery of certain linguistic features if carried out through activities that raise learners' awareness of rule-based representations. He argues that instructional activities need to provide an appropriate balance which, on the one hand, create opportunities for learners to notice key linguistic features and be aware of linguistic forms (c.f. Schmidt's 1990 'Noticing' hypothesis) and, on the other hand, provide extended opportunities to practise those features. Lyster's (2007) 'counterbalanced' approach aims to shift learners' attention towards linguistic form as a way of moving beyond their interlanguage forms and developing greater grammatical production accuracy.

Lyster, Collins, and Ballinger (2009) focus on the teacher–student interaction in early French immersion classrooms and, in particular, on cross-linguistic comparisons between French and English. More specifically, after the first year of observations in a study of four different French immersion classrooms, Lyster and colleagues noted that the two languages of these immersion pupils were kept separate—not allowing for any cross-linguistic comparisons. Nor were children encouraged to collaborate and support each other linguistically. As a result of these initial observations, Lyster et al. (2009) developed an experimental literacy-based unit of instruction aimed at promoting cross-linguistic awareness. The premise underlying this unit was that by promoting students' cross-linguistic awareness of French and English, students would acquire better developed linguistic representations in both L1 and L2. Lyster et al. also noted a very high level of motivation and interest among the students, when being read stories in both English and French, and very positive cross-curricular collaboration on the part of the teachers. However, this study did not examine whether there were significant improvements on key linguistic features as noted in Lyster (2002, 2004). This experimental intervention is important because it illustrates that there are a number of ways to draw learners' attention to linguistic form within immersion settings that do not detract from the communicative intent of the pedagogical activity.

The same premise underpinned Ballinger's (2013) study[3] in which children and teachers in French immersion programmes participated in a seven-week intervention for English and French dominant students, aimed at developing collaborative language learning strategies. As with Lyster et al. (2009), the children participated in a biliteracy project where the teachers read both English and French versions of different picture books. Students participated in collaborative literacy tasks following each reading in English-dominant and French-dominant dyads. The children also received instruction aimed at developing reciprocal language learning strategies, so that they could tap into their partner's expertise in the other language and, thus acquire greater language awareness and enhance their L2 production skills. Ballinger (2013) notes that working in both languages helped students develop deeper understanding of both content and language while at the same time promoting their cross-linguistic awareness. Her study illustrates the advantages of getting teachers to encourage students to tap into both languages during instructional tasks, an approach that has not usually been part of French immersion programmes—the two languages are typically kept separate. Lyster et al. (2009) and Ballinger (2013) illustrate the advantage of using both languages to develop and enhance linguistic awareness in order to advance learners' grammatical competence. This research is consistent with other contemporary ideas about the use of the L1 in an L2 foreign language classroom. Macaro (2009; see also Tian and Macaro, 2012; Macaro and Lee, 2012) advocates the judicious use of the L1 within L2 foreign language vocabulary pedagogy. Macaro and colleagues argue that this L1 use acts as a lexical focus-on-form which can have positive effects on linguistic development. As with these studies, Lyster et al. (2009) and Ballinger (2013) indicate that there may be very good reasons to incorporate pedagogy which draws from both languages in immersion contexts to promote grammatical accuracy and linguistic awareness. This pedagogical approach to use both languages, however, should be strategic and ensure that it truly enhances the effectiveness of the instruction, rather than simply translating difficult-to-learn material.

A similar approach to learning academic content within French immersion settings is described in Turnbull, Cormier, and Bourque (2011). In their study, Grade 7 French immersion students learning science were assigned to two groups—one that received the standard curriculum, and an experimental group that focused on questions of science following Lyster's (Lyster, 2007; Lyster and Mori, 2008) counterbalanced approach. In Turnbull et al.'s (2011) intervention study, some of the students studying the inner workings of volcanoes did so through an approach that involved negotiation of meaning in peer-to-peer collaborative group tasks, as well as shared reading and writing activities which also included the use of English (their L1) (see Tian and Macaro, 2012). Children's oral and written productions, and assessment of scientific knowledge (about volcanoes and seismic activity) were assessed pre- and post-intervention and revealed that the experimental group who had learned about these aspects of science through a literacy-based 'counterbalanced' (c.f. Lyster, 2007) approach made more progress both in French (the L2) and in science than the traditionally-taught comparison group. More specifically, the experimental group wrote longer texts in French with fewer errors, and seemed to demonstrate more knowledge of earthquakes and seismic activity than the comparison group. Furthermore, they found a positive relationship between use of English code-switching and the complexity of their utterances, their performance in written French, and their overall science knowledge. Therefore, it would appear that immersion students' L1 can act as an additional resource to scaffold their academic learning and bolster their

L2 learning. A further example of the effective use of the L1 in immersion contexts in relation to academic learning is found in Gearon (2011), who analysed the L1–L2 code-switched discourse of French immersion students in Australia studying medieval history. In Gearon's analysis, students' use of the L1 enabled negotiation of meaning and attention to linguistic forms—particularly vocabulary use—to allow them to complete the history-focused task (building a model medieval village).

These studies (and others like them), illustrate that immersion programmes with their significant levels of authentic input and focus on meaning may not be optimal in and of themselves to develop full grammatical (productive) mastery of some key linguistic features. However, introducing pedagogical techniques that draw learners' attention to linguistic form and offer opportunities for negotiation of meaning through collaborative task-based learning can be highly effective and lead to both short- and longer-term improvements in grammatical accuracy (see also Swain and Lapkin, 1998; 2000).

Cognitive effects of immersion

The discussion thus far has illustrated that majority language children participating in L2 immersion programmes can develop higher levels of functional L2 proficiency than students who receive traditional forms of L2 instruction, along with grade-appropriate levels of L1 language and academic achievement. These programmes promote bilingualism and, as was demonstrated in Chapter 2, there are a number of cognitive advantages in being bilingual. If immersion programmes promote bilingualism, then do children who participate in immersion programmes have any further cognitive advantages relative to children in non-immersion settings? In short, yes they do, both in terms of developing metalinguistic awareness (Hermanto, Moreno, and Bialystok, 2012) and in some aspects of executive function (Nicolay and Poncelet, 2013).

In Hermanto et al. (2012), 83 Grades 2 and 5 students participating in French immersion were assessed on a range of measures in both French and English, including receptive vocabulary and a sentence judgment task which required students to identify whether sentences were grammatically correct and which were in some cases semantically anomalous (for example, 'Where does a horse like to sail?'). Students were also assessed on a verbal fluency task where they were required to generate as many words from a particular category (such as clothing) as they could in a minute, a task that is believed to tap into formal linguistic knowledge and metalinguistic skill. The immersion children scored higher than the monolingual English-speaking children on the sentence judgment task and verbal fluency task by Grade 5. Hermanto et al. (2012) argue that the results illustrate that these emergent bilinguals benefit cognitively from participating in immersion education, since they had higher scores on the metalinguistic tasks.

Nicolay and Poncelet (2013) tested 106 native French-speaking 8-year-old children, some of whom were participating in an English immersion programme, while the rest were in non-immersion education. The children were assessed on a variety of language and attentional control tasks, including receptive vocabulary, divided attention, inhibition tasks, and mental flexibility tasks— all of which are believed to tap into the executive function skills discussed in Chapter 2. The children in the immersion setting (who were matched on socio-economic status and nonverbal IQ) outperformed the non-immersion children on a number of these executive function tasks, although not all did. The immersion children had better developed attentional skills, after only three years' participation in immersion education and despite the fact that they were not yet highly proficient bilinguals. Both the Hermanto et al. (2012) and Nicolay and Poncelet (2013) studies clearly demonstrate cognitive advantages for children in immersion settings.

In summary, the French immersion model is additive in that it promotes high levels of functional L2 proficiency, appropriate levels of literacy in both the L1 and L2, and grade-appropriate levels on academic content. The results of evaluation studies have overwhelmingly demonstrated that these programmes are successful on all counts—the exception being that children in immersion programmes often fail to achieve high levels of grammatical accuracy on some features of L2 grammar. However, other studies have shown that appropriate pedagogy which includes focus on corrective feedback and cross-linguistic comparisons that draw learners' attention to these features and promotes linguistic awareness, can go a long way to improving grammatical accuracy. Furthermore, participating in immersion education can also confer cognitive advantages to immersion students compared with matched children in non-immersion settings.

Two-way bilingual programmes

The second of the two models of bilingual education for majority language students considered in this chapter is the two-way immersion (TWI) or dual language model. These programmes aim to educate both minority and majority language students alongside each other. In effect, TWI programmes are an amalgamation of the immersion education model described above and models of bilingual education developed for minority language pupils discussed in Chapter 4[4]. Two languages are used for instruction, the minority language students' and the majority language students' native language. In the USA, the home of these programmes, where this model is offered extensively, the languages are often Spanish for the minority language learners and English for majority language students. However, there are many different language pairings in such programmes. TWI programmes provide content and language arts instruction in both languages for specific times during the school day and aim to promote additive bilingualism—high levels of functional oral proficiency and biliteracy in both languages, as well as grade-appropriate levels of academic achievement. A third aim of TWI models is affective, namely to develop high levels of self-esteem and positive inter-cultural sensitivity and behaviour. The development of self-esteem and identity is particularly relevant for the minority language learners, because in the absence of additive bilingual education, which promotes and supports ethnic minority students' L1, these children are at risk of developing negative self-image (Cummins, 2000). Participation in TWI models signals an important message to the minority language learners and society in general that the minority language is important, relevant, and of benefit to all members of society. In this chapter the focus will be on the majority language learners' development within these programmes, since minority language learners are the focus of Chapters 3 and 4.

The aims of these TWI models, therefore, are very similar to the one-way immersion model described earlier. The main difference is that the one-way immersion model is intended for only one group of learner—majority language learners, whereas the TWI model is intended for both minority and majority language students. Another important difference lies in the nature of the interactions in these classrooms. Given that TWI classrooms are made up of students who are native speakers of both instructional languages, development of the L2 is facilitated by interaction between 'novice' and 'expert' speakers of each language—for example, in Spanish/English TWI programmes, native English speakers benefit from interactions with native Spanish speakers during Spanish instructional times and vice versa. Both groups of students (minority and majority) can be both expert and novice depending on which language is being used during the day. Christian (1995) articulates a range of criteria she argues must be met in order for TWI programmes to be effective (see Table 5.2).

Characteristics of successful TWI programmes (Christian, 1995)
• Bilingual provision is made for at least 4–5 years.
• Focus of instruction is the same for TWI as for non-immersion programmes.
• Language input is optimal, comprehensible, interesting, and of high quantity. • Language arts instruction is provided in both languages. • Opportunities for output are maximized.
• Non-English target language is used for 50% of instruction time and 90% in the early grades. • Non-English target language is used for 90% in the early grades and English is provided at least 10% of the time.
• An additive bilingual environment is provided for *all* students to learn the L2 while continuing to develop their L1.
• Classrooms consist of an equal balance of minority and majority language students all participating in instructional activities together.
• Positive interactions between students are promoted through collaborative and cooperative learning activities.
• Programmes incorporate characteristics of effective schools, with high-quality professional pre- and in-service teacher training and home–school collaboration.

Table 5.2 Characteristics of successful two-way immersion programmes

In the USA, Spanish and English are the most common combination of languages in TWI programmes, however, there is a variety of different combinations including: Cantonese–English, French–English, Japanese–English, Korean–English, Navajo–English, Portuguese–English, and Russian–English (see www.cal.org for a list of programmes in the USA). As with most bilingual programmes throughout the world, there is a high degree of variability in the implementation of these programmes, as different schools are constrained by different pressures in their local communities—such as local policies about enrolment, the composition of staff in the schools, and the resources available to support the programmes. Programmes also differ in the age of entry to TWI immersion; however, most begin in Kindergarten or Grade 1 and continue until at least Grades 5 or 6 (Christian, 1995; Christian and Howard, 2008).

Two basic TWI models have been implemented in the USA. These are the 90:10 and the 50:50 model. In the 90:10 model, starting from Kindergarten or Grade 1, 90 per cent of the school day is spent in the minority language (Spanish or Cantonese in the USA) and 10 per cent is spent in the majority language (English in the USA). All academic curricular content is taught through the medium of the partner language while English is used to develop English oral language proficiency and pre-literacy skills. Instruction in reading is provided in the partner language to both groups of participating students. By Grade 3, approximately 80 per cent of the day is spent learning through the medium of the partner language and 20 per cent in English; at this point, reading instruction begins to include the majority language[5]. By Grades 4, 5, and 6, instruction is balanced between English and the partner language. In the 50:50 model, the instructional day is equally divided between English and the partner language throughout the primary school years. As mentioned earlier, there is variability as to how these models are actually implemented, particularly with respect to literacy instruction. Some schools separate minority from majority language learners: English reading instruction is provided to English native speakers first, and (for example) Spanish literacy instruction to Spanish speakers first, then both groups switch to develop literacy in both languages by approximately Grade 4. Other programmes, in contrast, provide instruction in literacy in both languages from the earliest grades to both groups of students simultaneously (Lindholm-Leary and Howard, 2008).

As with the one-way immersion model, participation in TWI programmes is voluntary, driven in large part by parental demand, although the precise reasons underlying parents' motivation may depend on whether the family is from an ethnic minority or not. Ethnic minority families are motivated by the concern that their children learn sufficient majority (English) language to get ahead in the world, while at the same time maintaining competence in the minority language and links to their heritage communities (Dorner, 2010; Whiting and Feinauer, 2011). The development of and participation in TWI programmes has been argued to be an effective way to reduce, or indeed close, the well documented achievement gap between minority and majority language learners[6] (Genesee and Lindholm-Leary, 2013). Thus, parents' decisions to enrol their children in TWI programmes is also motivated by the desire to mitigate against this trend for scholastic underachievement in minority language populations in the USA. Parents from the majority culture tend to be motivated by the same concerns as parents in the one-way immersion context—a recognition that being bilingual in the global economy can confer socioeconomic advantages to their child.

There have been a number of large-scale evaluations of these models in the USA with respect to students' language and academic achievement (Lindholm-Leary, 2001, Collier and Thomas, 2004, see also Genesee, Lindholm-Leary, Saunders, and Christian, 2006; August and Shanahan, 2008). The results of these evaluations have been remarkably consistent in showing that English majority native speakers in TWI programmes perform at or above grade level in academic curricular content in their L1, achieving standardized maths and reading test scores that are comparable to or even exceed those of peers not participating in TWI programmes. These findings have been consistent across a range of different studies (see Genesee et al., 2006) and across a range of different language pairs (for example, Cantonese–English, Korean–English, as well as Spanish–English). In short, there is no cost to the academic achievement of majority language students in TWI programmes resulting from participation in this form of bilingual education. Moreover, both majority and minority language learners make significant progress in acquiring both languages and have scores on oral language and literacy tests that are at or above grade when compared to peers in non-immersion programmes. These findings are also consistent for different proportions of TWI implementation, whether 90:10 or 50:50, and for children from different demographic and geographic districts within the USA (Lindholm-Leary and Block, 2010). Furthermore, an important benefit is that parents are generally positive about their children's learning and outcomes (Parkes and Ruth, 2011).

These evaluation studies were focused on standardized test performance of achievement in academic domains, in English and where possible, the non-native language. However, there are other dimensions to a child's performance in any educational programme, as aptly illustrated in Potowski's (2007) study of students' identity development and investment, as this cannot be captured by performance on a standardized test. Strengthened self-esteem and positive self-concept development are important objectives of TWI programmes. In her research, four children (two Spanish L1 minority and two Spanish L2 majority) students participating in a Spanish–English TWI programme were studied in Grade 5 and then again in Grade 8, using systematic observations, audio and video records of naturally occurring classroom language use, and standardized assessments of language proficiency. Interviews and participant observation methods were also employed to explore the relationship between students' identity investment and their classroom language use (identity investment is the extent to which the child identifies with being either a Spanish or English speaker). This is not unlike Gardner and Lambert's (1972) notion of 'integrative motivation' and to theories of motivation in second language acquisition research (Dörnyei, 2001). Potowski (2007) perhaps not surprisingly found that students with strong investments in Spanish—either because they felt it enriched their lives, sense of self, or status in their communities—used Spanish more often. She also found from her analyses of classroom discourse that while TWI programmes are largely successful, both majority and minority language students may not be using as much of the minority language as perhaps is assumed by educators and policy makers. Arguably, this imbalance between use of the minority and majority languages can be attributed to the high status and prevalence of the majority language outside of the school context. Even when use of Spanish is encouraged, the dominance of the majority language in the broader community has a profound impact on how children use both languages within the school context (Potowski, 2007). This is not to suggest that TWI programmes are not successful, but rather, as Potowski's study highlights, the importance of out-of-school factors in promoting (or indeed in inhibiting) full bilingual proficiency.

These findings are confirmed in a more recent study by Ballinger and Lyster (2011) who, like Potowski, examined the interactions in and use of Spanish in TWI Spanish–English classes. They recruited teachers and students in Grades 1, 3, and 8 and carried out a series of classroom observations, interviews, and questionnaires. As was observed by Potowski, the students in Ballinger and Lyster's study tended to prefer to use English. There was also a link between the amount of Spanish used and the language status of the child: children from Spanish-speaking homes tended to speak Spanish more in class and with peers than English-speaking children (see also Martin, 2012 for a study investigating similar issues in TWI programmes in Germany).

In summary, TWI programmes were developed to promote additive bilingualism, with full bilingual proficiency and biliteracy and grade-appropriate academic outcomes for minority and majority language learners together. A number of different models of these programmes have been implemented in the USA and elsewhere (see below). Results of large-scale evaluations are largely consistent in demonstrating levels of linguistic proficiency in both languages and levels of academic achievement for both majority and minority language learners equal to or better than those of students in mainstream, non-bilingual programmes.

These programmes, however, like one-way immersion programmes, do not produce fully balanced bilingual children. Majority language students tend to be less proficient in the minority language than minority language students, and even the minority language students tend to favour English in the higher grades, suggesting that neither group attains full bilingual proficiency[7]. It is important to note, however, that the L2 competence of majority language students in these programmes is not always characterized very precisely and therefore more research on the L2 competence of majority language learners in TWI programmes is required. It is worth emphasizing that one of the challenges in these TWI programmes is to encourage all students to use the minority language. Nonetheless TWI demonstrates clear advantages over traditional instructed L2 forms of education in developing linguistic proficiency and literacy skills in another language at no cost to academic achievement.

Content and language integrated learning

Content and Language Integrated Learning (CLIL) is a form of bilingual education for majority language speakers that is in many respects very similar to immersion programmes. At the core of a CLIL programme is the notion of integrating academic content with second language learning. This premise is one of the fundamental constructs underlying immersion programmes—the language to be learned is the medium of instruction of academic content. As a result, the boundary between immersion and CLIL programmes is sometimes very blurred, with some researchers suggesting that CLIL is the European implementation of immersion education, and others arguing that they are unrelated[8]. This section briefly considers the major features of CLIL programmes.

The term CLIL was adopted initially in the 1990s to describe an approach that is neither language teaching nor content learning alone, but an amalgam of both. It has been defined as '… a dual focused educational approach in which an additional language is used for the learning and teaching of both content and language' (Coyle et al., 2010, p. 1). While the focus on both content and language is interwoven, the emphasis may be on one or the other at any given point within specific classes or pedagogical activities. CLIL, therefore, clearly overlaps with immersion programmes; however, not all researchers accept that immersion and CLIL are instantiations of the same form of bilingual education (see Cenoz, Genesee, and Gorter (2013) for an extended discussion). In their introduction to a special issue of the journal *Language Teaching Research*, Lyster and Ballinger (2011) present a discussion of content-based language teaching in five different classroom contexts: a TWI setting in the USA, three different content-based English-medium classes in China, Malaysia, and Spain respectively, and a sheltered English immersion class for minority language learners in the USA. What these diverse educational settings have in common is the teaching of language through content; however, such content-based teaching can be implemented in a range of different educational approaches, thus perhaps leading to some terminological confusion in the literature.

Lasagabaster and Sierra (2010) present an attempt to articulate the precise differences between CLIL and immersion programmes as a reaction to the numerous different terms that are used to describe content-based language learning programmes in different countries (c.f. Eurydice, 2006). Table 5.3 presents five principles which Lasagabaster and Sierra (2010) argue are shared by both immersion and CLIL programmes.

Shared features of CLIL and immersion programmes (Lasagabaster and Sierra, 2010)
• Proficiency in *both* L1 and L2 at no cost to academic achievement is the final objective.
• Language as the medium of instruction is new and learning it is similar to L1 language development.
• Parents choose to opt in to the programme, finding it a more effective approach to learning an L2.
• Teaching staff are bilingual and able to implement the programme effectively to ensure all school activities can be carried out in L2.
• Communicative approach to learning is regarded as fundamental. • The objectives are to gain effective communication skills in the L2.
• The environment must stimulate and promote appropriate student interaction to foster linguistic progress.

Table 5.3 Five principles shared by both immersion and CLIL programmes

In addition to the similarities identified in Table 5.3, Lasagabaster and Sierra (2010) present what they consider to be a number of clear differences between immersion and CLIL programmes in:

1 the language of instruction
2 teachers (qualifications, teachers' proficiency in the additional language)
3 students' starting age
4 teaching materials
5 language objectives
6 immigrant students
7 research.

Lasagabaster and Sierra (2010) discuss these similarities and differences in the context of Spain, where a significant amount of research on CLIL has been carried out (for example, Ruíz de Zarobe and Jiménez Catalán, 2009; Cenoz, 2009) and argue that the examples they present from the Spanish context are generalizable to CLIL contexts elsewhere. While it is fairly clear that the shared objectives between CLIL and immersion presented in Table 5.3 are relatively unambiguous, it is far less clear that the differences articulated by Lasagabaster and Sierra (2010) are justified. For example, they argue that the language of instruction is foreign to students in CLIL programmes whereas the immersion language can be found in students' environment, be it home, society, or both. This claim, however, is not fully justified given that there are a number of immersion programmes throughout the world where the immersion language is not widely available outside of school. Take French immersion in Canada as one example—while Canada has a national policy on French and English, both languages are not equally present in all communities across this very large country. Indeed, children participating in French immersion programmes in British Columbia (western Canada) are more likely to hear an Asian language like Bangladeshi, Cantonese, Japanese, or Mandarin in the ambient environment than French. Yet these are still considered immersion programmes, and rightly so. Therefore, the putative difference between immersion and CLIL on the grounds of the nature of the language of instruction is not completely defensible (see also Cenoz, Genesee, and Gorter, 2013).

Lasagabaster and Sierra also claim that teachers in immersion programmes are bilingual, and indeed are meant to be fluently bilingual, whereas teachers in many CLIL programmes are not always trained appropriately nor have the same level of linguistic skills in the L2. Again Lasagabaster and Sierra (2010) evoke examples from Spain, where teachers receive extensive training to teach Spanish immersion programmes, while comparatively little pre-service teacher education is available for CLIL teachers. It is difficult to determine precisely the extent to which this position holds across geopolitical contexts, and undoubtedly there are many examples of immersion education in different contexts where teachers have had less than desirable training. With respect to starting age, Lasagabaster and Sierra (2010) suggest that CLIL programmes are more like examples of late immersion because few CLIL programmes described in the research literature have been aimed at young learners. They also argue that materials used in CLIL programmes tend to be edited (adapted or abridged) versions of authentic materials, in contrast to those they claim are used to teach students in immersion programmes. This issue is closely related to the expectation that the language in CLIL is 'foreign' but the additional language in immersion is meant to be somehow relevant to the child's environment. It is not clear, however, the extent to which this generalization applies across contexts of CLIL and/or immersion (Cenoz, Genesee, and Gorter, 2013).

While the goal of immersion education is unambiguous in terms of the desire to produce speakers with functional proficiency in both oral and written language, Lasagabaster and Sierra (2010) argue this is impossible in the CLIL context since (again in Spain) the stated government objectives of proficiency in, for example, Basque is at an intermediate level, not the higher, more advanced proficiencies expected of students in immersion programmes. Furthermore, in Spain, immigrant students tend to participate in immersion programmes but not CLIL; here Lasagabaster and Sierra (2010) cite the example of the Basque country where children from ethnic minority families are excluded from CLIL educational programmes. However, and contrary to Lasagabaster and Sierra's claim, children from ethnic minorities are indeed included in immersion programmes in Spain and other countries (for example, Canada) with growing evidence that they perform very well on tasks of literacy development in what is their L3 (Bérubé and Marinova-Todd, 2012).

The final feature on which Lasagabaster and Sierra (2010) distinguish immersion from CLIL programmes is research. They argue that CLIL programmes are still largely experimental whereas immersion programmes have been in place in several countries for a number of decades and therefore, they argue, CLIL programmes require more research to adequately evaluate their outcomes. This issue is particularly critical in the case of primary level learners who are less well represented in discussions of CLIL programmes, despite the fact that primary CLIL programmes are available in different settings. For example, in a relatively recent review of CLIL (Coyle et al., 2010) there is little or no discussion of evaluation of primary level CLIL programmes; instead the success of immersion at the primary level is invoked as an example that language learning through content-based programmes works for younger learners. The lack of focus on primary level CLIL programmes is also evident in Llinares, Morton, and Whittaker (2012) who review CLIL classroom interactions across four different European countries (Austria, Finland, the Netherlands, and Spain) but only one of the four databases analysed in their review is at the primary level.

Given the confusion, or at least the blurred boundaries, between CLIL and immersion, there clearly needs to be more systematic research examining the outcomes of CLIL programmes, particularly at the primary level (though see Dobson, Pérez Murillo, and Johnstone, 2010 for a review of primary CLIL in Spain). The detailed comparison between CLIL and immersion presented in Cenoz, Genesee, and Gorter (2013) leads to their conclusion '...that categorical distinctions between CLIL and immersion...are unsupported' (p. 13). Rather, Cenoz et al. (2013) argue that CLIL should be considered as an umbrella term such as 'Content-Based (language) Instruction' (CBI), one which includes a number of different examples of programme-types and learning opportunities. They further argue that immersion could likewise be considered a form of CLIL or CBI since immersion programmes share a number of characteristics with many forms of CLIL. More research critically evaluating the strengths and weaknesses of CLIL, together with a systematic research agenda examining all forms of student outcomes in CLIL programmes, including first and second language and academic outcomes, is required (Cenoz et al., 2013).

Immersion gone global

As a result of the resounding success of the one-way immersion programmes in Canada and the two-way immersion (TWI) programmes in the USA, educators around the world have adopted these models and extended and adapted them for use across a range of different linguistic and geopolitical contexts. Given that this volume adopts an international perspective, it is worth having a brief look at the different examples of immersion education as it has been extended and developed internationally. It is both interesting and important to identify how these programmes have been adapted to different linguistic contexts and also to identify the extent to which they are as successful as those discussed earlier. Note however, that this is a selective snapshot of some bilingual education programmes found internationally whose development was inspired by the immersion programmes in North America.

The Basque Country

Cenoz (2009) describes in detail the implementation of different educational programmes in the Basque country (or Basque Autonomous Community (BAC)) in northern Spain. In the BAC, three languages are used in education: Basque, Spanish, and English, where English is typically taught as a subject in mid- to later primary years, though many children as young as four are introduced to English, since over 90 per cent in the BAC attend pre-school where English is taught. Cenoz (2009) describes three different models in the Basque region:

1 The first was developed for native speakers of Spanish who are taught in Spanish, and where Basque is taught as a subject for 3–5 hours a week, and can also be used as the medium of instruction for some lessons. This model of Basque education is not really considered bilingual, since the majority language (Spanish) is the most common medium of instruction and Basque is typically only taught as a subject (like English). The aims of this model are for learners to acquire good comprehension skills in Basque, to develop basic productive fluency, to develop positive attitudes towards Basque, and to prepare students to interact in Basque environments.

2 This model was developed for native speakers of Spanish who wish to be bilingual in Basque and Spanish. Both languages are used for approximately 50 per cent of the time and both languages are also taught as school subjects, though there is significant variability as to how these proportions are implemented in schools. The aims of this model are for learners to acquire high levels of comprehension in Basque and good levels of production in Basque, and to prepare learners for further study in and about Basque.

3 The final model was developed as a language maintenance programme for native speakers of Basque, where the Basque language is the medium of instruction and Spanish is taught as a subject (like English). Basque is used approximately 75 per cent of the time. In this respect, this model is similar to the French immersion programmes described earlier. However, this model has developed to include a high proportion of children whose native language is Spanish. In consequence, it is also similar to the TWI programmes, in that both minority (Basque) and majority (Spanish) language students participate in the same programme. The aims of this model are for learners to strengthen their competence in Basque and enrich Basque language skills, to strengthen Basque speaking skills, and achieve a good functional proficiency in Spanish.

Cenoz (2009) reports significant differences in Basque proficiency across these three different models of bilingual education. Not surprisingly, students in model 3 are more proficient than those in model 2, who are in turn more proficient that those in model 1. Interestingly, however, there are no differences in terms of Spanish proficiency. Even children participating in model 3, where Spanish is taught as a subject for only approximately four to five hours a week develop high levels of proficiency in Spanish; this is undoubtedly due to the fact that Spanish is the majority language and these children are exposed to a significant amount of Spanish in their societal context. These educational programmes and the relative success of each in promoting full bilingual proficiency (in Basque and Spanish) speaks to the power of the school in developing plurilingual citizens through bilingual education. Importantly, there are no differences across the three models in terms of achievement in mathematics and science and, as described earlier, if students are not tested in the language in which they are instructed, they tend not to score as well (c.f. Genesee, 1987; 2008). Of these three models, the one that most closely resembles the immersion programmes described earlier achieves the best results in terms of bilingual proficiency with no cost to academic outcomes.

China

Early English immersion programmes have been implemented in mainland China; the development and success of these programmes are described in Knell, Haiyan, Miao, Yanping, Siegel, Lin, and Wei (2007), Siegel, (2011) and Qiang, Huang, Siegel, and Trube (2011). The implementation of these programmes was motivated by China's desire to develop the English language fluency of its citizens, since this was recognized as being critical to China's ability to develop a significant presence in the global economic context. Consequently, the French immersion model described above was adapted and implemented in mainland China, being first introduced in eight Kindergartens in the Autumn of 1997. The partial immersion model was applied in each of these settings, meaning the children were studying in English for 50 per cent of their time at school. Following this pilot, parents' and teachers' feedback was exceedingly favourable. Consequently, in 1998 this project was extended to five primary schools in Xi'an province in China. Test scores in both English and academic subjects were very positive, consistent with the research described earlier. As a result of the success in Xi'an, English immersion is currently available in many other regions in China and is now in at least 50 different schools, ranging from Kindergarten to secondary school in some settings. A range of studies have evaluated the effectiveness of these programmes, examining features such as language awareness, cognitive competence, English pragmatics, and academic performance. There are consistent advantages for the immersion students in terms of their English skills relative to non-immersion students, with no detriment to mathematics and other curricular subjects investigated (Knell et al., 2007; Qiang et al., 2011; Siegel, 2011). Unfortunately, however, bilingual education programmes developed to support ethnic minority groups in China have not been as successful recently: there has been a dramatic reduction in the number of available bilingual education programmes (Wang, 2011). This underscores Cummins' (2000) concern that the social status of the users of different languages (whether ethnic minorities or majority language learners) can have a significant impact on the nature of these programmes, their outcomes, and even the extent to which they are available.

Hong Kong

Immersion education in Hong Kong has been a subject of lively discussion and debate for some time (see Lin and Man, 2009; Hoare and Kong, 2008; Hoare, 2011 for detailed reviews). Hong Kong is a particularly interesting context, given its multilingual nature, where children may speak Cantonese, English, and/or standard Mandarin. Before 1997, when Hong Kong became a special administrative region of China, a large proportion of schools adopted an English Medium of Instruction (EMI) policy, since English was (and remains) a high-status language—fluent English is regarded as a prerequisite for economic and professional success. After the handover in 1997, language in education policy decisions changed. In 1998, the government adopted a compulsory mother-tongue policy up until the senior forms of secondary school (Grade 10 onwards), unless schools applied for and received exemption to remain English Medium of Instruction schools (EMI). Schools were allowed to remain EMI schools if they could demonstrate that the children were academically capable of being instructed through the medium of English and that the teachers had the necessary experience and expertise. There were 114 schools successful in their application to continue to provide EMI (Lo and Macaro, 2012). As a result, immersion in Hong Kong has been characterized as an 'elite' model.

Hong Kong primary school students' reading skills in Chinese are significantly superior to that of their skills in reading English texts, presumably in part a consequence of the reduced number of opportunities to learn to read in English, given the reduction in EMI programmes. This is an important finding, since English has such a high status in Hong Kong, and well developed skills in English are highly prized (Tse, Loh, Lam, and Lam, 2010; Poon, 2013)[9]. As a result, since 1998, the government of Hong Kong has 'fine-tuned' its language policy in light of:

1 parents' demand to allow more English medium of instruction programmes
2 the high status and perceived importance of English
3 the fact that six of the tertiary education institutions in Hong Kong are taught through the medium of English (Wang and Kirkpatrick, 2013).

Wang and Kirkpatrick (2013) outline models of trilingual education in Hong Kong primary schools established since this 'fine tuning' of language policy. They carried out a detailed case study of a government-funded school that adopted EMI for English, physical education, and visual arts from the first to sixth year of primary. Pǔtōnghuà (standard Mandarin Chinese) is the medium of instruction for the study of Chinese Language Arts and Literacy and Cantonese is the medium of instruction for maths, general studies, music, IT, and Chinese literacy. They analysed classroom discourse, interviewed staff, and used a questionnaire to gauge students' perceptions of their school's trilingualism model. Their analyses revealed that overall, students and staff were positive about the particular trilingualism model adopted in the case study school; teachers, however, varied in terms of the extent to which they felt able to maintain the school's language policy, particularly in terms of their use of English, since they substituted Cantonese in some cases (for example, for group discussions). Wang and Kirkpatrick argue for more focused guidelines on how to develop and implement trilingual education programmes and greater collaboration amongst teachers within trilingual schools.

Hong Kong is a linguistically diverse and educationally complex context. Research has indicated, however, that to the extent that immersion education can be properly implemented within Hong Kong schools, positive results ensue. For example, immersion contexts in Hong Kong are more effective at promoting different types of L2 vocabulary development (Lo and Murphy, 2010) and other aspects of English language learning (Hoare, 2011). However, immersion, and in particular EMI, is an elite form of education with the majority of children either being more academically able or being educated in private educational settings. Immersion education at primary level in Hong Kong schools is not as well represented as it is at secondary level, despite changes to educational policy and pressure from parents and society more generally. It will be most interesting to see how these multilingual educational programmes develop in Hong Kong in the coming years.

Singapore

Singapore has a population of approximately 3.6 million people, made up predominantly of people from Chinese (75 per cent), Malay (13.7 per cent), or Indian (8.7 per cent) backgrounds. While it is a Chinese-dominant society, English is also widely spoken, since English is the language of governance, commerce, education, and inter-ethnic communication. While a very broad definition of bilingualism is 'knowing two languages', in Singapore, it means specifically knowing English and either Chinese, Malay, or Tamil (Tupas, 2011). In school settings, English serves as the medium of instruction (starting in Grade 1) and also is taught as a subject, while Chinese, Malay, or Tamil are taught as mother tongues. In addition to English as the medium of instruction at Kindergarten, children learn their respective ethnic group's minority language for 20–25 per cent of the contact time in school (Dixon, 2010). Singapore's educational system has been described as 'stellar' and a model of multilingual education since children from primary schools in Singapore have been shown to outperform native English-speaking children (from majority language contexts such as New Zealand, the UK, the USA) in English reading (Mullis, Martin, Kennedy, and Foy, 2007). This finding is all the more compelling when considering that Singapore children tend to have lower scores on vocabulary and phonological awareness measures (Dixon, 2010). This advantage on English reading skill may reflect the nature of the pedagogical support students in Singapore receive. Additionally, bilingual education is viewed very positively in Singapore by teachers and society as a whole (Vaish, 2012). There are also numerous and significant opportunities for exposure to the immersion language outside of the school context—a feature not always typical of immersion setting—that again highlights the importance of out-of-school factors. All of these contribute to the success of bilingual education for majority language learners in Singapore.

Germany

TWI programmes have been implemented in Germany since as early as the 1960s and include TWI with German and a range of different languages, such as English, French, Portuguese, and Turkish. Other TWI programmes in Germany include German with autochthonous languages such as Danish or Sorbian (Meier, 2010). Meier notes that evaluations of TWI programmes are largely consistent with findings from other research—linguistic benefits to both minority and majority language learners as well as good standards of academic achievement. Like other researchers, she argues that students must participate in the TWI programme for long enough for these benefits to be acquired, and she further notes that while an ideal of TWI programmes might be balanced bilingualism for both minority and majority language learners, this is rarely achieved (Meier, 2010; see also Purkarthofer and Mossakowski, 2011 for a description of Slovene–German TWI programmes in Austria).

Latin America

There are a range of bilingual education models currently in place in Latin America with different linguistic and pedagogical aims. Some of these include elite forms of immersion found elsewhere (as in Hong Kong); however, some of the bilingual education programmes are particularly targeted at helping indigenous and more rural populations develop literacy skills in their community and majority languages. Among the diversity of programme models available, there are effectively two basic models: enrichment models which promote language development and additive bilingualism for majority language learners, and transitional and/or maintenance models for indigenous populations, which ultimately are subtractive[10] (King, 2005). The first type of model is the kind of bilingual education (immersion) model in focus in this chapter. In Latin America, these so-called elite enrichment models are aimed at children who speak the majority (usually Spanish) language and, as with the immersion models discussed earlier, they provide instruction in English (and in some cases in another European language along with Spanish). These programmes were originally designed for middle- and upper-middle class students to create further socioeconomic opportunities for these children.

However, bilingual schools have been established in more disadvantaged socioeconomic areas, leading to positive learning outcomes. As in Hong Kong and many other parts of the world, English enjoys a high social status in Latin America and therefore these models are most often provided in private bilingual schools for families living in urban areas. Historically, bilingual education in Latin America actually began in the 1910s and 1920s, pre-dating Lambert and Tucker's (1972) French immersion experiment. They were initially developed to support the children of representatives of multinational corporations who were seconded to Latin America to work, to allow their children to be educated bilingually and biculturally. These programmes were then extended to other Latin American citizens (de Mejía, 2005). For the most part, children participating in this form of bilingual education achieve high levels of proficiency in both the immersion and the home (usually majority) language, together with appropriate levels of oral proficiency and biliteracy skills (Simpson, 2005) and academic achievement (de Mejía, 2005). However, in some two-way immersion programmes there are asymmetries between the majority and minority language students in terms of oral proficiency in English in favour of the majority language speakers (Ordóñez, 2005), once again underscoring Cummins' (2000) concern about bilingual education favouring the elite members of society.

This brief global sketch of immersion programmes in different contexts highlights the prevalence and growth of this model internationally. There are numerous other examples of immersion education around the world, including Australia (de Courcy, 2002), Asia (Hamid, Nguyen, and Baldauf, 2013), Malaysia (Sua, Ngah, and Darit, 2013), South Korea (Jeon, 2012; Song, 2013), the Maldives (Mohamed, 2013), India (Bhattacharya, 2013), Nepal (Phyak, 2013), Timor-Leste (Taylor-Leech, 2013), and various countries in the European Union (Ó Muircheartaigh and Hickey, 2008); Södergård (2008); and see section on CLIL for more examples of bilingual education in Europe)[11]. It is well beyond the scope of this chapter to examine all of these instances of immersion education exhaustively and systematically. The programmes vary considerably in the way in which they are implemented, the ages at which education in more than one language begins, how far it continues throughout formal education, and in the amount of time allocated to different languages and for which subjects. Furthermore, the contexts in which these programmes are implemented vary with respect to degree of contact the pupils have with the immersion language outside of school. Not surprisingly, in cases where children do have a high degree of contact with the immersion language outside school, they tend to develop higher levels of oral language proficiency in comparison to those contexts where there is minimal exposure to the immersion language outside of school. The participants of these programmes also vary—sometimes they include only majority language learners (for example, French immersion in Canada, EMI in Hong Kong); but, at other times both minority and majority language learners are together in the same classroom (as in English immersion education in Latin America, which includes native (majority) Spanish speakers and ethnic minority students). The extent to which the original aims of the French immersion experiment (Lambert and Tucker, 1972) are achieved is influenced very much by these and other socioeconomic variables. Notwithstanding this variability, it is worthy of note how successful these programmes generally are in promoting bilingual proficiency and biliteracy in majority language contexts.

The age issue

Educational researchers have investigated the notion that 'younger is better' when it comes to L2 learning by comparing the outcomes of children participating in early vs. late immersion. If indeed younger is better, it could be assumed that starting immersion in Kindergarten would be preferable. This prediction is particularly relevant, given some claims that the offset of the critical period hypothesis is as early as six years of age (Herschensohn, 2007). Fortunately, there is evidence on this issue, with two major patterns of results emerging from these comparative studies.

The first pattern that emerges from studies comparing early vs. late immersion is that older learners can achieve comparable levels of L2 proficiency as those who start immersion in earlier grades. For example, Genesee (1981) and Adiv (1980: see Genesee, 1987) investigated the relative effects of starting immersion at different grades in French immersion programmes in Montréal, Canada. Children in early immersion programmes (beginning in Kindergarten) were compared with children in two-year late immersion programmes, where they participated in immersion in Grades 7 and 8 only (aged 12–13 years). Children in these two-year programmes would have already received instruction in French as an L2 as a part of the normal academic curriculum, so these children starting immersion in Grade 7 have had 6–7 years of French taught as a subject in school, beginning in Kindergarten. In these studies, performance on listening comprehension, oral production, reading comprehension, dictation, and writing was assessed. In both studies, there were no differences across the two types (early vs. late) of immersion programme on these measures. This finding is particularly compelling given that the children in the two-year immersion programme would have had significantly less exposure to French relative to the children in the early immersion programmes (1,400 hours for late immersion compared to 5,000 hours for early). However, even when the amount of exposure to French was equated (Genesee, 1987), the older learners were either similar to, or in some cases outperformed the early immersion students. Genesee (1981; 1987) suggests that the fact that these older children were no different from the early immersion ones implies faster learning on the part of the older students. These findings are compatible with research described in Chapter 6 on instructed foreign language learners (EFL), indicating faster rates of learning for older learners (Muñoz, 2006). Genesee (1987) further suggests that the advantage for these older learners may also stem from the fact that learning an L2 in school often requires the more cognitively demanding and context-reduced forms of communication that Cummins (1980) distinguishes (see Chapters 3 and 4), and which are more easily acquired by older learners as a result of their greater cognitive maturity. More advanced cognitive skills, and specifically the application of more explicit learning mechanisms is also argued by Muñoz (2006) to be one explanatory factor for superior L2 learning in older learners. Older immersion students are also literate in the native language and these L1 literacy skills facilitate the acquisition of literacy in the L2 (Genesee, Geva, Dresslel, and Kamil, 2006; Cárdenas-Hagan, Carlson, and Pollard-Durodola, 2007).

The second pattern from studies comparing immersion programmes with different starting grades suggests that early starters in immersion programmes do have an advantage over later starters. Genesee (1981) compared early and late immersion students (after one year of immersion in Grade 7) on tests of listening, speaking, reading, and writing and found that the early immersion children's performance was significantly higher than the late immersion students. This finding is particularly interesting because after two years of late immersion (after Grades 7 and 8), research has shown that there are no longer differences between the two groups of learners. Genesee (2004) argues that the relative advantage of starting late (or early) is therefore, linked to the amount of exposure. After only one year of exposure to immersion instruction the late starters do not show an advantage over the early immersion students; however, after two years, the late immersion children are comparable to the early immersion children. This finding, that it is the amount and nature of exposure the learners receive, not the age at which they begin learning the L2, is a consistent pattern that has emerged across each of the chapters in this volume.

In other studies and reviews the picture seems generally to favour early immersion students. For example, Wesche, Toews-Janzen, and MacFarlane (1996) present a comprehensive review of evaluations of early, middle, and late immersion programmes, and conclude that 'Early French immersion students consistently out-perform middle French immersion and late French immersion students overall...' (Wesche et al. 1996). Wesche et al. go on to note however, that the differences between these different groups of immersion students tends to diminish towards the end of secondary school, suggesting that even with less overall input, the older immersion learners are capable of catching up with the younger ones.

As indicated earlier, the success of early immersion programmes over later ones can result from a range of factors, such as students' natural language learning aptitude, positive attitudes towards learning, and increased exposure (Genesee, 2004). Other factors believed to account for an advantage of late immersion learners over early ones include having a well developed L1, in particular, well developed L1 literacy skills which can facilitate L2 development (Cummins 2000; Paradis et al., 2011). Self-selection can also be a factor in contributing to late immersion success. Immersion programmes (those studied in the research reviewed here) are voluntary and thus those learners and families who choose the immersion option tend to be very highly motivated. Academically advantaged children may also self-select for immersion programmes, which could lead to immersion classes made up of academically strong and highly motivated children, which in turn could account for their relative success (Genesee, 2004; Paradis et al., 2011).

The nature of the educational programme itself is also an important issue that might explain the differential success of early versus late immersion students. In Stevens (1983), late immersion learners who differed in terms of the amount of exposure they had to the L2 (French) were compared on a range of L2 measures. Somewhat surprisingly, the students who received 80 per cent of their school day instruction in French did not consistently score higher on these measures than other late immersion students who only spent 40 per cent of their school day in French. Stevens suggested that this somewhat surprising result was due to the pedagogical approach of the programme for the 40 per cent input students that allowed for a higher degree of choice and individual interaction with the language tasks, compared to the learners in the 80 per cent French day. This finding corresponds to Lyster's (2007) counterbalanced pedagogical approach discussed earlier, in that both the nature and level of engagement the children have with pedagogical activities can make important contributions to learning outcomes in immersion programmes.

In summary, studies that have directly compared younger versus older immersion learners differ in terms of outcomes, with some studies showing an advantage for younger learners, and others favouring older learners. In each of the studies, however, the age of the child is only one of a number of variables that contribute to L2 and academic outcomes in immersion education.

Educational implications

The focus of this chapter has been on specific forms of bilingual education available for speakers of the majority language. As the focus has been on education, the educational implications are in some respect self-evident. Children who are members of a language community that enjoys high status (often middle- to upper-class, and usually in more urban areas) and who participate in bilingual education fare extremely well. Note, however, that children from lower SES backgrounds also benefit from participating in immersion programmes (see Tedick, forthcoming). Learners in immersion programmes can achieve higher levels of L2 oral proficiency than students in traditional L2 programmes in which the L2 is taught for limited periods of time with a focus on explicit instruction in vocabulary and grammar; at the same time, they develop good literacy skills in both languages and meet or often exceed standard-level academic outcomes. Furthermore, there are a number of possible cognitive advantages (Hermanto et al., 2012; Nicolay and Poncelet, 2013), not to mention the socioeconomic benefits of participating in these forms of education. In short, there are no negative consequences to immersion that have been convincingly demonstrated through research.

Despite the resounding success of immersion education for majority language speakers, there are issues that still need to be addressed. One that has not yet received sufficient attention is the performance of minority language speakers in immersion education. For example, what happens to a child growing up in a Cantonese-speaking home, living in British Columbia, Canada, where the majority language is English, and who attends French immersion? Some research suggests that immersion can be an effective form of education for minority language speakers, just as it is for majority language children (Bild and Swain, 1989; Bérubé and Marinova-Todd, 2012). However, there are comparatively fewer studies investigating minority language learners in (one-way) immersion programmes. A second issue requiring further study concerns children who are at risk or who have special educational needs. Participation in immersion education is voluntary and in many cases self-selecting—children who participate are those who either wish to do so themselves and, thus, are intrinsically motivated, or children who have parents who decide for them, and in turn, support their child's education in productive and effective ways. What about children with learning difficulties, language impairments, or both? A recent review of research of at-risk children in immersion programmes is found in Tedick (forthcoming) who illustrates that children of lower academic ability, with special educational needs[12], lower L1 abilities, and from low SES backgrounds, all benefit from immersion education in that their performance on L1 measures and academic content is comparable to children from the same populations who are educated in the L1—yet they have higher scores in the L2. However, Tedick also argues that there is an urgency for more research on these populations to better determine the effectiveness of immersion education for at-risk students and to be in a stronger position to provide high-quality programmes for all learners.

Conclusions

This chapter has discussed two major forms of bilingual education available for majority language speakers, one-way, and two-way immersion. Both forms of education have been shown to be highly effective in promoting bilingual proficiency, intercultural sensitivity, and good academic outcomes. Indeed, these programmes have been so successful that they have been extended to many countries worldwide and have proved to be successful forms of education. More research is required to identify more effective pedagogical techniques, however. In particular, research is needed to show how best to use both the majority (L1) and the immersion language (L2) together in specific collaborative learning activities to promote L2 learning (see Ballinger, 2013 for an example). Furthermore, work that more closely identifies how to develop bilingual education for all learners is needed; such research would need to examine the suitability of immersion for students from a range of socioeconomic, linguistic, and cognitive backgrounds. Immersion education, at least in its modern incarnation, was developed in the 1960s, almost 50 years ago. An important goal in the next 50 years will be to further expand our understanding of the effectiveness of immersion education and pedagogy across a range of geopolitical contexts and for learners from very diverse backgrounds.

Notes

1 Note that minority language learners' linguistic and academic achievement in bilingual education programmes is discussed in Chapter 3 in the context of immersion models aimed at language maintenance or revitalization and in Chapter 4 in the context of the developing language and literacy skills in the (majority) L2.

2 See the discussion on transitional bilingual education models discussed in Chapter 4 as examples of subtractive bilingual programmes. These are programmes where children are educated in both their L1 and the majority L2 in the early years of their primary school experience, but who are then *transitioned* into education provided in the L2 only.

3 It is worth noting that Ballinger's (2013) study was carried out in an immersion context that included both native English- and French-speaking children. In other words, it was more like the dual immersion contexts described later in this chapter. It is worth remarking on Ballinger's (2013) study here as it relates in principle to Lyster et al.'s (2009) research.

4 See Genesee and Lindholm-Leary (2013) for a comprehensive review of learning outcomes in one-way and two-way immersion programmes for both minority and majority language learners.

5 Note, however, that in some implementations of TWI, this can occur earlier than Grade 3.

6 See also Chapters 3 and 4 for the discussion on minority language learners.

7 See also Chapter 3 for the discussion on the 'language shift' often observed in heritage (minority) language learners.

8 See Cenoz, Genesee, and Gorter (2013) for a comprehensive review of the boundary between CLIL and immersion.

9 Nayak and Sylva (2013) demonstrate that these early reading skills in English can be significantly improved with appropriate and targeted pedagogical support.

10 Note that these transitional models are discussed in Chapters 3 and 4.

11 See also Tedick, Christian, and Fortune (2011) for a relatively recent volume that covers a wide range of linguistic contexts in which immersion programmes have been implemented.

12 These include visual or hearing impairments, developmental delays, language impairments, autism, and specific learning disabilities.

6

Instructed foreign language learning in primary school

Introduction

An increasingly prevalent way in which primary school-aged children become multilingual is through the introduction of a foreign language (FL) taught as a subject within the primary curriculum. Governments around the world seem to be either introducing FL instruction into the primary curriculum where it might have previously been absent, or lowering the age at which FL instruction is introduced. In most countries, the FL of choice is English, and indeed Johnstone (2009) has suggested that the move to introduce English Language Teaching (ELT) to young learners represents '...a truly global phenomenon and possibly the world's biggest policy development in education' (p. 33). This chapter examines some of the major themes and issues that have emerged from the research literature investigating FL instruction at the primary level. The focus of this discussion is not on the specific interaction between teaching and learning in primary classrooms. In other words, this chapter is not about pedagogy and the way in which particular approaches to FL or L2 pedagogy (focus on form and explicit vs. implicit instruction, the importance of corrective feedback, interaction in the L2 classroom, etc.) might impact on L2 learning in primary school contexts. A number of excellent works have reviewed and examined the findings and implications of some of these more pedagogically-oriented discussions, many of which have been carried out in the context of primary school L2 FL learning (Philp, Oliver, and Mackey, 2008; Trofimovich, Lightbown, Halter, and Song, 2009; Spada and Tomita, 2010; Spada, 2011; Lyster, Saito, and Sato, 2013). This research tends to be oriented towards examining the effect of a particular pedagogical approach (for example, focus on form), on a specific outcome (such as question formation).[1] There will be no such meticulous discussion comparing different pedagogical approaches in this chapter. Nonetheless, in the general discussion of the nature of FL provision across different contexts, some reference will be made to different pedagogies and techniques that have been adopted in various FL contexts. Similarly, while some of the studies which do focus on pedagogy have been carried out within primary L2 or FL contexts, they do not tend to review the development of L2 FL learning across primary school in the context of relatively recent government decisions to lower the starting age at which young learners begin FL instruction. Therefore, the focus of this chapter is to provide a more holistic snapshot of some of the general issues surrounding FL instruction in primary contexts, in an attempt to provide a more overarching view of FL learning at the primary level.

The chapter begins with a brief illustration of how some countries have lowered the starting age at which children learn a FL through the primary curriculum and some of the policy decisions that have been made with respect to the provision and language(s) taught. Some of the main findings on the outcomes of FL instruction are then outlined. These outcomes include:

1 the extent to which young children make progress in their FL competence within the taught primary curriculum
2 the rate of progress they make
3 the extent to which individual differences factor in to their FL learning
4 children's motivation and attitudes towards FL learning
5 the role of the teacher
6 out-of-classroom factors that support of FL learning.

The chapter concludes with a discussion on what the FL context can reveal regarding the ease with which young children can learn L2s and how this relates to the complex interaction between the language learner's age and the nature of the input, instruction, and general support for L2 development.

Policy

As mentioned in Chapter 1, in 1999, the then Prime Minister of the UK, Tony Blair, claimed 'Everyone knows that with languages the earlier you start, the easier they are' (Sharpe, 2001). This statement came from the Romanes lecture he delivered at the University of Oxford and was made in the context of discussing the UK's National Curriculum and the various changes and developments his government intended to make. Indeed, reforms were made to the UK's National Curriculum that included the reintroduction of a taught foreign language into the primary National Curriculum by the year 2010 (after an absence of approximately 30 years). A change in government in the UK in the year FL instruction was intended to be reintroduced meant that this plan was subsequently halted. However, the present government has similarly resolved to introduce FL instruction into the primary curriculum as of 2014. This example is just one of many to be found in countries around the world, where governments are deciding that knowledge of a FL forms part of a set of so-called 21st century skills which (in part) aim to increase communication skills, and to promote the concept of global citizenry and intercultural sensitivity (Ananiandou and Claro, 2009). Some of the motivations underlying these decisions include the notion that FL learning can lead to improved L1 skills and greater sensitivity to other languages and cultures, in addition to actually developing L2 knowledge (Nikolov and Mihaljević Djigunović, 2011). These wider-ranging putative benefits of taught FL in primary school are reinforced by the Council of Europe (2007) which stated that the precise FL that is taught is somewhat less important than that children be exposed to and learn a FL.

Enever (2007) outlined some of the changes to policies on compulsory starting age for language learning in Europe and illustrated that 19 out of the 29 European Union member states had lowered the age at which an FL is introduced as a mandatory subject in the primary curriculum (see also Enever, 2009). A more recent discussion in Enever (2011a) illustrates that, at the time of writing, the number of member states of the European Union that have lowered the start age for FL learning currently stands at 27, 13 of which stipulate a start age of 7 or lower, 10 at 8 or 9 years, and 4 maintaining a start age of 10 or 11 years.

In Japan, the Ministry of Education, Culture, Science, and Technology (MEXT) proposed that English should be mandatory at Grades 5 and 6. However, initially it was stipulated that English should not be a formal taught academic subject like mathematics or Japanese language arts, but rather should be considered as part of 'general integrated studies' meaning there would be no formal evaluation of English L2 progress, nor would any grades be assigned to learners' performance. This proposal was fully implemented by the Japanese government in 2011 when English did become mandatory for all Grades 5 and 6 primary school children (ages 10–12) (Goto Butler, 2007).

In Turkey, a significant reform of primary education saw the implementation of a mandatory EFL start in Grade 4 (Uysal, Plakans, and Dembovskaya, 2007). A second foreign language (Chinese, French, German, Japanese, Russian, or Spanish) was introduced as an option in Grade 6 in an attempt to promote multiculturalism. Uysal et al. (2007) also outline the context in Latvia and report that FL learning starts in Grade 4, with a second FL introduced in Grade 6 (as in Turkey). This policy has since changed—Latvia is proposing to introduce a reform in 2013–2014, where the first foreign language learning will be compulsory, starting at age 7 (Eurydice, 2012). In Latvia, FL learning is so important that many children are also exposed to a taught FL in pre-school. The choice of which FL is taught is determined in part by what the children or parents decide, which corresponds to what Enever (2007) has referred to as 'parentocracy' (p. 219)—the notion that parents are a significant driving force behind the implementation of FL learning policies at primary school. In Latvia, as in many other countries, parents typically choose English. The final context reviewed by Uysal et al. (2007) is France, where they report that policy introduced in 2002 allows the introduction of FL learning in pre-school at age 5, and has resulted in an increase in the proportion of children studying an FL as part of the primary curriculum. As with the other two countries in focus in their paper, they note that 78.5 per cent of students choose English as the FL at primary school.

In Vietnam, EFL instruction as part of the primary curriculum was introduced in 2003 after the successful implementation of a pilot programme that had been introduced in a few cities in the 1990s (Nguyen and Nguyen, 2007). This decision meant that children in Grades 3–5 received two 40-minute English lessons every week. However, unlike some of the countries described above, English was an elective subject and implemented only when teaching expertise, materials, and parent and pupil demand were available. As a result of the success of this pilot programme, English was introduced as a compulsory subject in 2011 starting in Grade 3 (age 9) with four 40-minute classes per week (Nguyen, 2011).

In China, English was introduced as a compulsory subject in the taught primary curriculum in 2001 for children as young as six (Li, 2007). This reform was initially introduced into cities and suburban areas; rural areas of China being included in 2002. The policy, while focused on the promotion of English, also encouraged other FLs in some schools (Li, 2007). The extent to which children in rural schools receive the same amount or level of English instruction is not clear and indeed there is some evidence to suggest a large gap in the nature of the provision between urban and rural areas in China (Lu, 2003; see also Feng, 2011, 2012 for recent reviews).

Enever (2011b) outlines the policy issues relevant to the seven countries that participated in a recently completed large-scale three-year longitudinal study (Croatia, England, Italy, the Netherlands, Poland, Spain, and Sweden). A variety of schools in different settings (rural vs. urban) in each of the seven ELLiE (Early Language Learning in Europe) countries were visited at two or three points during each of the three years of this study, in which data were collected using a range of methods:

1 interviews with principals, teachers, and pupils
2 questionnaires administered to the pupils and parents
3 lesson observations focusing on both the teaching and the learners
4 different FL outcome measures such as listening, reading, and speaking tasks.

While each of these participating countries had FL policies regarding when children should be introduced to the FL, there was some variability in the formality with which the policies themselves were introduced and implemented, since it was frequently observed that FL learning began with schools and communities working together to promote FL learning in young learners—a more bottom-up (from the communities) than top-down (from the government) implementation. In the ELLiE study, the extent to which the FL policy is implemented effectively is very much dependent on the amount of funding available at both regional and national levels. Furthermore, as in many of the countries described in this chapter, some of the policies in the participating ELLiE countries included options to study more than one FL. For example, Croatia offers some choice of FL; England, the Netherlands, and Spain have policies where the local educational authorities can determine which FLs might be introduced and when; and finally, Sweden offers a choice of other FLs in addition to English (which is compulsory). When there is a choice of which FL to teach at primary level, communities and local educational authorities almost invariably choose English (Enever, 2011b). This finding is consistent across many other countries.

In the ELLiE study, the decisions of the seven participating countries on how much FL provision would be included in the primary curriculum varied considerably, and varied as a function of how much detail is specified about the amount of FL instruction in the respective policies. To illustrate, provision in the seven ELLiE countries ranged from one lesson per week in Grade 1 up to three or four lessons a week—with the amount of time spent in FL classes increasing across year grades in some of the countries (for example, Italy and Sweden). A potentially worrying trend where FL instruction was not considered as important a curricular subject as others (such as mathematics) was evident in some of the ELLiE countries, since occasionally the FL class would be cancelled or reduced if there were other school or class activities that were deemed more important (Enever, 2011a).

It is clear from this brief sketch of policy decisions in different countries that introducing FL instruction at younger ages in the primary curriculum seems to be a global phenomenon[2]. Enever and Moon (2010) discuss possible reasons underlying these decisions. One factor often articulated as a strong rationale for these policy decisions is the desire for citizens to develop proficiency in the FL (usually English), to enable them to engage more readily in international business and economic development. Indeed, China's policy decisions regarding a younger starting age for FL learning is motivated by a desire to improve the English language skills of China's population (Wang, 2002). Another, ever-present motivating factor behind such policies tends to be parental desire (Enever, 2007). The role of parents as instigators of specific language provision in primary school is also discussed in Chapters 3 and 5 in the contexts of heritage language learners and immersion education. Enever and Moon (2010) emphasize that in general, the underlying motivations for the development of such policies can be complex and varied, including the desire for economic advancement, respect for other languages and cultures, enhancement of communication across different ethnicities within a country, and as a global stance. These reasons for the implementation of different FL policies are consistent with Nguyen (2011), who notes that underlying Vietnam's decisions on FL policy are recognition of the importance of English in international communication, contribution to the economic and political strategic policy of Vietnam, a desire to keep up with the rest of the world, and to increase the language proficiency of Vietnamese citizenry.

Provision

Having identified that many countries are lowering the age at which FL instruction is introduced in the primary curriculum, it is worth examining some of the ways these decisions have been implemented. As indicated above, there is considerable variability across different geographical and educational contexts as to when FL programmes are introduced into the primary curriculum, how much time is allocated to FL learning, the specific type of curriculum that is implemented, the qualifications and training FL teachers have received, and whether FL instruction is delivered by generalist or specialist teachers (Nikolov and Mihaljević Djigunović, 2011). Within Europe, the time allocated to FL learning varies from one to several hours per week—as does whether the FL is introduced as a separately taught subject or whether it is part of the Content and Language Integrated Learning (CLIL) programmes where content is taught through the medium of a FL (Enever, 2011a; Nikolov and Mihaljević Djigunović, 2011)[3]. The most widely applied models of FL learning seem to be those where very general topics are introduced for FL learning (colours, leisure activities, family) or where topics from specific curricular subjects are used as the focus around which FL activities are developed. These approaches, however, are usually limited in a number of ways:

1 the amount of FL input and time allocated to FL learning
2 the teachers' qualifications (whether they have specialist FL training)
3 the level of proficiency the teachers have in the FL (Nikolov and Mihaljević Djigunović, 2011).

Not surprisingly, the nature of the FL outcomes are inextricably linked with the nature of the provision. If the provision is limited, one would predict the outcomes will be as well. This issue is discussed further below.

The importance of the school context in determining the effectiveness of FL instruction is highlighted in the ELLiE study (Lopriore and Krikhaar, 2011). The status of the FL in the school and the curriculum can have a considerable impact on effective provision of FL instruction. If the school allocates a sufficient amount of time to the FL classroom and if the FL is seen as a positive element of the overall curriculum (on the part of the teachers, parents, and learners) this can have a more positive impact on the provision. This point is consistent with Enever (2011b) who noted (also in the context of the ELLiE study) that some schools would cancel the FL lesson if it got in the way of other, presumably more important, school activities. The use of high-quality FL materials, and wider use of interactive whiteboards and computers can help arouse and maintain the interest of the pupils, and can also be an effective supplement to the FL pedagogy implemented by the teachers. Teachers should have available to them a variety of in-service professional development activities to help support and improve the pedagogical approach taken in the FL classroom. Finally, there should be wider participation in international projects, exchanges between schools and pupils to provide opportunities to use the FL outside of the school context, and reinforcement and support for the family–school connections often present in successful schools. The case studies that formed the ELLiE study therefore illustrate that FL provision is more successful if:

1 the FL policy is supported by schools and parents
2 support is in place for teachers
3 quality materials are accessible
4 there are sufficient out-of-class opportunities to use the FL (Lopriore and Krikhaar, 2011).

An examination of FL provision described in Harris and O'Leary (2009) has also yielded similar conclusions. In Ireland, the 'Modern Languages at Primary School' initiative was launched in 1998 in 270 schools and in 2009 had been introduced in nearly 400 schools representing approximately 12 per cent of schools in the country. Ireland is an interesting context to examine, because Irish is a regional minority language[4] and all children begin learning Irish when they start school. As a result, FL learning in Ireland constitutes a case of learning a third language. The Modern Languages at Primary School initiative introduces one and a half hours of instruction in one of four European languages (French, German, Italian, or Spanish). Harris and O'Leary (2009) outline the experience of participating in this initiative from the perspective of the pupils, parents, and teachers. Teachers in this FL programme can be regular members of staff, but are more commonly visiting, non-staff specialist teachers who receive additional in-service training to deliver FL instruction—a finding consistent with Nikolov and Mihaljević Djigunović, (2011). With respect to provision, pupils reported enjoying word games, raps, songs, language awareness activities, action games/sports, and drama the most. However, these FL activities were not the most frequent within the programme. Rather, whole class repetition of sentences and phrases was the most frequent activity, yet also the least preferred by the pupils. This issue of aligning classroom activities to reflect the interests of pupils more adequately is relevant in a number of different contexts (Enever and Watts, 2009).

A theoretical basis for using pedagogical activities which include rhymes and possibly raps and songs, preferred by pupils in the Harris and O'Leary (2009) study, can be found in Campfield and Murphy (2013). In their study, young Polish learners of EFL were randomly allocated into instructional groups that varied in whether the prosodic contours of English were made salient (as in the rhyme group) compared to a group with the same prose but no rhyme or a control group. The children in the rhyme salient group (who were given nursery rhymes as part of their FL provision) had higher metalinguistic knowledge of English word order than the other groups. The theoretical basis for this work rests on the prosodic 'bootstrapping' hypothesis developed in the domain of the L1, which argues that children use the prosodic contours of their L1 to help them support their L1 learning (to help them segment speech into grammatical units). Campfield and Murphy's (2013) study suggests that this idea is relevant to young EFL learners, since rendering these prosodic contours more salient in the input to young learners can have beneficial effects on FL learning.

Despite the increase in FL instruction around the world, there is relatively little available research reporting on the pedagogical approaches taken by teachers of FLs (Garton, Copland, and Burns, 2011). Garton et al. aimed to try and fill this gap by examining how ELT teachers teach English to young pupils[5]. They adopted a mixed-methods design which included a survey of perceptions of different pedagogical practices used from a global sample of ELT teachers of young learners and detailed case studies of classroom practice from five different teachers in different continents (Africa, Asia, Europe, Latin America, and the Middle East). The specific case studies carried out included:

1 a Grade 4 class in a low socioeconomic district in Colombia
2 one Grade 3 and two Grade 5 classes in a state school in a prosperous town in Northern Italy
3 mixed Grades 1 and 2 after-school classes outside the centre of Seoul in South Korea
4 a Grade 1 and a Grade 4 class in a rural state primary school in Tanzania
5 two Grade 6 classes (boys-only) state school in Abu Dhabi.

The inclusion of these different detailed case studies allowed Garton et al. (2011) to develop an understanding of the different types of ELT practices to young learners across a range of geographical, educational, and sociopolitical contexts. The results of the questionnaires revealed that teachers used a wide variety of different pedagogical activities in their English classes. The top five most frequently reported activities were:

1 repeating after the teacher
2 listening to tape-recorder/CD
3 pupils reading aloud
4 playing games
5 songs.

Garton et al. suggest that the somewhat surprising finding that listening to tape-recorders/CDs was a frequent activity due to the fact that ELT teachers in these contexts reported being under-confident in their own knowledge of and proficiency in English. They further note that absent from the list of reported activities was storytelling, which they note is consistently considered to be an effective pedagogical activity (Moon, 2000; Pinter, 2006). It is worth noting that storytelling also received a low rating in the ELLiE study (Enever, 2011a).

The only activity that was rarely used across these different case studies was translation. This is an interesting finding in light of the recent debates in the literature on the potential value of code-switching in the L2 classroom.

For example, Tian and Macaro (2012) argue that a teacher code-switching into the L1 when teaching vocabulary (which could be viewed as a form of translation), if executed judiciously, can lead to a lexical focus-on-form (c.f. Laufer and Girsai, 2008). In Tian and Macaro's study, adult EFL learners of English in China benefited from this lexical focus-on-form supporting the claim that there are times when use of the L1 can have a facilitative effect on L2 vocabulary development and thus constitute effective pedagogy. As Tian and Macaro's study was carried out within the adult EFL context it remains an empirical question whether these results are applicable to the young learner context. Nonetheless it would be interesting to identify whether and to what extent judicious use of translation as an example of lexical focus-on-form might be helpful for young learners. Macaro and Lee (2012) have indicated that young children tend not to prefer an L2-only classroom, so it is likely that translation as a pedagogical activity could have some benefits for young learners if used appropriately. Similarly, the work of Lyster (2007), Lyster, Collins, and Ballinger (2009) and Ballinger (2013) in immersion programmes also supports the use of the L1 to promote cross-linguistic awareness (see Chapter 5). Lesson observations collected in the context of the ELLiE study indicated that code-switching was widely used, however, the extent to which this was 'judicious' in that it was targeted or purposeful was less clear (Enever, 2011a)[6].

Garton et al. also report that teachers attempted to introduce communicative activities that were relevant to their specific cultural context, and cite the example of students in Abu Dhabi participating in interactive games involving matching sentences to pictures in response to locally relevant questions such as 'How many camels do you own'? Challenges faced and expressed by the teachers include dealing with large class sizes and mixed ability levels, together with the problems of promoting a positive attitude and strong motivation to learn a language which some pupils did not recognize as being relevant to them. Teachers also expressed a concern about whether or how to teach explicit grammar rules effectively to young learners, a problem for which Garton et al. note there is no consensus in the literature on the young learner population. While Garton et al.'s (2011) study was carried out with ELT young learners, and as such may not be generalizable to all contexts where FL instruction is being introduced to primary school pupils (for example, in Anglophone countries; see Tinsley and Comfort, 2012), the significant majority of countries and cases thus far studied have introduced English as a FL and possibly one or two additional FLs. It is likely, therefore, that these results are relevant across a wide range of contexts. Indeed, the variety of different activities used by FL teachers with primary school pupils described in Garton et al. (2011) were also found in the ELLiE study (Enever, 2011; and Harris and O'Leary, 2009), and further noted in Nikolov and Mihaljević Djigunović (2011).

Edelenbos, Johnstone, and Kubanek (2006) present a detailed report prepared for the European Commission that focuses on identifying the main pedagogical principles underlying the teaching of FLs to young pupils. Their report reviews research on teaching languages to young learners together with a summary description of what constitutes 'good practice' in the teaching of FLs to primary school children. This report also includes a set of pedagogical principles that are identified as being important as a basis on which effective L2 pedagogy can be developed.

Edelenbos et al. (2006) review a wide range of research addressing aspects of FL provision, including factors such as age, intensive programmes, continuity to secondary education, teachers' professional needs, and use of ICT (Information and Communications Technology). Their review reveals significant diversity in the types of FL programme available. Many programmes exemplify the more standard type of FL provision with one or two FL classes per week, as mentioned above. However, others take the form of intensive FL programmes where the amount of time spent in the FL is considerably increased relative to more standard programmes, such as the one described by Lightbown and Spada (1994) where French children learning English in Québec, Canada, spend five months of the year learning English (i.e. the entire day is spent in English class studying English, not content)[7] in *le bain linguistique* (the language bath) with the remaining half of the academic year spent learning academic content. Similarly, participation in immersion or partial immersion programmes or 'medium of instruction' provision where children are taught the content of the primary curriculum through the medium of another language (for example, Scottish Gaelic in Scotland; Welsh in Wales) can also have a facilitative effect on attitudes towards and outcomes from the L2 (see also Chapter 5 for an extended discussion).

Within the area of FL instruction and education there is a significant lack of research examining the continuity of FL provision available as children transition from end of primary to early secondary education (see Chesterton, Steigler-Peters, Moran, and Piccioli, 2004; and Cable, Driscoll, Mitchell, Sing, Cremin, Earl, Eyres, Holmes, Martin, and Heins, 2012, for notable exceptions). Those studies that have been carried out typically identify a lack of cohesion in FL provision in the transition from primary to secondary (Bolster, Balandier-Brown, and Rea-Dickens, 2004; Cable et al., 2012). Programmes focused specifically on aiming at greater coherence, however, can be quite effective as demonstrated by Schwob (2001; see Edelenbos et al., 2006). In the *Partenaire* programme, secondary and primary school teachers spend a week together in the FL classroom in addition to liaising outside the class to ensure a smooth transition to secondary education. Furthermore, high proportions of children achieve the target level of L2 performance (German, in the Schwob study; see Edelenbos et al., 2006) in this context, suggesting this effort to facilitate greater cohesion can contribute to effective provision.

Another factor related to provision and which was reviewed by Edelenbos et al. (2006) is the use of ICT. They reviewed three studies that explored the use of ICT in primary FL learning contexts. In Waschk (2004; see Edelenbos et al., 2006), children who used software such as video and/or audio sequences had improved oral fluency, whereas Nutta, Feyten, Norwood, Meros, Yoshi, and Ducher (2002) in a carefully matched study, did not find any advantages in attainment through the use of digital technologies. However there was greater interaction in the FL class when children used multimedia which, in turn, could have wider-reaching benefits. These mixed results are interesting and reflect the general findings in a current systematic review of the use of Computer-Assisted Language Learning (CALL) technologies in FL instruction at both primary and secondary level. Macaro, Handley, and Walter (2012) systematically reviewed and discussed CALL studies, examining the extent to which digital technology can promote different aspects of L2 learning (such as vocabulary, syntax, speaking, listening, reading skills, etc.). While there is somewhat mixed support for the use of CALL pedagogies in promoting specific features of L2 competence, there is evidence that the use of ICT can be facilitative in L2 vocabulary development and some aspects of speaking, listening, and reading skill (Macaro et al., 2012). Therefore, appropriate use of digital technologies in the FL classroom for young learners can be said to have a facilitative effect on different aspects of L2 development, and is worth considering in the context of designing effective FL provision.

Edelenbos et al. (2006) conclude their section on FL provision by highlighting a few key points that emerged from their review of the research literature. First, they argue for an early starting age (however, see the section below on whether 'younger is better' and elsewhere in this volume for a more detailed discussion on age). They argue that a younger starting age must also be associated with provision that offers adequate time and intensity of L2 exposure, together with an appropriate distribution of FL learning classes throughout the curriculum. Similarly, there should be appropriate continuity of FL provision across both the primary curriculum and on into secondary-level education. Finally, they argue for the judicious use of ICT activities to facilitate a wider range of input and interaction types, along with support from both national and local governmental organizations. In short, they point out that age is a variable that might contribute to the success of L2 and FL learning, but that this variable interacts with a number of other key features related to FL provision. From the more recent reviews of FL provision available in the ELLiE study (Enever, 2011), Nikolov's (2009) volume, and with the review in Nikolov and Mihaljević Djigunović (2011), the picture at present seems somewhat varied with respect to the extent to which FL programmes across the world are able to instantiate the features highlighted in Edelenbos et al. (2006).

Given that it is clear from the above discussion that there is an increasing global trend to lower the starting age at which FL instruction is introduced, together with a better understanding of some of the key features of FL provision that should be implemented, it is worth examining at this point the extent to which FL programmes have been successful at developing these 'plurilingual citizens' (c.f. Enever, 2009).

Outcomes

A range of different types of FL outcomes can be considered when identifying how effective FL instruction is, or what impact FL learning has had. In this section, different outcomes are discussed—competence in and progression of the FL, motivation and attitudes towards the FL, effect of the FL on aspects of the L1, individual or learner characteristics which influence FL learning, and how FL instruction impacts on the teacher. However, before examining these issues it is worth reflecting on the issue of assessment in young FL learners' development.

Assessment

Assessing FL learning in young learners is a challenge. It is difficult to pin down the construct being measured, particularly as there is such variety in the types of FL provision (Nikolov and Mihaljević Djigunović, 2011). Assessment should therefore be closely linked to the nature of the in-class activities; given that FL learning in children tends to develop slowly, whatever means of assessment is being used must be sensitive to this piecemeal growth. For example, in the context of the ELLiE study, after four years of FL instruction many of the children across the different countries were at the A1 level of the Common European Framework of Reference (CEFR) (Council of Europe, 2001) proficiencies (Enever, 2011a). This means then that they were still at the beginning stages of FL proficiency. Indeed, despite the fact that many studies of FL learning in primary school apply the CEFR criteria, doing so underlies a lack of understanding of how FL learning in the primary school context progresses—slowly and in a piecemeal fashion (Enever, 2009). Edelenbos and Kubanek-German (2004) advocate the idea that teachers develop *diagnostic competence*—the ability to interpret students' FL growth through appropriate assessments and to help students on the basis of this 'diagnosis'. This so-called diagnostic competence is another characterization of Sternberg and Grigorenko's (2002) 'assessment for learning', where learning is viewed in the context of readiness to develop. At present, there are very few standardized tests of language competence for young learners, and those that do exist tend to be relevant only to English.[8] Many research studies of FL learning in children either administer standardized tests developed for native-speaking populations (for example, the British Picture Vocabulary Scales to measure English receptive vocabulary (Dunn, Dunn, Whetton, and Pintilie, 1982)) or develop their own. Both approaches are problematic. For example, standardized tests may not be sensitive to slow development and may be norm-referenced on monolingual populations, yet provide good indices of reliability and validity. Bespoke tests however, may have little reliability and validity but might be more closely aligned to in-class activities[9]. Unfortunately, as yet there are few alternatives.

L2 outcomes and progression

Research that has examined young learner FL outcomes and progression is largely consistent on two main findings:

1 young learners can and do learn some formal features of the L2
2 they make relatively slow progress overall.

In the ELLiE study described earlier, the speaking, listening, and reading skills across the seven participating ELLiE countries were assessed, indicating overall significant variation both within and between different countries (Szpotowicz and Lindgren, 2011). To measure speaking performance, oral production tasks were set at the end of the children's second and third year of FL learning. Students were required to engage in a role-play 'in a restaurant', where children were prompted to use the FL in reaction to questions elicited by an 'interviewer'. For example, children would be asked a question such as: 'How did you like the food?' and the child was expected to respond appropriately in the FL. In coding their responses, the ELLiE team examined the amount of L2 produced together with the syntactic complexity of their productions. Their analyses clearly indicate steady growth in use of FL vocabulary with respect to both types and tokens. However, they note considerable variability across the seven countries in that the mean number of words produced across each country ranged from 7–17 words produced in Year 1 and from 9–36 in Year 2. Measures of lexical diversity and syntactic complexity indicated a steady increase across the three-year period of the ELLiE study. Furthermore, lexical diversity was positively correlated with syntactic complexity, suggesting that children were able to produce more syntactically complex utterances as a function of larger vocabulary knowledge (Szpotowicz and Lindgren, 2011).

Listening skill was measured by providing the children with a picture description task and, as with FL vocabulary, there was significant variation between the seven countries, as well as in the specific items on the test, with some items not consistently eliciting correct responses until the third year of the ELLiE study. However, the overall pattern is one of consistent growth, mitigated somewhat by the considerable variation across countries (Szpotowicz and Lindgren, 2011).

The reading task used in the ELLiE study was administered only in the final year of the study and consisted of a cartoon that was originally published in a children's magazine (hence authentic). Text from 8 out of 16 speech bubbles was erased and children were required to fill in these empty bubbles from a choice of three or four different options (presented visually). As with the other tasks, there was significant variation in the items; some items yielded an overall 32 per cent correct across the seven countries, while others yielded percentages as high as 84 per cent. Similarly, there was significant variability across the seven participating countries. Correlations across the tasks also were strong and positive showing that children who produce high scores in the listening task tended to produce higher scores in the reading and FL production tasks (see Szpotowicz and Lindgren, 2011).

The results from the ELLiE study show clear development of FL learning on these three measures (oral production, listening, and reading) across the three-year period of the project. They also show, however, very different patterns across different countries. These differences are argued to stem from a range of factors such as motivation, the teacher, the school, parents, and the extent to which the FL is supported outside of the school context (Szpotowicz and Lindgren, 2011). For example, contexts where exposure to FL is readily available and fairly frequent seem to do a better job in supporting in-class FL activities. The role of the teacher is paramount here—the teacher is the focal individual who can bring together these complex and interacting variables to form a bridge between home factors, learner characteristics, and FL pedagogy. The extent to which the FL teacher is able to create this bridging support depends very much on the availability of in-service professional development.

Harris and O'Leary (2009) similarly found that in the Modern Languages at Primary School FL programme implemented in Ireland, the majority of pupils receiving FL instruction made good progress in developing listening comprehension skills and in basic levels of spoken communication. They also note that girls tended to outperform boys on these measures.

Nikolov (2009) reports on a large-scale study investigating Hungarian children's learning of English and German. The children were in Years 6 and 10 (aged 12 and 16 respectively) and were given tests in either English or German, measuring their listening and reading comprehension as well as writing. A sub-sample of the children was also given an oral task. All of the tasks focused on meaning over form. The results of these measures indicated higher scores in English than in German for both year groups, and like the results in the ELLiE study, demonstrated a high degree of variability in the FL proficiency of the children. Nikolov notes a strong relationship between proficiency and the nature of the provision and argues that pedagogy that draws from grammar–translation methods and drills can be demotivating for young learners. She also argues that slow progress in developing FL proficiency in these learners is due in part to the use of these uninspiring pedagogical activities.

An evaluation of the 'Early Years Literacy Programme' (EYLP) is reviewed by Drew (2009). The EYLP was originally developed in Australia but was implemented in Grades 3 and 4 EFL classes in Norway. A school that introduced the EYLP to promote EFL in their learners was compared against schools that did not. Drew reported higher rates of progress in the school which implemented the EYLP, together with higher performance on the listening, reading, writing, and oral assessments that were given. Drew cautions, however, that the EYLP class also experienced other forms of teaching that the comparisons schools did not receive, hence it was not possible to attribute superior performance and faster rate of progress unequivocally to the EYLP itself. Nonetheless, he notes that the substantial amount of reading that forms part of the EYLP must have had a facilitative impact, because across the schools in the study all children spent a similar amount of time overall on EFL.

Orosz (2009) focused on FL vocabulary learning in the first two years of EFL in Hungarian schools. A cohort of 253 children aged 9–12 learning English in Grade 2 and receiving two lessons per week were given Meara and Milton's (2003) X-Lex vocabulary test, a computer-based assessment where children are required to identify real FL words in a mixed array of real and nonsense words. On average children learned approximately six words per contact hour during the first four years of English FL instruction, which represents consistent FL vocabulary growth. Vocabulary uptake, however, decreased at Grade 6, dropping to 3.4 words per contact hour. As with the other research discussed in this chapter, Orosz notes significant variability where some children were able to learn as many as 1,000 words in their first year of English instruction, while others only learned a handful.

Frequency of the vocabulary items was also a significant factor with higher-frequency words being learned more rapidly than lower-frequency items. Additionally, the extent to which a FL word can be associated with an L1 lexical item impacts on development of FL vocabulary in young learners (Szpotowicz, 2009).

Goorhuis-Brouwer and de Bot (2010) report on an evaluation of 'Early English Language Teaching' (EELT) in Dutch primary schools. As with the policy initiatives described above, EFL provision to young learners is increasing in the Netherlands (indeed the Netherlands is one of the seven participating ELLiE countries (Enever, 2011a). Goorhuis-Brouwer and de Bot examined the outcomes of four cohorts of children who had received EELT. The 2004 cohort consisted of 34 five-year-old Dutch children who were tested on English comprehension and production after a year of partial English immersion; the 2004–2005 cohort consisting of 123 children, were also tested on English comprehension and production after 6–18 months of partial English immersion; while the 2007 cohort, consisting of 93 Dutch speaking and 60 minority language learners were tested on English comprehension and production after a year of partial English immersion, and finally, the 2008 cohort consisting of 135 children were tested on English comprehension and production at age five (after a year of partial English immersion) and then retested at age six. For all of the cohorts, both the Dutch and minority language non-Dutch pupils, EELT had a positive impact on the development of English skills. Even after only six months of exposure, these children reached an average level of English proficiency similar to two-year-old native speakers. They conclude, therefore, that across these cohorts, drawn from different schools and regions of the Netherlands, consistent progress in English comprehension and production can be shown in these young learners. As with the other studies cited above, however, they note a considerable degree of variability with pupils and schools, where some develop rapidly, others more slowly.

One of the stated reasons for implementing FL instruction in the primary curriculum has been to increase intercultural sensitivity and to promote a positive attitude towards learning a second or foreign language and speakers of other languages (i.e. from other cultures). However, relatively few studies have attempted to actually examine the extent to which primary pupils develop intercultural sensitivity through participating in FL instruction. One exception is in Driscoll, Earl, and Cable (2013) who suggest that FL programmes might need to be more focused and coherent in delivering this particular outcome. In their three-year longitudinal study, they examined teaching approaches, staff attitudes towards teaching intercultural understanding, and pupils' attitudes, through lesson observations and interviews with head teachers, teachers, and teaching assistants. Forty different English primary schools varying in size and location (rural vs. urban) participated in the study. The teachers represented a range of levels of familiarity with the countries in which the FLs were spoken and most had received some form of language training. Over 50 per cent of the teachers in this study stated that developing intercultural sensitivity was a core aim of learning and teaching a FL at primary level. However, Driscoll et al. (2013) noted a general trend towards lack of systematic medium- to long-term planning for developing this intercultural sensitivity and an observable 'mismatch' between the stated importance of developing sensitivity towards other cultures in materials and curricular documents and the practice that Driscoll et al. observed. This conclusion was based on pupil comments stating they did not have much time in which to discuss or explore particular cultural factors that were of interest to them. Furthermore, the observed planned activities aimed at developing cultural awareness were largely incoherent with no 'shared understanding of defined cultural learning outcomes' (p. 13). Driscoll et al. suggest that pedagogy needs to harness children's enthusiasm to help develop both their own cultural identity, but also to improve their global awareness and appreciation of multiculturalism in general. While this study was based in the English primary school context and may not be generalizable to other geopolitical contexts, it does raise some important questions about how effective some FL programmes are at achieving their stated aims.

In summary, the evidence from research studies such as the few examples presented here is largely consistent, in that there is clear and credible evidence that young learners of a FL can make steady progress in FL learning in primary school across a range of different features of vocabulary, oral/aural tasks, comprehension, and production. The findings of these examples are also consistent with those studies reviewed by Edelenbos et al. (2006). However, in addition to manifest growth in L2 knowledge and competence, there is also significant variability within individuals, across schools, and regions. The source of this variability is likely due to a wide range of different factors such as the nature of the provision offered, professional development support for the teacher, parental support, and individual learner characteristics.

Motivation and attitudes

Overall, motivation to learn a FL has been shown to be reasonably high with positive attitudes both towards learning the FL and speakers of the FL (Nikolov and Mihaljević Djigunović, 2011). However, a worrying trend emerging from a number of studies is that this high motivation can decrease as children (particularly boys) progress through primary school. Furthermore, some evidence suggests that at the beginning stages of FL learning, young children might have a tendency to over-estimate their FL learning ability. As they become more cognitively mature, they develop more realistic expectations as to what they can reasonably achieve, and this perhaps affects their FL motivation (Nikolov and Mihaljević Djigunović, 2011). It could also be the case that when FL learning constitutes a case of L3 acquisition (for example, EFL learners in Catalonia, where primary school children are bilingual in Catalan and Spanish, anxiety might be lower compared to contexts where FL instruction constitutes the first experience young learners have with another language (Muñoz, 2006), as is the case for the majority of children in Anglophone countries.

Young children's feelings about learning the FL was explored in the ELLiE study (Mihaljević Djigunović and Lopriore, 2011). At the beginning of the three-year project, 71.01 per cent of the children surveyed had positive feelings about learning the FL. This figure dropped slightly to 68.1 per cent at the end of the study. Only 3.9 per cent of students expressed negative feelings towards learning the FL at the start of the project, a proportion that rose to 11.7 per cent at the end of the study. Pupil attitudes are associated with their FL outcomes. Learners with positive attitudes in the ELLiE study had higher lexical diversity in the oral production tasks—a finding that was consistent both at the beginning and at the end of the ELLiE project. Similarly, learners who reported preferring reading and speaking activities had higher listening comprehension scores, perhaps due to the fact that these require more focused attention on linguistic features, thus potentially resulting in higher linguistic competence (Mihaljević Djigunović and Lopriore, 2011).

The results from the ELLiE study are consistent with a number of other studies that have measured primary school pupils' attitudes and motivation towards learning a FL. For example, Harris and O'Leary (2009) report that in their evaluation of the 'Modern Languages at Primary School' initiative, the vast majority of pupils had or developed positive attitudes towards learning the language, as well as towards the European country in which the language was spoken. For example, 84 per cent of their sample agreed with the statement 'I am glad that I am learning X in primary school'. Similarly, children who were participating in a FL programme in the south of England indicated positive attitudes towards FL learning, though girls were identified as having more consistently positive attitudes than boys (Enever, 2009).

The extent to which children are motivated and positively disposed towards learning the FL can also interact with the particular FL being learned.

For example, Csizér and Kormos (2009) surveyed 1,777 Hungarian primary school pupils aged 13–14, who were learning either English (58 per cent of the sample) or German (38 per cent). Children learning English had more positive attitudes towards FL learning than those learning German, and also had higher reported levels of self-confidence. They argue that the pupils learning English had more support and opportunities to interact with English as an FL outside the classroom, which may have influenced the results.

Children's stated motivations and attitudes towards FL learning are also in part influenced by the conditions in which they are learning the FL. Mihaljević Djigunović (2009) describes a study where children in 'favourable' FL conditions were compared with children in 'less favourable' conditions. In Croatia, children in favourable conditions were learning EFL five days a week, one 45 minute-period per day in Grades 1 and 2, and four periods a week in Grades 3 and 4, and then three periods a week in Grade 5, until the end of primary school. Teaching was provided by specialist EFL teachers with university degrees and specific training in how to teach young learners. Pedagogy in these favourable conditions included storytelling, content learning, and Total Physical Response (TPR). The class size was never more than 15 pupils per group.

The sample from the less favourable settings included 138 children from four different towns in Croatia, who learned EFL under 'regular' conditions— two classes a week in Grade 1, in classes of up to 32 students, with teachers likely to have had only minimal training in how to teach young learners. Semi-structured oral interviews were administered to gauge students' attitudes towards English and native speakers of English; their motivation, perception of, and attitudes towards classroom activities; and self-assessment of their own EFL competence. The children in less favourable conditions were less likely to report saying English was a favourite subject in school, and reported enjoying age-appropriate in-class activities less frequently than the children in favourable conditions. They had less knowledge of English speakers and English culture than children in favourable conditions, and reported that they received less support from their parents. The children were less proficient in English and had lower confidence in learning English than children in favourable conditions. Mihaljević Djigunović (2009) concludes by highlighting the interaction between children's motivation and attitudes and the nature of the provision, and stresses the importance of getting the provision 'right' in FL learning at primary school.

Participating in a taught FL programme can in and of itself also boost learners' motivation to develop their FL knowledge. Barton, Bragg, and Serratrice (2009) describe an FL programme that is not so much focused on learning a specific FL, but rather on promoting language awareness in the primary years, to provide a solid basis upon which to build systematic FL competence in later secondary school. The motivation behind the 'Discover Languages' programme was based on Hawkins' (2005) idea that children cannot possibly know in primary school which L2s or FLs will be useful for them, and therefore instead of teaching a specific FL, it is better for children to learn the tools of how to learn a FL so that they can cope with the challenge later on. Barton et al. (2009) report that as a consequence of participating in this programme, children's extrinsic motivation to learn a FL was encouraged and developed.

In summary, this brief sketch of children's motivation and attitudes towards FL learning indicates that overall, children are motivated FL learners and report having positive attitudes towards their FL learning. However, this relatively positive outlook has been shown to wane over the primary school years in some cases. The reasons for this drop in motivation are complex and varied, including the nature of the provision itself, and support for the FL outside of classroom contexts.

Interaction with the L1

Researchers have long been interested in the relationship between developing L2 knowledge and the L1. Typically, however, the focus has been on identifying ways in which a given L1 might either facilitate or inhibit successful L2 learning (see Lado's (1957) Contrastive Analysis approach). Young FL learners' L1s are still developing in some aspects, therefore there could be ways in which developing knowledge of the L2 impacts on the L1 and vice versa. In their review, Nikolov and Mihaljević Djigunović (2011) report that even where the FL is actually a case of L3 learning, there seems to be harmonious growth with no negative consequences on the L1(s) as a result of FL learning. For example, Nikolov and Csapó (2010) demonstrate a strong relationship between developing L2 and L1 reading skills in children aged 12 and 14 learning English as a FL in Hungary. A somewhat similar study by Mihaljević Djigunović (2010) investigated the effect of an early vs. later start in FL learning on the development of listening and reading comprehension and writing in children learning Croatian as an L1 and English as an L2. A cohort of 414 students, aged between 14 and 15 years were recruited and divided into two groups according to when they began learning English: the early group began English before Grade 4 ($n = 125$) while the later group began English at Grade 4 or later ($n = 289$). There was a strong positive correlation between the L1 and L2 tests in the group who began EFL before Grade 4 (early learners): pupils who scored higher on the L1 tests had correspondingly high scores on the L2 versions. No such correlation was found for the later learners. Furthermore, the early learners outperformed the later learners on all tests, even in the L1, which may imply a possible advantage to the L1 development of the early learners resulting from their L2 learning. Although the design of the Mihaljević Djigunović (2010) study does not allow such a causal interpretation, this conclusion is consistent with her findings.

A study that directly addressed whether learning a FL in primary school has any facilitative effects on developing L1 skills was developed in Murphy, Macaro, Alba, and Cipolla (2014). In this study, 120 children in Years 3 and 4 (aged 7–9 years) were randomly assigned into one of three groups: L2 French, L2 Italian, or Control. Children assigned to the L2 French or L2 Italian groups received 15 hours of taught FL French or Italian, respectively. The instruction focused largely on vocabulary, with a few elements of grammar (for example, gender and plural assignment) and included activities in listening, speaking, reading, and writing. Children were tested on their English L1 literacy skills, using pre- and post-test standardized assessments before and after the 15 weeks of L2 instruction. Despite being matched on all tests at pre-test (the three groups were the same on the standardized measures of English spelling, phonological processing, single word reading, reading comprehension, and nonverbal IQ), children in the L2 French and Italian groups outperformed the control groups on measures of English single word reading and aspects of English phonological processing at post-test. Furthermore, the children who received the L2 Italian instruction scored higher than the children in the L2 French group on single word English reading and phonological awareness measures. Murphy et al. argue these results indicate that learning an L2/FL at primary school can have facilitative effects on developing L1 literacy skills. It also suggests that the extent to which the L2/FL is facilitative is likely to be related to how transparent the mapping is between phonemes and graphemes in both the L2 and L1. If the child speaks an L1 with an opaque Phoneme–Grapheme Correspondence (GPC) such as English, and learns an L2 with a transparent GPC, such as Italian, there may be stronger facilitative influences on the developing L1 literacy. In summary, introducing a taught FL into the primary curriculum can confer advantages on different aspects of the L1.

Learner variables

In considering the outcomes of participating in FL programmes in primary school, it is important to examine learner characteristics. In other words, do outcomes from FL learning at primary level depend on or interact with specific learner characteristics? In discussing motivation and attitudes above, it emerged that those learners with higher stated motivation and more positive attitudes are indeed more likely to have higher scores on various outcome measures. There are, however, other learner characteristics to consider.

The field of strategy use is vast (see Cohen and Macaro, 2007), but the amount of research carried out on L2 strategies in young primary school learners is significantly smaller and is worthy of more focused attention. Šamo (2009) investigated young FL learners' use of L2 reading strategies and compared this strategy use in 'good' and 'poor' learners. A cohort of 37 primary school children from Croatia, aged 13–14, were divided into groups in different ways. In one comparison, later learners (who had learned EFL for five years) were compared to early learners (who had learned EFL for eight years); in the other comparison good vs. poor EFL learners were compared and identified via an English proficiency test. Students were given three cloze tests, as well as a think-aloud procedure requiring the students to talk about their strategy use in completing the cloze passages. Good readers used a wider range of L2 reading strategies and used them more frequently than weaker readers. However, students who had been learning EFL for only five, as opposed to eight years, were no different in their L2 reading strategy use. Šamo concludes from this that while age is a variable to consider in examining FL outcomes and performance, it should be examined as only one of a number of possible factors contributing to L2/FL success. Similarly, Lan and Oxford (2003) show that while strategy use in young learners of EFL in Taiwan is associated with proficiency, gender and the extent to which the student enjoys EFL learning are also mitigating factors.

Macaro and Mutton (2009) have argued for a literacy-based component in FL instruction at primary level in light of their findings that giving young FL learners (aged 10–11) reading materials aimed to develop their inferencing strategies can lead to higher levels of reading comprehension. In their study, three groups of English children learning French as a FL were compared. One group received materials adapted from an English novel where the text was code-switched, in that French words were inserted into the English text and the children were encouraged (through strategy instruction) to infer the meaning of these novel French words. The second group was given the standard graded readers often used for FL learners at this level. The third group was given their normal FL teaching. The outcome measures were designed to evaluate whether the children learned new words and to assess their reading comprehension. The inferencing strategies group and the graded reader group outperformed the comparison group in reading comprehension. Additionally, the inferencing group outperformed the graded reading group on both inferencing the meaning of novel word forms and learning function words. These results demonstrate that strategy instruction can have beneficial effects for FL learning at the primary level and can be encouraged through the use of relevant materials.

Alexiou (2009) reports on the results of a three-year study examining the relationship between cognitive skills (aptitude) and success at EFL learning in 191 Greek learners of English aged 5–9. The aptitude measures included tests of memory—a short term memory for pictures and a semantic integration task which taps into recognition memory; and tests of analytic skills—inductive learning, visual perception tasks, reasoning ability (story sequencing), and spatial ability (jigsaw). Receptive and productive vocabulary knowledge was also assessed and was used as outcome measures in this study. The aptitude measures correlated positively with the children's English receptive and productive vocabulary measures. The discussion surrounding language learning aptitude and outcomes (Carroll, 1979; Skehan, 2002) is equally relevant in the case of FL learning in primary school and is useful for developing a child's learning profile at the beginning stages of FL learning. Developing an understanding of children's learning styles (i.e. aptitude) is beneficial for teachers and curriculum developers alike to meet the needs of their pupils. These findings are consistent with Sawyer and Ranta (2001), Kiss and Nikolov (2005), and Csapó and Nikolov (2009) who argue that inductive reasoning skills are important predictors of L2 outcomes.

In summary, a range of learner variables have been shown to predict and/ or impact on FL success at the primary level. Students' skills in the L1, their language learning aptitude (such as memory, reasoning ability, etc.) and their strategy use have all been shown to be relevant predictors of FL success. However, these learner-oriented characteristics interact with other variables, such as the nature of the FL provision and motivation to learn the FL.

Teachers

Arguably one of the most important variables in considering the nature of FL provision is the teacher. A number of FL learning studies have focused on the teacher, including reporting on their classroom practices, their uses of language, and their beliefs and attitudes towards FL learning at the primary level (Nikolov and Mihaljević Djigunović, 2011). In many contexts, FL teachers at primary level are expected to be proficient in the pupils' L1 and L2, as well as with the content and curriculum, at the same time as being experts in teaching young learners, and teaching languages in particular. The reality, as reported in Nikolov and Mihaljević Djigunović (2011), is that teachers are often unable to meet these expectations, and their actual roles in the FL classroom can vary to a great extent from classroom to classroom. For example, teachers can take on the role of bystander, translator, co-learner of the FL, or co-teacher. Some teachers may feel that they would rather be teaching older, more able FL learners than playing language 'games' with young children. Additionally, there is some evidence that FL teachers of young learners can rely heavily on the L1 (which is not in and of itself a negative practice when considered in light of some of the research on the possible use of code-switching as a pedagogical strategy) (Tian and Macaro, 2012). However it is not always obvious that teachers have this pedagogical aim in mind when using the L1.

The ELLiE study described earlier, explored the relationship between the teacher and successful FL classrooms, where a successful FL classroom was regarded as one that yielded high scores on the ELLiE language assessments[10] (Tragant Mestres and Lundberg, 2011). The main findings suggest that successful FL teaching can be found in a wide variety of situations and there is no one formula that leads to good FL performance. There was a considerable degree of variability across the schools on a number of factors, including use of the L1, the degree of teachers' FL proficiency and their pedagogical approach. The main common features with all these successful FL classes, however, were that the teacher reported enjoying the FL and teaching, had a fondness for the FL itself, and believed that learning the FL was beneficial to the children. Successful FL teachers were those who were able to create positive and supportive relationships with the children and most importantly, were able to keep the children focused on their FL learning. However, in these successful FL classes there was a fair degree of homogeneity (in that there were few children from immigrant families and parents tended to have high levels of education). This finding reinforces the need to consider a multitude of factors in attempting to understand the nature of successful FL learning in a range of contexts and learners (Tragant Mestres and Lundberg, 2011).

FL teachers' professional needs are considered as part of the Edelenbos et al. (2006) review. Issues that arose include how to establish the competencies required for successful FL learning, how to cope with teaching methodologies, ways of keeping children motivated and on task, and the need for appropriate in-service teaching support and professional development. These issues are also raised in Emery's (2012) review of teachers' qualifications and needs in the context of ELT for young learners. Questionnaires and interviews were carried out with teachers and head teachers from 89 countries, where 2,478 teachers responded to the questionnaire, while in-depth interviews were carried out with 85 teachers and head teachers from nine different countries. Emery found considerable variation in the different contexts; nonetheless there were identifiable global trends, some of which were positive, others less so. Class size was an identifiable problem with some teachers (in Cambodia) in classes with as many as 80 students sitting on the floor, as there were insufficient desks and chairs for the children. This was a concern in a number of countries and Emery notes that '... while in some countries we talk about the *maximum number* of pupils allowed in a class, in other countries it is the *minimum number* allowable.' (p. 10). In some countries, teacher shortages create additional burdens for the teachers already in place. With respect to qualifications, 38 per cent of the sample indicated they held a degree, 25 per cent held a Masters Degree. Of the total number of respondents, 35 per cent had no qualifications to teach primary, while 21 per cent were not specifically trained to teach FL. However, 85 per cent reported they had attended a training course of some kind, many of which were organized by governmental agencies in their respective countries, and 79 per cent responded that they wished to take further professional development courses. Respondents also felt that having good English language skills was the most important criterion in making a 'good primary school English teacher', followed by having experience with children, teaching experience and knowledge, an understanding personality, and good qualifications. Knowledge of syllabus, ability to keep discipline, and knowing the rules of English grammar were not considered important. Emery's (2012) recommendations stemming from her review range from ensuring the reduction of class sizes, providing sufficient teacher training opportunities and professional development for teachers, enhancing their job satisfaction, and offering opportunities for promotion. Given the prevalence of FL learning at primary level, where English is the main FL being taught, along with the recognized relationship between FL outcomes and the quality of the teaching and teacher, ensuring that teachers are well supported in their professional endeavour is critical.

Out-of-school factors

A final variable to consider in examining FL outcomes referred to in many of the discussions above is the context beyond the FL class itself, and the extent to which this—home and the wider society—supports FL learning. When research on FL learning and outcomes attempts to measure the out-of-class context, there is invariably an identifiable relationship between out-of-school factors and FL learning. This issue is discussed in some detail in Lindgren and Muñoz (2013) and while their study focused solely on the seven participating ELLiE studies, a number of studies have shown a similar relationship. It is reasonable to assume that these findings will also apply to other countries. In their qualitative review of the seven ELLiE countries, parents, teachers, and children highlighted the positive impact of exposure to the FL outside the school, notably of subtitled television programmes and movies, as being supportive of their in-class learning. Parental support emerged as a very important variable in children's FL development, where the parents' level of education and their personal relationship with the FL (if there is one) positively impacts on children's FL skills. For example, if the parent knows the FL or uses the FL in the workplace, not surprisingly this will have a positive effect on the child's FL learning. As with all the other studies above, Lindgren and Muñoz note considerable variation across and within different countries. Some children in some countries are exposed to the FL daily (as in Sweden and the Netherlands) whereas others (for example, England) rarely encounter the FL outside of school. Where there is no exposure to the FL outside the classroom, schools can effectively compensate by providing much higher levels of contact with the FL through the school. While socioeconomic status does have an impact on FL outcomes, good quality teaching can mitigate against economic disadvantage. Lindgren and Muñoz conclude by arguing that non-school factors need to be considered by policy makers and practitioners to help develop curricula appropriately balanced to help compensate for out-of-school factors (see also Muñoz and Lindgren, 2011).

In summary, non-school factors play an important role in children's FL outcomes and should be considered alongside FL pedagogy, learner characteristics, and FL provision.

The age issue

The discussion in this chapter has highlighted some of the main issues and findings on FL learning in children. However, what has not yet been addressed is the extent to which studies specifically aimed at comparing younger and older starters achieve the same level of FL competence. A few studies have been carried out that address these issues; however, they have yielded mixed results.

In their review, Edelenbos et al. (2006) suggest that a tendency to be more successful at learning the FL will be associated with an early starting age. This was their recommendation based on their review of 11 different studies that addressed the younger vs. older issue. However, only a small number of these 11 studies systematically compared young and older starters, controlling for amount of input. One such study is found in the comprehensive series of investigations reported in Muñoz (2006).

Muñoz presents a range of studies investigating the effect of age on EFL in Catalan/Spanish bilingual children learning English in school as part of the Barcelona Age Factor (BAF) project. Systematic comparisons were made on a number of different variables including foreign language perception and production, vocabulary, morphosyntax, learner strategies, and writing development across children who learned English at different ages. Muñoz (2006b), for example, compared four different groups of subjects who differed in age of onset (AO) of learning English as a foreign language. The specific AOs included were 8, 11, 14, and 18+ years. Students were compared after 200 hours, 416 hours, and 726 hours of English instruction, respectively. Dictation tests, cloze tests, listening comprehension, grammar, written composition, oral tasks, and phonetic imitation and discrimination assessments were administered. The 18+ learners had the highest scores after 200 hours of instruction, but their learning slowed between 200 and 416 hours of English in relation to the other groups. Students who began learning at age 14 had statistically higher scores and a more rapid rate of learning than the younger learners (8 and 11). Those whose AO was 11 years also had statistically higher scores than the youngest group at Time 2 (after 416 hours of English instruction). This study indicates that older starters had overall more successful scores than early starters. Furthermore, with a handful of exceptions (for example, in aural perception) overall the younger learners did not surpass the older learners in terms of their scores. There is, therefore, a complex interaction between rate, age, and task type/linguistic skill. Muñoz concludes by suggesting that it is the interaction between the learners' stage of cognitive development and the kind and amount of exposure they receive (whether instructed or not) that will determine the point at which the younger learners catch up with the older ones.

García Mayo and García Lecumberri (2003) present a very similar picture. In this volume, research is presented that examines the effect of age on EFL in terms of the children's code-switching patterns and attitudes to learning, competence in morphosyntax, English pronunciation, English writing, and strategy use. A clear picture emerges from the García Mayo and García Lecumberri volume: the notion of 'younger is better' is not substantiated in a context where the language being learned is being taught as a subject, and where the learners' exposure to it is largely restricted to the school context. Larson-Hall (2008) also demonstrates that Japanese speakers who started learning EFL at younger ages do not score higher than later learners on measures of morphosyntax. Similarly, Marinova-Todd, Marshall, and Snow (2000) argue that older learners can be as successful at learning a foreign language as younger learners.

However, despite these studies arguing that either older learners have the advantage, or that at least older learners are not disadvantaged, there are also studies which argue younger starters have an advantage. For example, Pinter (2011) argues that the quality of the materials used in the Muñoz's (2006) BAF project were not evaluated, and that other research that factored in high-quality input and teaching indicates a possible advantage of younger over older learners (Mihaljević Djigunović and Vilke, 2000). In this eight-year project in Croatia, Mihaljević Djigunović and Vilke report that young learners (aged 6–7) who were taught English, French, German, or Italian, compared against a group who started their L2 instruction at age 10, were significantly better at pronunciation, orthography, and vocabulary than the older starters. They further outperformed the older learners on tasks tapping in to implicit learning processes. The authors suggested that the most important variable to account for the younger learners' success was the quality of the input and teaching. This assertion speaks to the importance of ensuring that high-quality pedagogical resources are in place to support the L2 learning process effectively in young learners.

In summary, in looking (only) at studies comparing older vs. younger learners in instructed FL contexts, there is at best equivocal evidence in support of an early vs. late start in FL learning. What is clear from the discussion above, is that young FL learners can learn aspects of the FL, albeit slowly, and that a complex interaction involving a number of different variables (not just age) contribute to the success of FL learners in developing L2 knowledge.

Educational implications

What then can we learn from the instructed FL context in terms of how young children learn an L2/FL? It is clear that young children can and do make slow but steady progress on a range of different FL measures; that they have generally positive attitudes and high levels of motivation to learn the FL, particularly in the initial stages of learning; and that successful FL learning is determined by a complex range of variables including individual learner characteristics, quality of and support for teaching, as well as exposure and support for the FL learning outside of the classroom context. It is also clear, however, that young FL learners are by no means fast and rapid L2 learners soaking up language 'like a sponge'. FL learning in primary school is effortful, for both the learner and the teacher, an idea reinforced in Marinova-Todd et al. (2000). This is not to say introducing FL instruction into the primary curriculum is misguided. There is good evidence that FL learning not only develops[11], but that FL learning can have positive influences on other aspects of young children's developing L1 skills (Murphy et al., 2014). The benefits of primary FL learning are particularly salient when considered from the point of view of language awareness training (Hawkins, 2005). FL instruction and learning at primary school can serve as the basis on which targeted and focused FL study can proceed in secondary level education.

It is not entirely clear whether and to what extent the decisions made by governments to lower the starting age for FL instruction at the primary level have been made in the knowledge of the issues described above. One fears, for example, that policy makers may not be conscious of the significant complexity associated with determining success in FL learning in primary education. The issues raised in this chapter highlight a multi-faceted constellation of factors that contribute to determining first, whether and to what extent a young learner will acquire proficiency in the FL and second, continue to develop their competence in the FL over time. The issue of assessment, only briefly touched on here, is critical as well. However, determining the most effective means of measuring FL learning and progress in young learners is a considerable challenge. Presumably, policy makers will want to evaluate the success of their decisions to introduce FL into primary curricula. How will they do so? If they apply the CEFR framework to assess young learners' FL proficiency, they may decide that FL provision at primary level does not work, since learners do not typically advance beyond the early stage at A1 level. Consequently, they may decide to withdraw FL provision from already overcrowded primary curricula. If this were to happen then potentially one of the most significant policy developments in the world could also turn out to be one of the biggest U-turns in policy making (Johnstone, 2009).

There are, therefore, real and significant consequences for failing to appreciate the complexity of FL learning in primary schools. While younger learners may not be fast learners, there are a host of benefits to learning a FL as part of the primary curriculum, both in terms of learning the FL, developing some inter-cultural awareness, as well as potentially having positive impacts on the learners' developing L1 literacy skills, to name only a few. FL learning through primary education can also provide a solid foundation upon which FL learning can develop when the child is older and can apply their more advanced explicit learning mechanisms to the task (c.f. Muñoz, 2006).

Conclusions

This chapter has explored some of the major themes and issues emerging from research examining instructed FL learning, arguably the most prevalent means by which primary school-aged children are exposed to and begin to develop L2/FL skills. A key issue emerging from this research is one of substantial variability in the nature of FL provision, in the outcomes reported in various studies from different countries worldwide, in the interaction between in- and out-of-class factors and, finally, in relation to the degree of confidence one can have in the assertion that younger is better for FL learning.

The discussion in this chapter highlights that it is at best simplistic and at worst inaccurate to argue that young learners are somehow better learners than older ones. Nonetheless there are numerous positive consequences of introducing FL instruction through the primary curriculum, and researchers and practitioners alike need to work together to move towards a shared understanding of good practice in FL education.

Notes

1 See Lightbown and Spada (1994) as an example of research in primary school contexts where specific aspects of the input (focus-on-form) are manipulated to determine the effect on features of L2 learners' language (such as adjective placement or inflectional morphology).

2 See also the *EL Gazette*, July 2013 for a description of some FL instructional programmes targeted for young learners in Latin America.

3 Note that CLIL as a context of L2 learning in primary school is discussed in Chapter 5.

4 Note that Irish is a regional minority language in the sense that it is the regional or indigenous language of Ireland, but English is the majority language. Ireland is a relatively unique context since Irish is a regional minority language, but is widely taught as a subject in primary school. Few countries provide such widespread instruction of regional language(s).

5 See also Rixon (2013).

6 A possible explanation for why translation was not indicated as a pedagogical activity could also derive from the fact that primary teachers may not view translation as an activity *per se* but rather as a natural part of classroom interaction to promote meaning (c.f. Enever, personal communication).

7 For a more detailed discussion of intensive programmes see Muñoz (2012).

8 An example is Cambridge Young Learners English (YLE) test, which was originally designed for use in private language school contexts and as a result is likely not an appropriate test for all English L2 contexts for young learners.

9 As one example, in Murphy (2000) the school in which her study was carried out used an in-house proficiency measure which suggested Murphy's sample consisted of three different proficiency bands in ESL whereas the standardized test Murphy administered did not discriminate between these three groups—indicating that the results of bespoke and standardized assessments are often very different.

10 Note, as mentioned in the introduction to this chapter, that there are many examples of rigorous examinations of the nature of L2 instruction on L2 outcomes in younger learners. The focus here is not on a detailed examination of the interaction between L2 pedagogy and outcomes, but rather on a more holistic understanding of some teacher variables.

11 As only one example of this successful L2 learning in younger learners see Muñoz (2012), which includes a number of chapters on younger learners.

7

Trends, implications, and conclusions

Introduction

The overarching aim of this volume is twofold. One goal is to provide a review of major themes and issues that have emerged from different contexts in which primary school-aged children are exposed to another language and through which they could become bilingual (or multilingual). Chapters 2–6 presented these reviews for each of their respective contexts—bilingualism, heritage language learners, minority language learners, immersion, and instructed foreign language learning. The second main goal of this volume is to evaluate what these reviews of the literature can tell us with respect to whether and to what extent 'younger is better' in child L2 learning at the primary level, and the extent to which other variables in addition to age might contribute to child L2 outcomes. This cross-context analysis will be the focus of the discussion in this concluding chapter. To that end, the main findings emerging from the review of the different contexts will be summarized; the extent to which current educational provision does or does not support the development of bi- or multilingualism will be discussed, together with implications of future directions both in terms of research and educational policy. However, first, let us revisit the age issue.

Theoretical assumptions regarding age and L2 learning

The discussion of the Critical Period Hypothesis (CPH) in Chapter 1 identified that the CPH contends that children need exposure to the to-be-learned language(s) within a 'critical' or 'sensitive' period in their development, otherwise they are likely to be unable to develop full grammatical proficiency in those language(s). There is an undeniable relationship between the age of a learner and their ultimate L2 attainment (Muñoz and Singleton, 2011). However, what is less clear is the extent to which age in and of itself *predicts* L2 attainment. In other words, what is the role and explanatory power of other variables in determining L2 attainment? Muñoz and Singleton (2011) critically review a number of research studies, some of which highlight age of L2 onset as the 'crucial' variable, while other linguistic and/or contextual variables are either ignored or inadequately discussed. The purpose of this chapter, and indeed this entire volume, is to look more closely at the context: the setting in which the child is exposed to the L2, in terms of quantity of exposure and the nature of the interactions the child may have with the L2 in given contexts. It is not the purpose of this volume to try and resolve the debates about the CPH. However, as DeKeyser (2013) notes, a break in the Age-of-Acquisition → Ultimate Attainment function that is explained by variables other than age (including motivation, attitude, identity, input, schooling in the L2) would indicate there is no critical period (p. 53). In other words, the CPH would predict that as the learner gets older, ultimate attainment becomes increasingly less native-like[1]. If failure to reach native-like levels of proficiency can be attributed to something other than age of onset, then this raises a serious challenge to the validity of the CPH. The reviews in this volume therefore make a contribution to the debates surrounding the CPH given that, as I argue, the variability in the extent to which children actually become bilingual seems to be determined more by context, not age. This conclusion does not provide a definitive resolution to the CPH debate, because older learners, operating outside the putative offset of the CPH (whenever that might be), have not been included in this review of research, nor do the discussions in Chapters 2–6 allow for a controlled comparison which partials out variability due to age alone relative to these other factors. Therefore, the discussion here is more holistic in nature, perhaps offering a suitable starting point to begin examining in greater detail the relative contribution of different variables that are typically confounded with age of acquisition.

The children whose L2 development is discussed in Chapters 2–6 can all be argued to be operating within the critical period. While there is some debate as to when the offset of the critical period might be (Muñoz and Singleton, 2011)—ranging anywhere between one year and adolescence—many research-ers investigating the CPH would concede that children from each of the different populations represented in Chapters 2–6 operate within a 'sensitive' period at least, if not a critical one. If this is true, then variability in outcome may not be exclusively explained away by the CPH. As mentioned earlier, the focus of this volume is not to resolve the debate. Nonetheless, given that each population constitutes a learner younger than age ten, variability in terms of L2 or bilingual outcomes are arguably more powerfully explained by the dif-ferences in the linguistic input and the environment experienced by children within each of the different contexts described in this volume, and not by the Age-of-Acquisition → Ultimate Attainment continuum endorsed by some researchers (Hyltenstam and Abrahamsson, 2003).

Trends across contexts

Attainment and rate

The main themes emerging from each of the five contexts reviewed in this volume related to linguistic outcomes and rate of language development will be presented in Tables 7.1–7.4, each presenting the main issues along four dimensions. Attainment and rate (Table 7.1) reflects the evidence on how much L2 (or L1 in the case of heritage language learners) is learned by the child, along with a discussion of rate of learning where possible. The main findings that address the role of parents, school, and community/society in shaping or influencing L2 outcomes are presented in Tables 7.2–7.4 respectively.

Table 7.1 highlights some of the key findings on linguistic outcomes across the five different L2 learning contexts discussed in this volume. One of the first issues to note is that *all* children can either become bilingual and/or learn aspects of a second language. This might seem a somewhat superficial observation, but importantly, there was no evidence in any of the contexts discussed in this volume of negative consequences to learning an L2—that is, it does not retard either children's rate of L1 learning, or their academic achievement. The only caveat here is the possible smaller vocabulary size and the slight lag on some aspects of morphosyntax discussed in the context of BFLA. However, even with these two examples, there is corresponding evidence that BFLA children can quickly catch up with monolingual norms. The cognitive architecture of young children is more than adequately equipped to tackle the challenge of learning multiple languages. Indeed, it often does not seem to be a challenge at all. Within the BFLA context, even at just a few days old, babies' brains are accommodating linguistic input from more than one language. BFLA children achieve the same milestones as monolingual children overall, in roughly the same time period. Furthermore, being bilingual seems to have cognitive advantages, advantages that were also observed in the context of immersion.

In terms of ultimate attainment in the L2 (or at least as 'ultimate' as can be observed in a child who is still developing) there is no single, clear pattern demonstrating increased L2 proficiency or degree of bilingualism as a function of context. While it is unambiguously clear that children make the least progress in L2/bilingual development in the context of FL instruction, it is more difficult to identify which of the remaining contexts is the most facilitative in producing fluent bilinguals. The FL context is input-limited in comparison to all of the other contexts, which are comparatively input-rich. Even without closer examination of the nature of the input, at a simplistic level, the amount of exposure clearly has a powerful impact. Children developing in the BFLA context make solid, substantial gains in both languages. However, the extent to which they develop full oral proficiency and biliteracy skills is very much dependent upon a range of different factors. These include whether and to what extent the child receives instruction through the medium of and/or on the language, what the status of the language is in the society at large, and the degree of exposure and opportunities for interaction in each of the languages. Many minority language learners begin their language learning as BFLA children, but experience a language shift when they begin formal education through the medium of the majority L2 (see Chapter 3). Some of the research in the minority language learner context has identified that even when minority language learners participate in dual immersion programmes

Bilingual first language acquisition (Chapter 2)

- Bilingual-to-be babies' brains are able to discriminate between phonological contrasts in ambient languages.
- Bilingual children achieve the same linguistic milestones as monolinguals in approximately the same time frame.
- Bilingual children manifest the same patterns of linguistic development as monolinguals.
- Bilingual children code switch frequently for many different reasons.
- Bilingual children typically become dominant in one of their two languages.
- Cross-linguistic influence is typical of bilingual first language acquisition.
- Bilingualism may provide a range of cognitive advantages.
- Bilingual children may have smaller vocabulary size in both languages.
- A lag in rate of development in one of the two languages is possible.
- Bilinguals rarely develop balanced proficiency.

Heritage language learners (Chapter 3)

- HL learners may be learners of an ethnolinguistically minority language or a language not widely spoken in the community.
- HL learners often begin life as BFLA children, but typically experience a language shift to the majority language.
- Policy decisions on the language of education for HL learners may be transitional.
- HL learners may outperform L2 learners of the same language, especially on implicit and phonologically-oriented tasks.
- HL learners typically do not achieve full bilingual proficiency where their HL either does not develop completely and/or aspects of the HL attrite.
- Competence in the HL typically falls somewhere between L1 and L2.

Minority language learners (Chapter 4)

- There is a consistent achievement gap in academic outcomes between many minority language learners and native-speaking children.
- The achievement gap may be due to lagging behind NS peers on measures of reading comprehension.
- Vocabulary knowledge is a predictor of reading comprehension skills, and minority language learners often have lower scores on vocabulary assessments.
- Interventions for improving minority language learners' vocabulary knowledge have been largely successful.
- There are a number of different types of vocabulary knowledge, and more work is needed to more closely examine the relationship between different dimensions of vocabulary knowledge and literacy skill.
- There are many non-linguistic variables that influence minority language learners' academic and linguistic outcomes, including cultural norms, maternal education, and socioeconomic status.

Immersion and CLIL (Chapter 5)

- Immersion education aims to provide content through the L2 at least 50% of the school day, up to late primary school and sometimes into the secondary school years.
- The primary aim of immersion is to promote additive bilingual and biliteracy development.

- One-way immersion is intended for majority language students; two-way immersion includes minority and majority language students in the same class, where content-based instruction is provided through both minority and majority languages.
- Immersion programmes are highly successful; immersion students have higher levels of L2 oral proficiency and literacy than L2 learners in traditional L2 instruction; students still struggle with certain grammatical and socio-pragmatic features.
- Use of immersion students' L1 can help raise cross-linguistic awareness, thus improving immersion students' L2 outcomes.
- The success of immersion programmes in North America has led to the adaptation and extension of immersion programmes worldwide.
- CLIL is arguably an instantiation of immersion education.
- Older children beginning immersion may achieve comparable L2 outcomes as younger starters.
- Immersion education is beneficial for minority language learners for whom the immersion language is a third language.

Instructed foreign language learning (Chapter 6)

- More children worldwide are being taught a foreign language at younger ages.
- FL programmes vary in how and when they are introduced worldwide.
- Young FL learners make slow but steady progress in FL.
- FL outcome assessment is challenging and should be linked to classroom activities.
- FL learning in young learners can have positive effects on aspects of the L1.
- Young FL learners have positive attitudes and motivation; these may wane by the end of primary school.
- Primary school FL learning can increase language awareness.
- There is mixed evidence on outcomes of FL instruction at younger ages; but FL instruction in primary education is a good basis for later rapid progress.

Table 7.1 Summary of the main themes in each of the five language learning contexts

and have opportunities to be educated (in part) through the medium of their (minority) L1, they still nonetheless interact more in the L2, presumably because the L2 has higher status and is more prevalent in the ambient community (see for example, Potowski, 2007, in Chapter 5).

This finding underscores Cummins' (1996, 2000) concern about the manner in which interactions within formal education reinforce power relations in the wider society. If the minority language is perceived as low status, then it is more likely that educators and the students themselves will reinforce the subordinated power relations within the school context. As a result, both minority and majority language speakers in TWI programmes speak more of the majority than the minority language. Therefore, despite the fact that children may start out learning two languages within the BFLA context, they may not develop balanced proficiency in both languages. The most facilitative context for promoting bilingualism is undoubtedly a BFLA context where both languages have equal status in and outside of the home, where both languages are used fairly equally in the wider society, and in which children can receive some formal education in both languages. Unfortunately, contexts such as these are comparatively rare. It is important to note, however, that even in such exceptional contexts, it is still unlikely that a child will develop equal proficiency and biliteracy skills across both languages. The discussion in Chapter 2 demonstrated that children are typically dominant in one of their two languages. Again, the environment in which the child is developing determines patterns of linguistic dominance.

Children in immersion contexts can make very rapid progress in the immersion (L2) language, and indeed have consistently been shown to outperform peers who participate in traditional L2 instructional programmes (Genesee, 2004). However, without some focus on linguistic form in the context of immersion classrooms, students often fail to develop some grammatical aspects of the L2 (Harley and Swain, 1984). This problem can be remedied somewhat, however, by the pedagogical approach taken within immersion settings (Lyster, Collins, and Ballinger, 2009). It may not be sufficient, therefore, for children to be instructed through the medium of the L2—there still needs to be an appropriate targeted focus on some aspects of the L2 to help them develop greater L2 knowledge and skills. In other words, although being immersed in the L2 can yield very positive outcomes in terms of L2 oral proficiency and biliteracy skills, appropriate pedagogical support can enhance these learning outcomes.

In terms of rate of development, again it is easy to identify that the slowest progress in L2 learning is in the input-limited instructed FL context. However, it is not easy to establish which of the remaining contexts facilitate fastest growth. It is tempting to argue it is in the BFLA context, but as discussed above, rate of bilingual learning is very much dependent on the extent to which children's BFLA environment can be sustained once they begin formal education. In the context of minority language learners, rapid progress is observed on context-supported conversational skills (BICS) (as above). However, minority language learners might make very slow progress in their home (heritage) language if it is an indigenous language with relatively few speakers and few opportunities for engaging and interacting with the HL. Minority language learners who speak immigrant minority languages might also experience significantly reduced progress in their HL development when they begin formal education. They may no longer perceive their HL as being important and may identify with speakers of the higher status majority language. These factors are implicated in Montrul's (2008) 'incomplete acquisition' hypothesis. HL learners develop rapidly initially, but their rate of HL development slows down and then stalls before the complete system is developed. Similarly, they develop knowledge of the majority L2 relatively rapidly (BICS) but it can take many years for them to develop the same level of vocabulary knowledge as majority language learners, which may have negative consequences on their L2 reading comprehension skills (Genesee et al., 2006). Again, the factors that contribute to rate of development are the context—how much exposure the child receives in both languages, the status of the minority language, and the extent to which the minority language is supported in educational contexts. Additionally, child-internal factors such as motivation and attitudes are predictive of both rate and ultimate attainment in the two languages.

Children who participate in immersion programmes make good progress in their L2 competence, despite the fact that in many cases of immersion, the only exposure to the L2 is through the school setting (Genesee, 2004). This finding illustrates the power and indeed the need for the school to support bilingual development. Interestingly, children who participate in late immersion programmes can also quickly catch up with children who began learning the L2 through immersion at younger ages. Genesee (1987) has suggested that older students' explicit learning mechanisms and more advanced cognitive skills ensure faster progress in late immersion programmes, enabling them to catch up.

In summary, we see from Table 7.1 that there is no simple formula to develop bilingual children. The limited exposure to the L2 in a foreign language context yields the least amount of L2 knowledge and bilingualism that develops the most slowly. However, this is perfectly reasonable. One cannot realistically expect highly proficient speakers of an L2 in only a few hours' worth of exposure each week (if that). In the UK, for example, the school year lasts for a minimum of 190 days (or 380 sessions). In such an environment it will be exceedingly difficult to enable the child to develop anything other than basic FL skills. At the other end of the spectrum, where the child receives significant exposure to both languages from birth (the BFLA context), the extent to which BFLA children go on to become proficient in both languages, with full oral proficiency and biliteracy skills, is determined by both child-internal (motivation, identity) and child-external (exposure, input, education) factors. Indeed, these child-internal and child-external factors are relevant to L2 achievement in each context reviewed in this volume.

Parents

Table 7.2 summarizes the main themes emerging from each context with respect to the role of the parents in supporting the child's bilingualism and/or L2 development.

Table 7.2 illustrates that parents have a pivotal role in each of the five contexts reviewed in this volume, in that parental support for the bilingual development determines outcomes. Parents in the BFLA context support both languages in the home, by providing the primary source of exposure to both languages. Young BFLA children may model the same codes-switching behaviour that they observe in their parents (c.f. Genesee, Nicoladis, and Paradis, 1995). Similarly, Paradis and Navarro (2003) reported higher than expected use of overt subjects in a Spanish–English bilingual child who was exposed to a dialect of Spanish that itself had higher than typical rates of overt subjects. The input the parents provide in the BFLA context, therefore, is exceedingly powerful in shaping both L2 outcomes and interactional patterns

---

Bilingual first language acquisition (Chapter 2)

- Parents provide input to both languages.
- Parents model code-switching patterns.

Heritage language learners (Chapter 3)

- Parents provide input in the HL.
- They may be apprehensive about educational programmes supporting the HL; they may fear children will not develop sufficient proficiency in the majority language.
- The importance parents place on learning the HL is a predictive factor in HL outcomes.

Minority language learners (Chapter 4)

- Parents provide input in the minority L1 and the L2 as well in cases of BFLA.
- Parents may not help develop the L1 as much as the L2, out of desire for children to develop proficiency in the L2.
- Parents can nonetheless choose bilingual education programmes if available to promote both the minority L1 and the majority L2 (e.g. TWI immersion).
- Parents can also enrol children in complementary education to facilitate L1 development.

Immersion (Chapter 5)

- Parents can exert pressure to establish immersion programmes if none are available.
- Parents have a role in deciding to enrol the child in immersion.

Instructed foreign language learning (Chapter 6)

- Parents can exert pressure to set up instructed FL as part of the curriculum.
- Parents can support FL policy and practice.
- Parents may help support FL learning if they are knowledgeable in the FL themselves.
- Parents can provide increased exposure to the FL with holiday visits, exposure to TV, films, and online programmes in the FL.

Table 7.2 The role of parents in each of the five language learning contexts

in children. In the HL context, as with BFLA, the home is the major (if not the only) source of exposure to the heritage language. Parents in HL contexts may also enrol their children in complementary education programmes to provide the child with instruction in the heritage or home language. Participation in these complementary schools may sometimes be the only means through which HL learners receive any language arts instruction in the home language (García, Zakharia, and Otcu, 2013). Parents in the HL context may also inadvertently impede bilingual development in cases where they are concerned that participating in HL education programmes might slow down their child's rate of L2 learning. The research described in Chapter 3 presented some examples of settings where parents had less positive attitudes about mother tongue education programmes due to their concern that such instruction might delay the child's L2 (English learning) (Iyamu and Aduwa Ogiegbaen, 2007). The parents' role is similarly powerful in the minority language learning context, since they are the primary source of the home language, and may opt to enrol their child in either complementary programmes or in particular forms of available bilingual education.

Finally, the role of the parent in supporting instructed FL learning was woven throughout Chapter 6—often in the example of parents being the driving force underlying the development of different FL programmes (see Enever's, 'parentocracy', 2007). In summary, not surprisingly, parents are a major contributing variable in determining bilingual and L2 outcomes across each of the contexts reviewed in this volume.

The school

The school, the class, and the teacher are three very powerful variables in supporting bi- or multilingualism in the contexts discussed in Chapters 3–6. The school is a less powerful predictor of outcomes for the bilingualism

---

Bilingual first language acquisition (Chapter 2)

- The school is less influential in BFLA contexts. However, pre-school provision can support bilingual development where available.

Heritage language learners (Chapter 3)

- Education for most HL learners is subtractive; the school's aim is to stress majority language, not to develop full bilingual proficiency/biliteracy.
- Transitional educational programmes imply that the home language is not relevant to the wider society.
- Dual language immersion programmes provide good results in developing L1 and L2 language and literacy skills.

Minority language learners (Chapter 4)

- Interventions that focus on oral language skills have been largely successful in improving vocabulary and reading skills in minority language learners.

Immersion (Chapter 5)

- The school is the primary source of the immersion language for many children in immersion programmes.
- Pedagogy promoting cross-linguistic awareness appears to help children develop comprehensive L2 grammars.

Instructed foreign language learning (Chapter 6)

- The school/class provides the only exposure to the FL for many primary school children.
- The quality of teaching is a significant predictor of FL outcomes.
- FL classes that arouse enthusiasm and create positive, enjoyable experiences for the children are the most successful with respect to FL learning.
- Large class sizes are not conducive to successful FL learning.
- Teachers need appropriate pre-and in-service professional training.

Notes: Statements relevant to heritage language learners are also applicable to minority language learners.

Table 7.3 The role of the school in each of the five language learning contexts

context discussed in Chapter 2 simply because children in the BFLA context are too young to be in school. However, in the remaining contexts, the school is critical. For minority language learners, the school can either reinforce the stereotypes and attitudes of the wider society, or, where they are negative, actively serve to fight against them. Cummins (1996, 2000) has argued that if a minority language learner comes from a subordinated societal group, the educational provision can either reinforce that subordination or challenge it:

> ...subordinated group students will succeed academically to the extent that the patterns of interaction in the school challenge and reverse those that have prevailed in the society at large (2000, p. 49).

The school, therefore, can actively empower minority language learners through appropriate in-class interaction, including use of their home language; it can also promote developing reading skills in the home language of minority language learners by providing a balanced reading programme. It is an unfortunate reality that many minority language learners come from lower-income families, which is also associated with maternal education, and the number of experiences and opportunities to engage with print-related activities in the home (Cummins, 2012). The school, therefore, can step in to the breach and provide support for children's developing literacy skills both in and outside the home—by cultivating learners' interest in reading, and indeed where possible, by providing the books as well as the instruction. As was discussed in Chapters 3 and 4, it is not always possible for teachers to draw from the students' L1 if they are in linguistically diverse communities. However, even in these situations it is possible to develop pedagogical activities that reinforce and value children's home language(s) (Cummins, 1996, 2005; Issa and Hatt, 2013). Ideally, minority language learners participate in dual language immersion programmes where they receive formal instruction through the medium of their home language in addition to the majority L2. However, in many communities this is not always possible. Nonetheless, in settings where there are high numbers of minority language pupils, teachers should receive appropriate training to help them best support the needs of all their learners.

In immersion settings the school is equally powerful, as the school is the primary source of the L2. Indeed, immersion programmes were developed in part due to the recognition of the importance and benefits of being bilingual—which was difficult to achieve in linguistically homogenous contexts (i.e. for majority language speakers). The school, therefore, is often the primary means through which the child experiences and interacts with the L2. Immersion programmes have been shown to be highly successful in developing good oral proficiency and biliteracy skills at no cost to academic outcomes—outcomes that are achieved primarily through the school context. The same is also true for children in instructed FL programmes. Typically throughout the world, children being taught a FL have less exposure to the FL outside of the school.

As with immersion programmes, therefore, the school is the primary resource that supports L2 learning in these children and therefore has the most immediate and pronounced impact on the extent to which the child will develop knowledge of the FL. Undeniably, therefore, the school, including the general support for L2 learning throughout the school culture, the quality of the teaching, and the extent to which teachers are supported with appropriate in service professional development, are all significant determinants of L2 learning across each of the contexts reviewed in this volume.

The school has a pivotal role then in each context because formal education allows the child to develop literacy skills and academic language in each language. Immersion programmes are the only educational programmes that do this adequately—supporting biliteracy skills and bilingual oral proficiency. An important educational implication from this review, therefore, is that the most successful educational programmes for developing bi- and/or multilingualism are immersion programmes, and specifically, TWI immersion programmes for minority language learners. In short, any programme that is subtractive (i.e. transitional programmes) do not adequately support the child's bilingual proficiency and biliteracy. The school is also critical in terms of offering the child exposure that might otherwise not be available in the ambient environment—notable in some immersion and in FL contexts.

The community

Table 7.4 summarizes the main themes to emerge from the discussion in Chapters 2–6 which address the role of the community/society in supporting bi- or multilingualism.

The degree to which the language is present and valued in the community is significant. The community, as with the school, plays a considerable role in the way the two languages are perceived. Unequal experience or exposure to two languages will contribute to dominance patterns in bilingual children. In the context of minority language learners, children from linguistic groups that are perceived as being of lower status will likely struggle in formal education, therefore if the community values the language(s) the child is more likely to be able to participate in educational programmes which support the development of both (as in two-way immersion programmes). Similarly, for children who are majority language speakers being taught a foreign language—the opportunities the child has to engage and interact with the FL impacts on the development of the FL.

Tables 7.1–7.4 tease out the major issues that have emerged from the discussions in Chapters 2–6. Despite the fact that all the learners discussed in this volume are young learners, and should therefore be readily able to acquire and develop competence in more than one language, Tables 7.1–7.4 illustrate significant variability both within and across contexts. This variability is influenced by a number of factors, including the role of the school, parents, and community.

Bilingual first language acquisition (Chapter 2)
• The community is vital in developing bilingual proficiency in that: if the community/ society values both L1 and L2, children are more likely to develop balanced bilingual proficiency and biliteracy skills.

Heritage language learners (Chapter 3)
• HL communities can support development of HL through community-based programmes.   • The wider L1 society can negatively impact HL development by treating the HL community as subordinate.

Minority language learners (Chapter 4)
• The majority society can negatively impact L1 and L2 development by not valuing the HL community.   • The community can facilitate bilingual development if children identify positively with being bilingual.

Immersion (Chapter 5)
• The wider community plays a minimal role in immersion in contexts where there is little opportunity to interact with the immersion language outside of school.

Instructed foreign language learning (Chapter 6)
• The wider community can support FL learning to the extent that the FL is available outside of school (e.g. on television, radio. etc.).   • School and society can encourage parents' support of children's access to the FL; additional exposure and interaction outside the school context can positively impact FL outcomes.

Table 7.4 The role of the community/society in each of the five language learning contexts

Theoretical perspectives

Arguably the most obvious theoretical approach to understanding language development that could account for this variability is the usage-based approach introduced in Chapter 1. Usage-based approaches view language develop-ment as arising out of specific individual experiences that the child has with the language, experiences which shape the developing linguistic system, and which ultimately converge on an abstracted set of grammatical principles (Tomasello, 2003: Lieven and Tomasello, 2008; Ambridge and Lieven, 2011; Bybee 2007, 2008. 2010; Ellis, 2008; Ellis, O'Donnell, and Römer, 2013). Underlying this view is the notion that language is a complex adapted system which has at its core, a social function—i.e. it is used in the context of human interaction and the nature of this interaction, along with our cogni-tive architecture, enables us to converge on a grammatical system (Beckner,

Blythe, Bybee, Christiansen, Croft, Ellis, Holland, Ke, Larsen-Freeman, and Schoenemann, 2009; Larsen-Freeman and Cameron, 2008). The usage-based, or constructivist, approach has been gaining prominence in the context of child L1 acquisition as more and more complex and elaborated constructivist theories have been put forward to help explain how the child comes to learn the complexity that is language (Ambridge and Lieven, 2011). Usage-based explanations have been argued to account for a variety of different features of linguistic competence, including phonology, speech perception, morphosyntax, compounding, constituent structure, and speech processing (Newton, 2012; Ambridge and Lieven, 2011; Nicoladis and Krott, 2007; Beckner and Bybee, 2009; Christiansen and MacDonald, 2009). Children's development of linguistic features such as negation, for example, have been found to follow the frequency with which specific negation patterns are available in the input, where the most frequent negation markers available in the input are the first to emerge in child speech (Cameron-Faulkner, Lieven, and Theakston, 2007). Similarly, children's development of argument structure has been closely linked with the frequency of verbs in the input. Specifically, the frequency with which specific lexical items appear in the input is associated with the development of grammatical knowledge (Kidd, Lieven, and Tomasello, 2010). In their study, 60 children aged between 4;0 and 4;11, and 30 children aged between 5;9 and 7;0 participated in a task that required them to recall test sentences containing low- or high-frequency complement-taking verbs (verbs which take a sentential complement). For example, the verb 'say' is a complement-taking verb in the sentence 'Mickie says Minnie is wearing a lovely dress'. Children were more accurate at recalling sentences with high-frequency than low-frequency complement-taking verbs. Furthermore, their recall of target sentences was more likely to be influenced by a high-frequency lexical prime than a low-frequency one, results that illustrate that children's knowledge of complementation (a syntactic feature) is associated with their knowledge of individual lexical items, specifically, verbs which take sentential complements (Kidd et al., 2010). Thus, as described in Chapter 1, the *frequency* of specific features of language is an important determinant in the developmental trajectory of linguistic features. Additionally, support for the usage-based approach in understanding the development of L1 has been found in languages other than English (Krajewski, Theakston, Lieven, and Tomasello, 2011).

Increasingly, this usage-based approach has been adopted to help explain features of L2 development (in both adult and child L2). Goldberg and Casenhiser (2008), Ellis (2008), Tyler (2010), and Ellis et al. (2013) are examples of ways in which the basic tenets of usage-based approaches to understanding language acquisition can, and should, be applied to L2 development. Within the usage-based paradigm, studies on L2 acquisition have examined a diverse range of L2 phenomena including the development of verb argument structure (Ellis and Larsen-Freeman, 2009), the development of formulaic language (Millar, 2011; Eskildsen, 2008), L2 negation (Eskildsen, 2012), morphosyntax

(Paradis, Nicoladis, Crago, and Genesee, 2011; Blom, Paradis, and Duncan, 2012;) and L2 writing (Geluso, 2013; Verspoor, Schmidt, Xu, 2012). Young French–English bilinguals' use of the past tense has been conceptualized within the usage-based paradigm in Paradis et al. (2011) where four-year-old French–English bilinguals were compared against four-year-old French monolinguals on past tense formation, specifically to examine how exposure in the home might influence bilinguals' accuracy in producing past tense forms. Past tense formation was measured through an elicitation task, and home language use was measured through the administration of a questionnaire completed by the child's parents, who recorded the child's language learning history and parents' use of English and/or French. The child's exposure to and use of French and English in the home was used to categorize the children into different input-groupings—those who had more English or more French—and analyses of past tense forms were carried out along these dimensions. Importantly, differential levels of exposure to each of the two languages had an impact on the extent to which children were accurate in either English or French in relation to monolinguals. In other words, acquisition rates were sensitive to variation in the input to which the children were exposed, a finding consistent with the usage-based approach.

Similar findings were reported in Blom, Paradis, and Duncan (2012), who investigated the development of the third person -*s* in children learning English as a second language (ESL). Factored in to the analyses were a range of other variables believed to impact on the development of this inflectional morpheme (such as frequency, allomorphic variation—different realizations of the -*s* agreement marker—vocabulary size, and the child's L1. Their results indicated that ESL children's use of the -*s* third person marker was influenced by each of these different variables—children were more inaccurate using the -*s* with high-frequency words (illustrating an effect of frequency); children who had L1s with inflectional morphology were more accurate than children who came from other L1 backgrounds (illustrating the influence of L1 background); larger lexicon was associated with greater accuracy (demonstrating an effect of vocabulary size); and finally, children with more exposure to English had higher scores (demonstrating the effect of the input). These findings underscore the importance of including multiple variables in investigations of different aspects of L2 learning since:

> . . . a range of factors simultaneously impact language development, and . . . a usage-based approach . . . can successfully account for the factors that determine L2 children's accuracy . . .
>
> (Blom et al., 2012, p. 990).

The usage-based approach, therefore, meticulously examines the relationship between the linguistic environment and L2 knowledge the child internalizes. Many studies in the L1 and L2 domains have identified how the complexity of the linguistic input to which children are exposed can shape, influence, and ultimately determine linguistic outcomes. It seems perfectly reasonable, if not likely, therefore, that such an approach will underpin the bilingual development described in each of these contexts. Indeed a number of the studies that have been carried out within the L2 domain advocating a usage-based approach have been carried out within these contexts. The work of Paradis et al. (2011), for example, was carried out in the simultaneous bilingual context, while the work of Blom et al. (2012) recruited children who were minority language learners, but at an early point in their development, between the ages of three and eight years.

More research that closely examines the relationship between exposure to specific input patterns and outcomes is needed. This is particularly important in the contexts described in Chapters 4, 5, and 6, where children are learning key features of their L2 in formal education. For example, minority language learners often receive the first initial significant exposure to the majority L2 through formal education. While there have been evaluations of L2 outcomes in minority language learners, these typically address more holistic aspects of L2 competence—addressing such issues as vocabulary size, oral proficiency, and literacy skills. Usually the point of these studies is to identify whether and to what extent children participating in particular programmes make L2 gains relative to children in other programmes or L2-only education. As an example, Collier and Thomas (2004) and Genesee, Lindholm-Leary, Saunders, and Christian (2006) describe the outcomes of large-scale evaluations of different types of bilingual education for minority language learners in North America. The outcomes of these evaluations have demonstrated that children who participate in two-way immersion programmes do as well as or better in both L1 and L2 outcomes than children who participate in L2-only education. However, there have not been very many large-scale longitudinal studies which investigate the precise relationship between the input children receive in the classroom, and their L2 learning. In other words, just as Blom et al. (2012) and Paradis et al. (2011) were able to specifically attribute particular developmental patterns to the input, so research in primary classroom contexts needs to more carefully examine the nature of classroom discourse, and identify the precise ways in which this classroom interaction shapes L2 learning. Eskildsen (2012) for example, carried out a longitudinal investigation of adult L2 English learning in a classroom context within a usage-based approach. He recorded classroom interaction experienced by two adult learners of English and examined the relationship between the input, classroom interaction, and the learners' development of L2 negation. More research like Eskildsen's is required in the child L2 classroom, focusing on discrete aspects of L2 competence (like negation in Eskildsen's study) and which maps the trajectory of L2 development on to the linguistic input.

There are numerous benefits to such an approach in the child L2 classroom. It would allow for further careful studies examining the usage-based approach and its predictions, and test the limits of the theory. Adopting the usage-based paradigm in young L2 learner contexts will help address questions that identify the extent to which the input in classroom-based interaction shapes and determines ultimate L2 knowledge and representation, and in what ways. Furthermore, the input itself is highly variable across, and even within, each of the contexts. For example, in the instructed FL context, arguably the input is severely limited in scope and breadth—when many children receive not much more than an hour per school week either working in or learning about the FL. Consequently there will be significantly reduced opportunities for young children to use their implicit learning mechanisms to abstract underlying lexical and grammatical principles from this input-limited environment. In the immersion contexts reviewed in Chapter 5, however, children spend a significant proportion of their school day using the L2—engaged in meaningful, authentic interaction. These are comparatively input-rich environments that afford the child many opportunities to use the L2 in specific ways, enabling them to construct their L2 lexical and grammatical competence. The precise manner in which the linguistic environment in classroom situations facilitates L2 outcomes in a usage-based approach is not yet clear due to a lack of research in this area. One of the advantages of learning a language primarily in a classroom-based context is that the linguistic environment can be manipulated through different pedagogical techniques. If frequency, for example, is a predictive variable in L2 learning (as usage-based theories suggest), then frequency is something that can be manipulated in L2 primary-level classrooms. This is a rather simplistic portrayal—however, it serves to illustrate the point. Pedagogy and provision can only be enhanced with a greater understanding of the *precise* way in which environmental factors shape bi- and multilingual development in primary school contexts.

Research could examine these issues more carefully in relation to minority language learners and the extent to which their home language is supported by participating in TWI programmes. It is clear from the research described in Chapter 4 that minority language learners benefit from participating in TWI programmes. However, the comparisons that have demonstrated this have been focused on more broad-based L2 outcomes, such as those that form part of the language arts curriculum, which typically focuses on pre-literacy skills such as phonemic awareness. In considering the work of Montrul and colleagues described in Chapter 3, it would be interesting to compare HL learners who are participating in TWI programmes against those who are not, with respect to the same focused linguistic investigations examining the morphosyntactic interface. To what extent do HL learners who participate in TWI programmes show the same 'incomplete' acquisition patterns described in Montrul (2008) at the vulnerable morphosyntactic interface? How does the environment in the TWI classroom help prevent HL grammars from fossilizing? These are the sorts of questions that require greater consideration, and which might most profitably be addressed from a usage-based perspective.

Educational implications and conclusions

There is no biological impediment to bilingualism in young children, and no negative consequences of becoming bilingual or learning aspects of a second or foreign language. However, just being a young learner does not guarantee success in developing knowledge of more than one language. There is substantial variability across each of the contexts observed throughout Chapters 2–6 and, while some contexts are generally more or less successful in yielding bilingual outcomes, we do not observe equal bilingual development across these contexts. Nor do we see consistency in an individual context. The observed variability is manifest in the same areas across each context, however. In other words, what varies is the extent to which the child will develop knowledge and skills in both languages and develop biliteracy skills. Age as a factor predicting this variability is not particularly helpful given that most of the children across the five language learning contexts in this volume are of a similar age range. Therefore, other factors must be at work, causing this variability in outcomes. The most important of these, in general terms, is the linguistic input to which the child is exposed—in instructed FL contexts the child is learning the FL in input-limited environments. In immersion or minority language learner contexts, the child is developing L2 or bilingual knowledge in input-rich environments. Not surprisingly, therefore, we see greater gains in immersion and minority language learners' bilingual development than in instructed FL settings. However, the precise manner in which the input shapes and determines L2 outcomes has not yet been adequately examined; further research carried out in a usage-based paradigm will be helpful here.

With reference to Tony Blair's statement in Chapters 1 and 6, which implies that everyone knows learning languages is easy in childhood—the contexts reviewed in this volume suggests that this statement is at worst inaccurate, and at best simplistic. Undoubtedly there are manifest age-of-acquisition effects such as those described in DeKeyser (2013). However, it seems naive to suggest that it is 'easy' to learn language when minority language learners have been shown to lag behind native-speakers on vocabulary, for example, even at the end of primary school after many years of input-rich exposure to the L2. Promoting L2 learning and bilingual development in primary school contexts is unquestionably a good idea—as demonstrated in each of the chapters in this volume, there are few (if any) negative consequences of so doing. However, it is important to understand the context in which bilingual development takes place, to better appreciate the limits on what is realistic, and identify ways in which the educational provision can help support those features of bilingual development known to be a challenge to young learners. For example, understanding that key aspects of vocabulary (such as academic vocabulary) are important for young learners has led to the development of highly successful academic vocabulary interventions (Carlo et al., 2004) which have had positive effects on reading outcomes, for both native-speaking and minority language students.

The most successful educational programme for promoting bilingual development in young children is the immersion context—either one- or two-way. immersion programmes have been highly effective throughout the world, and with many different languages. Based on this evidence, one way to think about developing future educational provision is for policy makers to examine more closely how bilingual education, and immersion in particular, might be expanded to even further geopolitical contexts, languages, and learners. Such a proposal, however, may not be universally feasible as it will not always be clear within a given context which language(s) would be the most appropriate for an immersion education programme. It would be useful, therefore, if educators could expand and improve on the provision that is already being implemented. In the heritage language learner context, the research reviewed in Chapters 3 and 4 clearly identified the powerful, facilitative, and supportive role of use of the child's L1 in the majority language classroom. Where it is not feasible to develop two-way immersion programmes for such contexts, it would at least be useful if educators could learn more about the benefits of using the child's L1 in different pedagogical activities. As previously identified, even in classrooms where children come from different linguistic backgrounds (i.e. many L1s), teachers can still nonetheless engage in pedagogical activities which make connections to the children's home languages (Cummins, 2005; Issa and Hatt, 2013). Teacher education programmes and in-service professional development can guide teachers as to the most effective ways in which to draw upon the child's home language as a resource. Furthermore, materials developers could include activities and guidelines for how teachers might be able to connect pedagogy to the child's home language environment. In the FL context, one of the greatest challenges will be to identify which languages should be prioritized. With increasing global migration and greater numbers of children placed in schools in new language contexts (minority language learners) the question of which language should be taught as a foreign or second language becomes ever more relevant and interesting. FL learning for minority language learners amounts to a case of taught L3 where the L2 is being learned through the medium of instruction. Decision-making, therefore, about which language(s) to include as the FL need to take this into consideration. Furthermore, as FL instruction is increasingly widespread internationally, advances can be made, using usage-based empirical research, to examine the effectiveness of different aspects of provision, materials development, and support for FL learning in the whole school, home, and community.

It is a great gift to be bilingual, one that is not just a luxury, but more and more a necessity for professional and economic advancement. Education is meant to prepare young people to tackle the world—to equip them with the skills and knowledge they will need to go forth and contribute positively to society, to create a better future for all present generations, and generations to come. In order to achieve these goals, in today's climate of rising global migration and the increasing internationalization of commerce, our schools need to be able to produce bilingual citizens. Understanding the trends in bilingual and L2 learning across different contexts is a beginning to help schools accomplish this mammoth but critically important task.

Note

1 Though see Muñoz and Singleton (2011) for a detailed discussion of the merit of using the native speaker as a point of comparison here.

Bibliography

Aarts, R. & **Verhoeven, L.** (1999). Literacy attainment in a second language context. *Applied Psycholinguistics*, *20(3)*, 377–393.

Adegbija, E. (2004). Language policy and planning in Nigeria. *Current Issues in Language Planning*, *5*, 181–246.

Alexiou, T. (2009). Young learners' cognitive skills and their role in foreign language vocabulary learning. In (Ed.). *Early learning of modern foreign languages: Processes and outcomes.* Bristol: Multilingual Matters.

Ambridge, B. & **Lieven, E.** (2011). *Child language acquisition: Contrasting theoretical perspectives.* Cambridge: Cambridge University Press.

Ananiandou, K. & **Claro, M.** (2009). 21st century skills and competences for new millennium learners in OECD countries. *OECD Education Working Papers*, *41*. http://dx.doi.org/ 10.1787/218525261154

Andrews, R. (2009). *Review of research in English as an Additional Language (EAL).* London: NRDC Institute of Education.

Armon-Lotem, S. (2012). Introduction: Bilingual children with SLI – the nature of the problem. *Bilingualism: Language and Cognition*, *15(1)*, 1–4.

August, D. & **Shanahan, T.** (Eds.) (2008). *Developing reading and writing in second-language learners: Lessons from the report of The National Literacy Panel on language-minority children and youth.* New York: Routledge/CALL.

Baker, C. (2006). *Foundations of bilingual education and bilingualism, 4th Edition.* Clevedon: Multilingual Matters.

——. (2011). *Foundations of bilingual education and bilingualism, 5th Edition.* London: Multilingual Matters.

Bale, J. (2010). International comparative perspectives on heritage language education policy research. *Annual Review of Applied Linguistics*, *30*, 42–65.

Ball, J. (2009). Supporting young Indigenous children's language development in Canada: A review of research on needs and promising practices. *The Canadian Modern Language Review*, *66(1)*, 19–47.

Ballinger, S. (2013). Towards a crosslinguistic pedagogy: Biliteracy and reciprocal learning strategies in French immersion. *Journal of Immersion and Content-Based Language Education*, *1(1)*, 131–148.

——. & **Lyster, R.** (2011). Student and teacher oral language use in a two-way Spanish/English immersion school. *Language Teaching Research*, *15(3)*, 289–306.

Bartlett, L. & **García, O.** (2011). *Additive schooling in subtractive times.* Nashville: Vanderbilt University Press.

Barton, A., **Bragg, J.** & **Serratrice, L.** (2009). 'Discovering Language' in primary school: An evaluation of a language awareness program. *Language Learning Journal*, *37(2)*, 145–164.

Beckner, C. & **Bybee, J.** (2009). A usage-based account of constituency and reanalysis. *Language Learning*, *59(1)*, 27–46.

——., **Blythe, R.**, **Bybee, J.**, **Christiansen, M.H.**, **Croft, W.**, **Ellis, N.C.**, **Holland, J.**, **Ke, J.**, **Larsen-Freeman, D.** & **Schoenemann, T.** (2009). Language is a complex adaptive system: Position Paper. *Language Learning*, *59(1)*, 1–26.

Bedore, L.M., Peña, E., Summers, C.L., Boerger, K.M., Resendiz, M.D., Greene, K., Bohman, T.M. & Gillam, R.B. (2012). The measure matters: Language dominance profiles across measures in Spanish–English bilingual children. *Bilingualism: Language and Cognition*, *15(3)*, 616–629.

Ben-Zeev, S. (1977). Mechanisms by which childhood bilingualism affects understanding of language and cognitive structures. In P.A. Hornby (Ed.). *Bilingualism: Psychological, social and educational implications*. New York: Academic Press.

Bernardini, P. & Schlyter, S. (2004). Growing syntactic structure and code-mixing in the weaker language: The Ivy Hypothesis. *Bilingualism: Language and Cognition, 7(1)*, 49–69.

Bérubé, D. & Marinova-Todd, S.H. (2012). The development of language and reading skills in the second and third languages of multilingual children in French Immersion. *International Journal of Multilingualism, 9(3)*, 272–293.

Bhattacharya, U. (2013). Mediating inequalities: Exploring English-medium instruction in a suburban Indian village school. *Current Issues in Language Planning, 14(1)*, 164–184.

Bialystok, E. (1986). Factors in the growth of linguistic awareness. *Child Development, 57*, 498–510.

——. (1991). Metalinguistic dimensions of bilingual language proficiency. In E. Bialystok (Ed.). *Language processing in bilingual children*. Cambridge: Cambridge University Press.

——. (2001). *Bilingualism in development: Language, literacy and cognition*. Cambridge: Cambridge University Press.

——. & Barac, R. (2013). Cognitive Effects. In F. Grosjean & P. Li (Eds.). *The psycholinguistics of bilingualism*. Chichester: Wiley.

——., Barac, R., Blaye, A. & Poulin-Dubois, D. (2010). Word mapping and executive functioning in young monolingual and bilingual children. *Journal of Cognition and Development, 11(4)*, 485–508.

——., Craik, F.I.M., Klein, R. & Viswanathan, M. (2004). Bilingualism, aging, and cognitive control: Evidence from the Simon task. *Psychology and Aging, 19(2)*, 290–303.

——., Luk, G., Peets, K.F. & Yang, S. (2010). Receptive vocabulary differences in monolingual and bilingual children. *Bilingualism: Language and Cognition, 13(4)*, 525–531.

——. & Miller, B. (1999). The problem of age in second-language acquisition: Influences from language, structure and task. *Bilingualism: Language and Cognition, 2*, 127–145.

Bild, E.R. & Swain, M. (1989). Minority language students in a French programme: Their French proficiency. *Journal of Multilingual and Multicultural Development, 10*, 255–274.

Birdsong, D. (Ed.) (1999). *Second language acquisition and the critical period hypothesis*. Mahwah, NJ: Erlbaum.

Blom, E., Paradis, J. & Duncan, T.S. (2012). Effects of input properties, vocabulary size and L1 on the development of third person singular -s in child L2 English. *Language Learning, 62(3)*, 965–994.

Bloomfield, L. (1933). *Language*. New York: Holt.

Bolonyai, A. (2007). (In)vulnerable agreement in incomplete bilingual L1 learners. *International Journal of Bilingualism, 11(1)*, 3–23.

Bolster, A., Balandier-Brown, C. & Rea-Dickens, P. (2004). Young learners of modern foreign languages and their transition to the secondary phase: A lost opportunity? *Language Learning Journal, 30*, 35–41.

Bonnesen, M. (2009). The status of the 'weaker language' in unbalanced French/German bilingual language acquisition. *Bilingualism: Language and Cognition, 12(2)*, 177–192.

Bortfeld, H. & Whitehurst, G.J. (2001). Sensitive periods in first language acquisition. In D.B. Bailey, J.T. Bruer, F.J. Symons & J.W. Lichtman (Eds.). *Critical thinking about Critical Periods*. Baltimore/London: Paul H. Brookes.

Bosch, L. & Sebastián-Gallés, N. (2001). Evidence of early language discrimination abilities in infants from bilingual environments. *Infancy, 2(1)*, 29–49.

——. (2003). Simultaneous bilingualism and the perception of a language-specific vowel contrast in the first year of life. *Language and Speech, 46(2/3)*, 217–243.

Bowers, P.G. (1993). Text reading and rereading: Determinants of fluency beyond word recognition. *Journal of Reading Behavior, 25*, 133–153.

Brutt-Griffler, J. & Makoni, S. (2005). The use of Heritage Language: An African perspective. *The Modern Language Journal, 89(4)*, 609–612.

Burgoyne, K., Kelly, J.M., Whiteley, H.E. & Spooner, A. (2009). The comprehension skills of children learning English as an additional language. *British Journal of Educational Psychology, 79*, 735–747.

Burgoyne, K., Whiteley, H.E. & Hutchinson, J.M. (2011). The development of comprehension and reading-related skills in children learning English as an additional language and their monolingual English-speaking peers. *British Journal of Educational Psychology, 81*, 344–354.

Burns, T.C., Werker, J.F. & McVie, K. (2003). Development of phonetic categories in infants raised in bilingual and monolingual environments. In B. Beachley, A. Brown and F. Conlin (Eds.). *Proceedings of the 27th Annual Boston University Conference on Language Development*. Cascadilla Press.

Burstall, C. (1975a). Factors affecting foreign language learning: a consideration of some recent research findings. *Language Teaching and Linguistics Abstracts, 8*, 5–125.

——. (1975b). Primary French in the balance. *Foreign Language Annals 10(3)*, 245–252.

Bybee, J. (2007). *Frequency of use and the organization of language*. Oxford: Oxford University Press.

——. (2008). Usage-based grammar and second language acquisition. In P. Robinson & N. Ellis (Eds.). *Handbook of cognitive linguistics and second language acquisition*. New York: Routledge.

——. (2010). *Language, usage and cognition*. Cambridge: Cambridge University Press.

Byers-Heinlein, K., Burns, T.C. & Werker, J. (2010). The roots of bilingualism in newborns. *Psychological Science, 21(3)*, 343–348.

Cable, C., Driscoll, P., Mitchell, R., Sing, S., Cremin, T., Earl, J., Eyres, I., Holmes, B., Martin, C. & Heins, B. (2012). Language learning at Key Stage 2: Findings from a longitudinal study. *Education 3–13, 40(4)*, 363–378.

Cain, K., Oakhill, J., & Bryant, P. E. (2004). Children's reading comprehension ability: Concurrent prediction by working memory, verbal ability, and component skills. *Journal of Educational Psychology, 96*, 31–42.

Cameron, L. (2002). Measuring vocabulary size in English as an Additional Language. *Language Teaching Research, 6(2)*, 145–173.

Cameron-Faulkner, T., Lieven, E. & Theakston, A. (2007). What part of *no* do children not understand? A usage-based account of multiword negation. *Journal of Child Language, 33*, 251–282.

Campbell, R. & Sais, E. (1995). Accelerated metalinguistic (phonological) awareness in bilingual children. *British Journal of Developmental Psychology, 13*, 61–68.

Campfield, D.E. & Murphy, V.A. (2013). The influence of prosodic input in the second language classroom: Does it stimulate child acquisition of word order and function words? *Language Learning Journal*, DOI: 10.1080/09571736.2013.807864.

Cárdenas-Hagan, E., Carlson, C.D. & Pollard-Durodola, S.D. (2007). The cross-linguistic transfer of early literacy skills: The role of initial L1 and L2 skills and language of instruction. *Language, Speech and Hearing Services in Schools, 38*, 249–259.

Carlisle, J., Beeman, M., Davis, L. & Spharim, G. (1999). Relationship of metalinguistic capabilities and reading achievement for children who are becoming bilingual. *Applied Psycholinguistics, 20*, 459–478.

Carlo, M., August, D., McLaughlin, B., Snow, C., Dressler, D., Lippman, D., Lively, T. & White, C. (2004). Closing the gap: Addressing the vocabulary needs of English language learners in bilingual and mainstream classrooms. *Reading Research Quarterly, 39*, 188–206.

Carreira, M. (2004). Seeking explanatory adequacy: A dual approach to understanding the term 'Heritage Language Learner'. *Heritage Language Journal, 2(1)*, 1–25.

——. & **Kagan, O.** (2011). The results of the National Heritage Language Survey: Implications for teaching, curriculum design, and professional development. *Foreign Language Annals*, *44(1)*, 40–64.

Carroll, J.B. (1979). Psychometric approaches to the study of language abilities. In C.J. Fillmore, D. Kempler and W.S-Y Wang (Eds.). *Individual differences in language ability and language behaviour*. New York: Academic Press.

Castles, S. (2013). The forces driving global migration. *Journal of Intercultural Studies*, *34(2)*, 122–140.

Cenoz, J. (2009). *Towards multilingual education: Basque educational research from an international perspective*. Bristol: Multilingual Matters.

——., Genesee, F. & **Gorter, D.** (2013). Critical Analysis of CLIL: Taking stock and looking forward. *Applied Linguistics*, doi:10.1093/applin/amt011.

Chall, J. (1983). *Learning to read: The great debate*. New York: Wiley.

Chen, X., Ramirez, G., Luo, Y.C., Geva, E. & **Ku, Y.M.** (2012). Comparing vocabulary development in Spanish and Chinese-speaking ELLs: The effects of metalinguistic and sociocultural factors. *Reading and Writing*, *25*, 1991–2020.

Chesterton, P., Steigler-Peters, S., Moran, W. & **Piccioli, M.T.** (2004). Developing sustainable language learning pathways: An Australian initiative. *Language, Culture and Curriculum*, *17(1)*, 48–57.

Chimbutane, F. (2011). *Rethinking bilingual education in postcolonial contexts*. Clevedon: Multilingual Matters.

Chomsky, N. (1965). *Aspects of the theory of syntax*. Cambridge, MA: MIT Press.

——. (2007). Approaching UG from below. In U. Sauerland & H.M. Gärtner (Eds.). *Interfaces + Recursion = Language: Chomsky's Minimalism and the view from Syntax-Semantics*. Berlin: Morton de Gruyter.

Christian, D. (1995). Two-way immersion education: Students learning through two languages. *The Modern Language Journal*, *80*, 66–76.

——. & **Howard, E.R.** (2008). Language development and academic achievement in two-way immersion programs. In T.W. Fortune & D.J. Tedick (Eds). *Pathways to multilingualism: Evolving perspectives on immersion education*. Clevedon: Multilingual Matters.

Christiansen, M.H. & **MacDonald, M.C.** (2009). A usage-based approach to recursion in sentence processing. *Language Learning*, *59(1)*, 126–161.

Cohen, A.D. & **Macaro, E.** (Eds.) (2007). *Language learner strategies: Thirty years of research and practice*. Oxford: Oxford University Press.

Collier, V. P. (1992). A synthesis of studies examining long-term language minority student data on academic achievement. *Bilingual Research Journal*, *16*, p. 187–212.

——. & **Thomas, W.P.** (2004). The astounding effectiveness of dual language education for all. *NABE Journal of Research and Practice*, *2(1)*, 1–20.

Comanaru, R. & **Noels, K.A.** (2009). Self-determination, motivation and the learning of Chinese as a heritage language. *The Canadian Modern Language Review*, *66(1)*, 131–158.

Cook, V. (1991). The poverty-of-the-stimulus argument and multi-competence. *Second Language Research*, *7(2)*, 103–117.

——. (1999). 'Going beyond the native speaker in language teaching'. *TESOL Quarterly*, *33(2)*, 185–209.

Cortina, R. (2014). *The education of indigenous citizens in Latin America*. London: Multilingual Matters.

Council of Europe (2001). *Common European framework of reference for languages: Learning, teaching, assessment*. Cambridge: Cambridge University Press.

——. (2007). *From linguistic diversity to plurilingual education: Guide for the development of language education policies in Europe main version*. Strasbourg, France: Council of Europe, Language Policy Division. Retrieved from http://ec.europa.eu/education/doc/official/keydoc/actlang/act_lang_en.pdf.

Coyle, D., Hood, P. & **Marsh, D.** (2010). *Content and language integrated learning*. Cambridge: Cambridge University Press.

Csapó, B. & Nikolov, M. (2009). The cognitive contribution to the development of proficiency in a foreign language. *Learning and Individual Differences, 19*, 209–218.

Csizér, K. & Kormos, J. (2009). An investigation into the relationship of L2 motivation and cross-cultural contact among elementary school students. In M. Nikolov (Ed.). *Early learning of modern foreign languages: Processes and outcomes*. Bristol: Multilingual Matters.

Cummins, J. (1976). The influence of bilingualism on cognitive growth: A synthesis of research findings and explanatory hypotheses. *Working Papers on Bilingualism, 9*, 1–43.

——. (1981). The role of primary language development in promoting educational success for language minority students. In California State Department of education (Ed.). *Schooling and language minority students: A theoretical framework*. Los Angeles: Evaluation, Dissemination and Assessment Center; California State University.

——. (1984). *Bilingualism and special education: Issues in assessment and pedagogy*. Clevedon: Multilingual Matters.

——. (1996). *Negotiating identities: Education for empowerment in a diverse society, 2nd Edition*. Los Angeles, CA: CABE (California Association for Bilingual Education).

——. (2000). *Language, power and pedagogy: Bilingual children in the crossfire*. Clevedon: Multilingual Matters.

——. (2005). A proposal for action: Strategies for recognizing heritage language competence as a learning resource within the mainstream classroom. *The Modern Language Journal, 89(4)*, 585–592.

——. (2009). Pedagogies of choice: Challenging coercive relations of power in classrooms and communities. *International Journal of Bilingual Education and Bilingualism, 12*, 261–272.

——. (2012). The intersection of cognitive and sociocultural factors in the development of reading comprehension among immigrant students. *Reading and Writing, 25*, 1973–1990.

Curtiss, S. (1977). *Genie: A psycholinguistics study of a modern-day 'wild-child'*. New York: Academic Press.

——., Fromkin, V., Krashen, S., Rigler, R. & Rigler, M. (1974/2004). The linguistic development of Genie. In B. Lust & C. Foley (Eds.). *First language acquisition: The essential readings*. Oxford: Blackwell.

Davis K.F., D'Odorico P., Laio F. & Ridolfi L. (2013). Global Spatio-Temporal Patterns in Human Migration: A Complex Network Perspective. *PLoS ONE 8(1)*: e53723. doi:10.1371/journal.pone.0053723.

de Bot, K. (1992). A bilingual production model: Levelt's 'speaking' model adapted. *Applied Linguistics, 13*, 1–24.

——. & Gorter, D. (2005). A European perspective on heritage languages. *The Modern Language Journal, 89(4)*, 612–616.

de Courcy, M. (2002). *Learners' experiences of immersion education: Case studies of French and Chinese*. Clevedon: Multilingual Matters.

de Groot, A.M.B. (2013). Bilingual memory. In F. Grosjean & P. Li (Eds.). *The psycholinguistics of bilingualism*. Chichester: Wiley.

De Houwer, A. (1995a). Early bilingual acquisition: Focus on morphosyntax and the separate development hypothesis. In J. Kroll & A. de Groot (Eds.). *The handbook of bilingualism*. Oxford: Oxford University Press.

——. (1995b). Bilingual language acquisition. In P. Fletcher & B. MacWhinney (Eds.). *The handbook of child language*. Oxford: Blackwell.

——. (2007). Parental language input patterns and children's bilingual use. *Applied Psycholinguistics, 28*, 411–424.

——. (2009). *Bilingual first language acquisition*. Clevedon: Multilingual Matters.

de Mejía, A. (2005). Bilingual education in Colombia: Towards an integrated perspective. In A. de Mejía (Ed.). *Bilingual education in South America*. Clevedon: Multilingual Matters.

184 *Bibliography*

DeKeyser, R.M. (2000). The robustness of critical period effects in second language acquisition. *Studies in Second Language Acquisition*, 22(4), 499–533.

DeKeyser, R.M. (2013). Age effects in second language learning: Stepping stones toward better understanding. *Language Learning*, 63(1), 52–67.

DeKeyser, R.M., Alfi-Shabtay, I. & Ravid, D. (2010). Cross-linguistic evidence for the nature of age effects in second language acquisition. *Applied Psycholinguistics*, 31, 413–438.

DeKeyser, R.M. and Larson-Hall, J. (2005). What does the Critical Period really mean? In J. Kroll and A.M.B. de Groot (Eds.). *Handbook of bilingualism: Psycholinguistic approaches*. New York: Oxford University Press.

Department for Education (2013). *Consultation report: Foreign languages at Key Stage 2*.

——. (2012). *Consultation report: Making languages statutory at Key Stage 2*.

Deuchar, M. & Quay, S. (2000). *Bilingual acquisition: Theoretical implications of a case study*. Oxford: Oxford University Press.

Diaz, R.M. (1983). Thought and two languages: The impact of bilingualism on cognition. In E.W. Gordon (Ed.). *Review of research in education*, X, Washington, DC: AERA.

Ding, H. & Yu, L. (2013). The dilemma: A study of bilingual education policy in Yi minority schools in Liangshan. *International Journal of Bilingual Education and Bilingualism*, 16(4), 451–470.

Dixon, L.Q. (2010). The importance of phonological awareness for the development of early English reading skills among bilingual Singaporean kindergartners. *International Journal of Bilingual Education and Bilingualism*, 13(6), 723–738.

Djité, P.G. (2008). *The sociolinguistics of development in Africa*. Clevedon: Multilingual Matters.

Dobson, A., Pérez Murillo, M. D. & Johnstone, J. (2010). *Bilingual education project Spain—Evaluation report*. British Council.

Dockrell, J.E., Stuart, M. & King, D. (2010). Supporting early oral language skills for English language learners in inner city preschool provision. *British Journal of Educational Psychology*, 80, 497–516.

Döpke, S. (1992). *One parent one language: An interactional approach*. Amsterdam: John Benjamins.

——. (1998). Competing language structures: The acquisition of verb placement by bilingual German–English children. *Journal of Child Language*, 25, 555–584.

Dorner, L.M. (2010). English and Spanish 'para un futuro'—or just English? Immigrant family perspectives on two-way immersion. *International Journal of Bilingual Education and Bilingualism*, 13(3), 303–323.

Dörnyei, Z. (2001). *Teaching and researching motivation*. Harlow: Pearson Education.

Drew, I. (2009). Using the early years literacy programme in primary EFL Norwegian classrooms. In M. Nikolov (Ed.). *Early learning of modern foreign languages: Processes and outcomes*. Bristol: Multilingual Matters.

Driscoll, P., Earl, J. & Cable, C. (2013). The role and nature of the cultural dimension in primary modern languages. *Language, culture and curriculum*, 26(2), 146–160.

Droop, M., & Verhoeven, L. (1998). Background knowledge, linguistic complexity and second language reading comprehension. *Journal of Literacy Research*, 30(2), 253–271.

——. (2003). Language proficiency and reading ability in first- and second-language learners. *Reading Research Quarterly*, 38(1), 78–103.

Duarte, J. (2011). Migrants' educational success through innovation: The case of the Hamburg bilingual schools. *International Review of Education*, 57, 631–659.

Duff, P.A. (2008). Heritage language education in Canada. In D.M. Brinton, O. Kagan & S. Bauckus (Eds.). *Heritage language education: A new field emerging*. New York: Routledge.

——. & Li, D. (2009). Indigenous, minority, and heritage language education in Canada: Policies, contexts and issues. *The Canadian Modern Language Review*, 66(1), 1–8.

Dunn, L.M. (1965). *Peabody picture vocabulary test*. Minnesota: American Guidance Service.

——., ——., Whetton, C. & Pintilie, D. (1982). *British Picture Vocabulary Scale*. Windsor: NFER-Nelson.

Edelenbos, P., & Kubanek-German, A. (2004). Teacher assessment: The concept of 'diagnostic competence'. *Language Testing*, 21, 259–283.

Edelenbos, P., Johnstone, R. & Kubanek, A. (2006). *The main pedagogical principles underlying the teaching of languages to very young learners*. Final Report of the EAC 89/04, Lot 1 study. European Commission. http://europa.eu/languages/en/document/97/7.

Ehrlich, M., Kurtz-Costes, B. & Loridant, C. (1993). Cognitive and motivational determinants of reading comprehension in good and poor readers. *Journal of Reading Behaviour*, 25(4), 365–381.

Eilers, R.E., Pearson, B.Z. & Cobo-Lewis, A.B. (2006). The social circumstances of childhood bilingualism: The Miami experience. In P. McCardle, & E. Hoff (Eds.). *Childhood bilingualism*. Clevedon: Multilingual Matters.

Ellis, N.C. (2008). Usage-based and form-focused language acquisition: The associative learning of constructions, learned attention, and the limited L2 endstate. In P. Robinson & N. Ellis (Eds.). *Handbook of cognitive linguistics and second language acquisition*. New York: Routledge.

——. & Larsen-Freeman, D. (2009). Constructing a second language: Analyses and computational simulations of the emergence of linguistic constructions from usage. *Language Learning*, 59(1), 90–125.

Ellis, N. C., O'Donnell, M. B. & Römer, U. (2013). Usage-based language: Investigating the latent structures that underpin acquisition. *Currents in Language Learning*, 1, *Language Learning*, 63: Suppl. 1. 25–51.

——. & Sagarra, N. (2011). Learned attention in adult language acquisition: A replication and generalization study and meta-analysis. *Studies in Second Language Acquisition*, 33 (4), 589–624.

Emery, H. (2012). *A global study of primary English teachers' qualifications, training and career development*. ELT Research Papers. The British Council.

Emmorey, K. (2002). *Language, cognition and the brain: Insights from sign language research*. Mahwah, NJ: Erlbaum.

Enever, J. (2007). Yet another early start language policy in Europe: Poland this time! *Current Issues in Language Planning*, 8(2), 208–221.

——. (2009). Can today's early language learners in England become tomorrow's plurilingual European citizens? In M. Nikolov (Ed.). *Early learning of modern foreign languages: Processes and outcomes*. Bristol: Multilingual Matters.

——. (Ed.) (2011a). ELLiE: *Early language learning in Europe*. London: The British Council.

——. (2011b). Chapter 1: Policy. In J. Enever (Ed.). ELLiE: *Early language learning in Europe*. The British Council.

——. & Moon, J. (2010). *A global revolution? Teaching English at primary school*. The British Council.

——. & Watts, C. (2009). Primary foreign language pathfinders: The Brighton and Hove experience. *Language Learning Journal*, 37(2), 219–232.

Eskildsen, S.W. (2008). Constructing another language – Usage-based linguistics in second language acquisition. *Applied Linguistics*, 30(3), 335–357.

——. (2012). L2 negation constructions at work. *Language Learning*, 62(2), 335–372.

Eurydice (2006). *Content and Language Integrated Learning (CLIL) at school in Europe*. Brussels: European Commission.

——. (2012). *Key data on teaching languages at school in Europe*. Brussels: Education, Audiovisual and Culture Executive Agency (EACEA P9 Eurydice and Policy Support).

Feng, A. (2011) (Ed.). *English language education across greater China*: Multilingual Matters.

——. (2012). Spread of English across greater China. *Journal of Multilingual and Multicultural Development*, 33(4), 363–377.

Fortune, T.W. & Tedick, D.J. (2008). One-way, two-way and indigenous immersion: A call for cross-fertilization. In T.W. Fortune & D.J. Tedick (Eds.). *Pathways to multilingualism: Evolving perspectives on immersion education*. Clevedon: Multilingual Matters.

Francis, N. (2011). Imbalances in bilingual development: A key to understanding the faculty of language. *Language Sciences, 33*, 76–89.

Galambos, S. & Goldin-Meadow, S. (1990). The effects of learning two languages on levels of metalinguistic awareness. *Cognition, 34*, 1–56.

García, E. (1991). *Education of linguistically and culturally diverse students: Effective instructional practices*. Educational practice report number 1. Santa Cruz, CA and Washington, DC: National Center for Research on Cultural Diversity and Second Language Learning. (ERIC Document Reproduction Service No. ED 338 099).

García Mayo, M. & García Lecumberri, M. (Eds.) (2003). *Age and the acquisition of English as a foreign language*. Clevedon: Multilingual Matters.

García, O. (2005). Positioning heritage languages in the United States. *The Modern Language Review, 89*, 601–605.

——. (2009). *Bilingual education in the 21st Century: A global perspective*. Chichester: Wiley-Blackwell.

——., Zakharia, Z. & Otcu, B. (Eds.). (2013). *Bilingual community education and multilingualism: Beyond heritage languages in a global city*. Bristol: Multilingual Matters.

Gardener, R.C. & Lambert, W.E. (1972). *Attitudes and motivation in second language learning*. Rowley: Newbury House.

Garton, S. Copland, F. & Burns, A. (2011). *Investigating global practices in teaching English to young learners*. The British Council.

Gathercole, V.M., & Thomas, E.M. (2009). Bilingual first-language development: Dominant language takeover, threatened minority language take-up. *Bilingualism: Language and Cognition, 12*, 213–237.

——., ——., Jones, L., Guasch, N.V, Young, N. & Hughes, E.K. (2010). Cognitive effects of bilingualism: Digging deeper for the contributions of language dominance, linguistic knowledge, socio-economic status and cognitive abilities. *International Journal of Bilingual Education and Bilingualism, 13(5)*, 617–664.

Gearon, M.M. (2011). The bilingual interactions of late partial immersion French students during a history task. *International Journal of Bilingual Education and Bilingualism, 14(1)*, 39–48.

Geluso, J. (2013). Phraseology and frequency of occurrence on the web: native speakers' perceptions of Google-informed second language writing. *Computer Assisted Language Learning, 26(2)*, 144–157.

Genesee, F. (1981). A comparison of early and late second language learning. *Canadian Journal of Behavioral Science, 13*, 115–127.

——. (1987). *Learning through two languages: Studies of immersion and bilingual education*. Cambridge: Newbury House.

——. (1989). Early bilingual development: One language or two? *Journal of Child Language, 16*, 161–179.

——. (2004). What do we know about bilingual education for majority language students? In T.K. Bhatia & W. Ritchie (Eds.). *Handbook of bilingualism and multilingualism*. Malden, MA: Blackwell.

——. (2006). Bilingual first language acquisition in perspective. In P. McCardle & E. Hoff (Eds.). *Childhood bilingualism: Research on infancy through school age*. Clevedon: Multilingual Matters.

——. (2008). Dual language in the global village. In T.W. Fortune & D.J. Tedick (Eds). *Pathways to multilingualism: Evolving perspectives on immersion education*. Clevedon: Multilingual Matters.

——., Boivin, I. & Nicoladis, E. (1996). Talking with strangers: A study of bilingual children's communicative competence. *Applied Psycholinguistics, 17*, 427–442.

——., Geva, E., Dressler, C. & Kamil, M. (2006). Synthesis: Cross-linguistics relationships. In D. August & D. Shanahan (Eds.). *Developing literacy in second language learners*. Mahwah, NJ: Erlbaum.

——. & Lindholm-Leary, K. (2013). Two case studies of content-based language education. *Journal of Immersion and Content-Based Language Education, 1(1)*, 3–33.

——., Lindholm-Leary, K., Saunders, W.M. & Christian, D. (Eds.) (2006). *Educating English language learners: A synthesis of research evidence*. Cambridge: Cambridge University Press.

——., Nicoladis, E. & Paradis, J. (1995). Language differentiation in early bilingual development. *Journal of Child Language, 22(3)*, 611–631.

Gervain, J. & Werker, J.F. (2008). How infant speech perception contributes to language acquisition. *Language and Linguistics Compass*, 2, 1149–1170.

Geva, E. (2000). Issues in the assessment of reading disabilities in L2 children—beliefs and research evidence. *Dyslexia, 6(1)*, 13–28.

——. & Farnia, F. (2012). Developmental changes in the nature of language proficiency and reading fluency paint a more complex view of reading comprehension in ELL and EL1. *Reading and Writing*, 25, 1819–1845.

Goetz, P.J. (2003). The effects of bilingualism on theory of mind development. *Bilingualism: Language and Cognition, 6(1)*, 1–15.

Goldberg, A.E. & Casenhiser, D. (2008). Construction learning and second language acquisition. In P. Robinson & N. Ellis (Eds.). *Handbook of Cognitive Linguistics and Second Language Acquisition*. New York: Routledge.

Goorhuis-Brouwer, S. & de Bot, K. (2010). Impact of early English language teaching on L1 and L2 development in children in Dutch schools. *International Journal of Bilingualism, 14(3)*, 289–302.

Goto Butler, Y. (2007). Foreign language education at elementary schools in Japan: Searching for solutions amidst growing diversification. *Current Issues in Language Planning, 8(2)*, 129–147.

Gough, P., Hoover, W. & Patterson, C. (1996). Some observations on a simple view of reading. In C. Cornoldi & J. Oakhill (Eds.). *Reading comprehension difficulties: Processes and intervention* (pp. 1–13). Mahwah, New Jersey: Lawrence Erlbaum.

——. & Tunmer, W. (1986). Decoding, reading and reading disability. *Remedial and Special Education*, 7, 6–10.

Green, D.W. (1986). Control, activation and resource. *Brain and Language*, 27, 210–223.

——. (2011). Bilingual Worlds. In V. Cook & B. Bassetti (Eds.). *Language and Bilingual Cognition*. New York: Psychology Press.

Grosjean, F. (1989). Neurolinguists, beware! The bilingual is not two monolinguals in one person. *Brain and Language*, 36, 3–15.

——. (2008). *Studying bilinguals*. Oxford: Oxford University Press.

Guèvremont, A. & Kohen, D.E. (2012). Knowledge of an Aboriginal language and school outcomes for children and adults. *International Journal of Bilingual Education and Bilingualism, 15(1)*, 1–27.

Hakuta, K. (2001). A critical period for second language acquisition? In D.B. Bailey, J.T. Bruer, F.J. Symons and J.W. Lichtman (Eds.). *Critical thinking about Critical Periods*. Baltimore/London: Paul H. Brookes.

——., Bialystok, E. & Wiley, E. (2003). Critical evidence: A test of the critical period hypothesis for second-language acquisition. *Psychological Science*, 14, 31–38.

——. & Diaz, R.M. (1985). The relationship between degree of bilingualism and cognitive ability: A critical discussion and some new longitudinal data. In K.E. Nelson (Ed.). *Children's language*. Hillsdale, NJ: Erlbaum.

——., Ferdman, B.M. & Diaz, R.M. (1987). Bilingualism and cognitive development: Three perspectives. In S. Rosenberg (Ed.). *Advances in applied psycholinguistics: Reading, writing and language learning*. New York: Cambridge University Press.

——., Goto Butler, Y.G. & Witt, D. (2000). *How long does it take English learners to attain proficiency?* Linguistic Minority Research Institute (Available at LMRI website: http://www.lmri.ucsb.edu/resdiss/pdffiles/hakuta.pdf).

Hamid, M.O., Nguyen, H.T.M. & Baldauf, R.B. (2013). Medium of instruction in Asia: Context, processes and outcomes. *Current Issues in Language Planning, 14(1)*, 1–15.

Harley, B., & Swain, M. (1984). An analysis of verb form and function in the speech of French immersion pupils. *Working Papers in Bilingualism, 14*, 31–56.

Harris, J. (2007). Bilingualism and bilingual education in Ireland North and South. *International Journal of Bilingualism and Bilingual Education, 10, (4)*, 359–368.

——. & O'Leary, D. (2009). A third language at primary level in Ireland: An independent evaluation of the Modern Languages in Primary Schools initiative. In M. Nikolov (Ed.). *Early learning of modern foreign languages: Processes and outcomes.* Bristol: Multilingual Matters.

Harrison, B. (1998). Te Wharekura o Rakamangamanga: The development of an indigenous language immersion school. *Bilingual Research Journal, 22(2/4)*, 297–316.

Hart, B. & Risley, T.R. (1995). *Meaningful differences in the everyday experience of young American children.* Baltimore: Brookes.

Hatcher, P. J. & Hulme, C. (1999). Phonemes, rhymes and intelligence as predictors of children's responsiveness to remedial reading instruction: Evidence from a longitudinal intervention study. *Journal of Experimental Child Psychology, 72*, 130–153.

Hauser, M., Chomsky, N. & Fitch, W.T. (2002). The faculty of language: What is it, who has it, and how did it evolve? *Science, 298*, 1569–1579.

Hawkins, E. (2005). Out of this nettle, drop-out, we pluck this flower, opportunity: Re-thinking the school foreign language apprenticeship. *Language Learning Journal, 32*, 4–17.

Hayashi, Y. & Murphy, V.A. (2013). On the nature of morphological awareness in Japanese–English bilingual children: A cross-linguistic perspective. *Bilingualism: Language and Cognition, 16(1)*, 49–67.

He, A.W. (2010). The heart of heritage: Sociocultural dimensions of heritage language learning. *Annual Review of Applied Linguistics, 30*, 66–82.

Heredia, R.R. (2008). Mental models of bilingual memory. In J. Altarriba & R.R. Heredia (Eds.). *An introduction to bilingualism: Principles and processes.* London: Lawrence Erlbaum.

Hermanto, N., Moreno, S. & Bialystok, E. (2012). Linguist and metalinguistic outcomes of intense immersion education: How bilingual? *International Journal of Bilingual Education and Bilingualism, 15(2)*, 131–145.

Herschensohn, J. (2007). *Language development and age.* Cambridge: Cambridge University Press.

Hirsh-Pasek, K. & Golinkoff, R.M. (1996). *The origins of grammar: Evidence from early language comprehension.* Cambridge, MA: MIT Press.

Hoare, P. (2011). Context and constraints: Immersion in Hong Kong and mainland China. In D.J. Tedick, D. Christian & T.W. Fortune (Eds.). *Immersion education: Practices, policies, possibilities.* Bristol: Multilingual Matters.

——. & Kong, S. (2008). in T.W. Fortune & D.J. Tedick (Eds.). (2008). *Pathways to multilingualism: Evolving perspectives on immersion education.* Clevedon: Multilingual Matters.

Hoff, E. (2003). Causes and consequences of SES-related differences in parent-to-child speech. In M.H. Bornstein & R.H. Bradley (Eds.). *Socioeconomic status, parenting and child development.* Mahwah, NJ: Lawrence Erlbaum Associates.

——., Core, C., Place, S., Rumiche, R., Señor, M. & Parra, M. (2012). Dual language exposure and early bilingual development. *Journal of Child Language, 39*, 1–27.

——. & Naigles, L. (2002). How children use input in acquiring a lexicon. *Child Development, 73*, 418–433.

Holm, A. & Dodd, B. (1999). A longitudinal study of the phonological development of two Cantonese–English bilingual children. *Applied Psycholinguistics, 20,* 349–376.

Hornberger, N. (1997). Literacy, language maintenance, and linguistic human rights: Three telling cases. *International Journal of the Sociology of Language, 127,* 87–103.

——. (2005). Opening and filling up ideological and implementational spaces in heritage language education. *The Modern Language Journal, 89,* 605–609.

Hulk, A. & Müller, N. (2000). Bilingual first language acquisition at the interface between syntax and pragmatics. *Bilingualism: Language and Cognition, 3(3),* 227–244.

Hunt, V. (2011). Learning from success stories: Leadership structures that support dual language programs over time in New York City. *International Journal of Bilingual Education and Bilingualism, 14(2),* 187–206.

Hutchinson, J.M., Whiteley, H.E., Smith, C.D. & Connors, L. (2003). The developmental progression of comprehension-related skills in children learning EAL. *Journal of Research in Reading, 26(1),* 19–32.

Hyltenstam, K. & Abrahamsson, N. (2003). Maturational constraints in second language acquisition. In C.J. Doughty & M.H. Long (Eds.). *Handbook of second language acquisition.* Oxford: Blackwell.

Issa, T. & Hatt, A. (2013). *Language, culture and identity in the early years.* London: Bloomsbury.

Iyamu E.O.S. & Aduwa Ogiegbaen, S.E. (2007). Parents and teachers' perceptions of mother-tongue medium of instruction policy in Nigerian primary schools. *Language, Culture and Curriculum, 20,* 97–108.

Jean, M. & Geva, E. (2009). The development of vocabulary in English as a second language children and its role in predicting word recognition ability. *Applied Psycholinguistics, 30,* 153–185.

Jeon, M. (2012). English immersion and educational inequality in South Korea. *Journal of Multilingual and Multicultural Development, 33(4),* 395–408.

Johnson, C.E. & Lancaster, P. (1998). The development of more than one phonology: A case study of a Norwegian–English bilingual child. *International Journal of Bilingualism, 2,* 265–300.

Johnstone, R. (2009). An early start: What are the key conditions for generalized success? In J. Enever, J. Moon & U Raman (Eds.). *Young learner English language policy and implementation: International perspectives.* Reading: Garnet Education.

Jones, C. & Nangari, J.C. (2008). Issues in the assessment of children's oral skills. In J. Simpson & G. Wigglesworth (Eds.). *Children's language and multilingualism: Indigenous language use at home and school.* London: Bloomsbury.

Jongejan, W., Verhoeven, L. & Siegel, L.S. (2007). Predictors of reading and spelling abilities in first- and second-language learners. *Journal of Educational Psychology, 99(4),* 835–851.

Jule, A. (2010). A case study of Mrs Smith's words and her quiet girls. In R.M. Jiménez Catalán (Ed.). *Gender perspectives on vocabulary in foreign and second languages.* Basingstoke: Palgrave Macmillan.

Jusczyk, P.W. (1997). *The discovery of spoken language.* Cambridge, MA: MIT Press.

Kame'enui, E.J. & Simmons, D.C. (2001). Introduction to this special issue: The DNA of reading fluency. *Scientific Studies in Reading, 5(3),* 203–210.

Kidd, E., Lieven, E.V.M. & Tomasello, M. (2010). Lexical frequency and exemplar-based learning effects in language acquisition: Evidence from sentential complements. *Language Sciences, 32,* 132–142.

Kieffer, M. & DiFelice Box, C. (2013). Derivational morphological awareness, academic vocabulary and reading comprehension in linguistically diverse sixth graders. *Learning and individual differences, 24,* 168–175.

——. & Lesaux, N.K. (2012). Direct and indirect roles of morphological awareness in the English reading comprehension of native English, Spanish, Filipino and Vietnamese speakers. *Language Learning, 62(4),* 1170–1204.

——. & **Vukovic, R.** (2013). Growth in reading-related skills of language minority learners and their classmates: More evidence for early identification and intervention. *Reading and Writing, 26,* 1159–1194.

King, K. (2005). Language policy and local planning in South America: New directions for enrichment bilingual education in the Andes. In A. de Mejía (Ed.). *Bilingual education in South America.* Clevedon: Multilingual Matters.

Kiss, C. & Nikolov, M. (2005). Developing, piloting and validating an instrument to measure young learners' aptitude. *Language Learning, 55(1),* 99–150.

Knell, E., Haiyan, Q., Miao, P., Yanping, C., Siegel, L.S., Lin, Z. & Wei, Z. (2007). Early English immersion and literacy in Xi'an, China. *The Modern Language Journal, 91,* 395–417.

Kohnert, K., Bates, E. & Hernandez, A. (1999). Balancing bilinguals: Lexical-semantic production and cognitive processing in children learning Spanish and English. *Journal of Speech, Language and Hearing Research, 42,* 1400–1413.

Kondo-Brown, K. (2010). Curriculum development for advancing heritage language competence: Recent research, current practices and a future agenda. *Annual Review of Applied Linguistics, 30,* 24–41.

Kovács, A.M. (2009). Early bilingualism enhances mechanisms of false-belief reasoning. *Developmental Science, 12(1),* 48–54.

Krajewski, G, Theakston, A.L., Lieven, E.V.M. & Tomasello, M. (2011). How Polish children switch from one case to another when using novel nouns: Challenges for models of inflectional morphology. *Language and Cognitive Processes, 26(4/5/6),* 830–861.

Kuo, L.J. & Anderson, R.C. (2006). Morphological awareness and learning to read: A cross-language perspective. *Educational Psychologist, 41,* 161–180.

Lado, R. (1957). *Linguistics across cultures: Applied linguistics for language teachers.* Ann Arbor: University of Michigan Press.

Lam, K., Chen, X., Geva, E., Luo, Y.C. & Li, H. (2012). The role of morphological awareness in reading achievement among young Chinese-speaking English language learners: A longitudinal study. *Reading and Writing, 25,* 1847–1872.

Lambert, W.E. & Tucker, G.R. (1972). *The bilingual education of children: The St. Lambert experiment.* Rowley, MA: Newbury House.

Lan, R.L. & Oxford, R. (2003). Language learning strategy profiles of elementary school students in Taiwan. *IRAL, 41,* 339–379.

Lanza, E. (1992). Can bilingual two-year olds code-switch? *Journal of Child Language, 19,* 633–658.

Larsen-Freeman, D. & Cameron, L. (2008). *Complex systems and applied linguistics.* Oxford: Oxford University Press.

Larson-Hall, J. (2008). Weighing the benefits of studying a foreign language at a younger starting age in a minimal input situation. *Second Language Research, 24(1),* 35–63.

Lasagabaster, D. & Sierra, J.M. (2010). Immersion and CLIL in English: More differences than similarities. *ELT Journal, 64(4),* 367–375.

Laufer, B. & Girsai, N. (2008). Form-focused instruction in second language vocabulary learning: A case for contrastive analysis and translation. *Applied Linguistics, 29,* 1–23.

Lenneberg, E.H. (1967). *Biological foundations of language.* New York: Wiley.

Leopold, W. (1949). *Speech development of a bilingual child (vol. 4).* Evanston, IL: Northwestern University Press.

Lesaux, N. K., Crosson, A., Kieffer, M. J., & Pierce, M. (2010). Uneven profiles: Language minority learners' word reading, vocabulary, and reading comprehension skills. *Journal of Applied Developmental Psychology, 31,* 475–483.

——., **Geva, E., Koda, K., Siegel, L.S. & Shanahan, T.** (2008). Development of literacy in second-language learners. In D. August & T. Shanahan (Eds.). *Developing reading and writing in second-language learners: Lessons from the report of The National Literacy Panel on language-minority children and youth.* New York: Routledge/CALL.

——., Koda, K., Siegel, L. & Shanahan, T. (2006). Development of literacy. In D. August & T. Shanahan (Eds). *Developing literacy in second language learners: Report of the national literacy panel on language minority children and youth.* Mahwah, NJ: Lawrence Erlbaum.

——., Lipka, O. & Siegel, L.S. (2006). The development of reading in children who speak English as a second language. *Developmental Psychology, 39 (6),* 1005–1019.

——., Rupp, A.A. & Siegel, L.S. (2007). Growth in reading skills of children from diverse linguistic backgrounds: Findings from a 5-year longitudinal study. *Journal of Educational Psychology, 99(4),* 821–834.

Lieven, E. & Tomasello, M. (2008). Children's first language acquisition from a usage-based perspective. In P. Robinson & N. Ellis (Eds.). *Handbook of cognitive linguistics and second language acquisition.* New York: Routledge.

Li, M. (2007). Foreign language education in primary schools in the People's Republic of China. *Current Issues in Language Planning, 8(2),* 148–160.

Lightbown, P.M. & Spada, N. (1994). An innovative program for primary ESL students in Québec. *TESOL Quarterly, 28(3),* 563–579.

Lin, A.M.Y & Man, E.Y.F. (2009). *Bilingual education: Southeast Asian perspectives.* Hong Kong: Hong Kong University Press.

Lindgren, E. & Muñoz, C. (2013). The influence of exposure, parents, and linguistic distance on young European learners' foreign language comprehension. *International Journal of Multilingualism, 10(1),* 105–129.

Lindholm-Leary, K. J. (2001). *Dual language education.* Clevedon: Multilingual Matters.

Lindholm–Leary, K. & Block, N. (2010). Achievement in predominantly low SES/Hispanic dual language schools. *International Journal of Bilingual Education and Bilingualism, 13(1),* 43–60.

——. & Howard, E. (2008). Language and academic achievement in two-way immersion programs. In T. Fortune & D. Tedick (Eds.). *Pathways to bilingualism: Evolving perspectives on immersion education.* Bristol: Multilingual Matters.

Lipka, O. & Siegel, L.S. (2007). The development of reading skills in children with English as a second language. *Scientific Studies of Reading, 11 (2),* 105–131.

Llinares, A., Morton, T. & Whittaker, R. (2012). *The role of languages in CLIL.* Cambridge: Cambridge University Press.

Lo, Y.Y. & Macaro, E. (2012). The medium of instruction and classroom interaction: Evidence from Hong Kong secondary schools. *International Journal of Bilingual Education and Bilingualism, 15(1),* 29–52.

——. & Murphy, V.A. (2010). Vocabulary knowledge and growth in immersion and regular language-learning programmes in Hong Kong. *Language and Education, 24(3),* 215–238.

Lopriore, L. & Krikhaar, E. (2011). Chapter 3: The School. In J. Enever (Ed.). ELLiE: *Early language learning in Europe.* The British Council.

Lu, Z. (2003). Zhongguo waiyu jiaoyu zhengce de shiran fenxi yu yingran shexiang. [An analysis of China's foreign language policies and tentative suggestions.] *Jichu Yingyu Jiaoyu Yanjiu* [Journal of Basic English Education], *(1),* 6–12.

Lyster, R. (1994). The effect of functional–analytic teaching on aspects of French immersion students' sociolinguistic competence. *Applied Linguistics, 15,* 263–287.

——. (2002). Negotiation in immersion teacher–student interaction. *International Journal of Educational Research, 37,* 237–253.

——. (2004). Research on form-focused instruction in immersion classrooms: implications for theory and practice. *French Language Studies, 14,* 321–341.

——. (2007). *Learning and teaching languages through content: A counterbalanced approach.* Amsterdam: John Benjamins.

——. & Ballinger, S. (2011). Content-based language teaching: Convergent concerns across divergent contexts. *Language Teaching Research, 15(3),* 279–288.

——., Collins, L. & Ballinger, S. (2009). Linking languages through a bilingual read-aloud program. *Language Awareness, 18,* 366–383.

——. & **Mori, H.** (2008). Instructional counterbalance in immersion pedagogy. In T.W. Fortune & D.J. Tedick (Eds.). *Pathways to multilingualism: Evolving perspectives on immersion education.* Clevedon: Multilingual Matters.

——., **Saito, K.** & **Sato, M.** (2013). Oral corrective feedback in second language classrooms. *Language Teaching, 46(1),* 1–40.

Macaro, E. (2009). Teacher use of codeswitching in the second language classroom. In M. Turnbull & Dailey-O'Cain (Eds.). *First language use in second and foreign language learning.* Clevedon: Multilingual Matters.

——. & **Lee, J.H.** (2012). Teacher language background, Codeswitching, and English-only instruction: Does age make a difference to learners' attitudes? *TESOL Quarterly,* DOI: 10.1002/tesq.74.

——., **Handley, Z.** & **Walter, C.** (2012). A systematic review of CALL in English as a second language: Focus on primary and secondary education. *Language Teaching, 45(1),* 1–43.

——. & **Mutton, T.** (2009). Developing reading achievement in primary learners of French: Inferencing strategies versus exposure to 'graded readers'. *Language Learning Journal, 37(2),* 165–182.

MacArthur Communicative Development Inventory (1989). San Diego: University of California, Center for Research in Language.

Mackey, W.F. (1962). The description of bilingualism. *Canadian Journal of Linguistics, 7,* 51–85.

Malone, S. & **Paraide, P.** (2011). Mother tongue-based bilingual education in Papua New Guinea. *International Review of Education, 57,* 705–720.

Mancilla-Martinez, J. & **Lesaux, N.** (2011). The gap between Spanish speakers' word reading and word knowledge: A longitudinal study. *Child Development, 82(5),* 1544–1560.

Manis, F. R., Lindsey, K. A., & **Bailey, C. E.** (2004). Development of reading in grades K–2 in Spanish-speaking English language learners. *Journal of Learning Disabilities Research and Practice, 19,* 214–224.

Marinova-Todd, S. (2012). 'Corplum is a core from a plum': The advantage of bilingual children in the analysis of word meaning from verbal context. *Bilingualism: Language and Cognition, 15(1),* 117–127.

——., **Marshall, D.B.** & **Snow, C.** (2000). Three misconceptions about age and L2 learning. *TESOL Quarterly, 34(1),* 9–34.

Martin, B. (2012). Coloured language: Identity perception of children in bilingual programmes. *Language Awareness, 21(1),* 33–56.

Martin, K.I. & **Ellis, N.C.** (2012). The roles of phonological STM and working memory in L2 grammar and vocabulary learning. *Studies in Second Language Acquisition, 34(3),* 379–413.

Martin-Jones, M., Blackledge, A. & **Creese, A.** (Eds.) (2012). *The Routledge handbook of multilingualism.* London: Routledge.

Martinez, R. & **Murphy, V.A.** (2011). Effect of frequency and idiomaticity on second language reading comprehension. *TESOL Quarterly, 45(2),* 267–290.

Marx, A.E. & **Stanat, P.** (2012). Reading comprehension of immigrant students in Germany: Research evidence on determinants and target points for intervention. *Reading and Writing, 25,* 1929–1945.

May, S. (2013). Indigenous immersion education: International developments. *Journal of Immersion and Content-Based Language Education, 1(1),* 34–69.

McIlwraith, H. (Ed.) (2013). *Multilingual education in Africa: Lessons from the Juba Language-in-Education Conference.* London: The British Council.

McKendry, M.G. (2013). Investigating the relationship between reading comprehension and semantic skill in children with English as an additional language: A focus on idiom comprehension. Unpublished Doctoral Dissertation, University of Oxford.

——. & **Murphy, V.A.** (2011). A comparative study of listening comprehension measures in English as an additional language and native English-speaking primary school children. *Evaluation and Research in Education, 24(1),* 17–40.

McLaughlin, B. (1978). *Second language acquisition in childhood.* Hillsdale, NJ: Lawrence Erlbaum.

Meara, P. (1992). *EFL vocabulary tests*. Swansea: Centre for Applied Language Studies.

——. & Milton, J. (2003). *X-Lex: The Swansea levels test*. Newbury: Express Publishing.

Mehler, J., Jusczyk, P.W., Lambertz, G., Halsted, G., Bertoncini, J. & Amiel-Tison, C. (1988). A precursor of language acquisition in young infants. *Cognition, 29,* 143–178.

Meier, G.S. (2010). Two-way immersion education in Germany: Bridging the linguistic gap. *International Journal of Bilingual Education and Bilingualism, 13(4),* 419–437.

Meisel, J. (2007). The weaker language in early child bilingualism: Acquiring a first language as a second language? *Applied Psycholinguistics, 28,* 495–514.

Menken, K. & Kleyn, T. (2010). The long-term impact of subtractive schooling in the educational experiences of secondary English language learners. *International Journal of Bilingual Education and Bilingualism, 13(4),* 399–417.

Merino, B.J. (1983). Language loss in bilingual Chicano children. *Journal of Applied Developmental Psychology, 4,* 277–294.

Mihaljević Djigunović, J. (2009). Impact of learning conditions on young FL learners' motivation. In M. Nikolov (Ed.). *Early learning of modern foreign languages: Processes and outcomes.* Bristol: Multilingual Matters.

——. (2010). Starting age and L1 and L2 interaction. *International Journal of Bilingualism, 14(3),* 303–314.

——. & Lopriore, L. (2011). Chapter 2: The learner: Do individual differences matter? In J. Enever (Ed.). *ELLiE: Early language learning in Europe.* London: The British Council.

——. & Vilke, M. (2000). Eight years after: Wishful thinking versus facts of life. In J. Moon and M. Nikolov (Eds.). *Research into teaching English to young learners.* Pécs: University of Pécs Press.

Millar, N. (2011). The processing of malformed formulaic language. *Applied Linguistics, 32(2),* 129–148.

Mohamed, N. (2013). The challenge of medium of instruction: A view from Maldivian schools. *Current Issues in Language Planning, 14(1),* 185–203.

Montrul, S. (2004). Subject and object expression in Spanish heritage speakers: A case of morpho-syntactic convergence. *Bilingualism: Language and Cognition, 7,* 125–142.

——. (2008). *Incomplete acquisition in bilingualism: Re-examining the age factor.* Amsterdam: John Benjamins.

——. (2009). Knowledge of tense-aspect and mood in Spanish heritage speakers. *International Journal of Bilingualism, 13(2),* 239–269.

——. (2010a). How similar are adult second language learners and Spanish heritage speakers? Spanish clitics and word order. *Applied Psycholinguistics, 31,* 167–207.

——. (2010b). Current issues in heritage language acquisition. *Annual Review of Applied Linguistics, 30,* 3–23.

——. (2013a). Bilingualism and the heritage language speaker. In W. Ritchie & T. Bhatia (Eds.). *The handbook of bilingualism.* Malden, MA: Wiley-Blackwell.

——. (2013b). *El bilingüismo en el mundo hispanohablante.* [Bilingualism in the Spanish-speaking World]. Malden, MA: Wiley-Blackwell.

——. & Sánchez-Walker, N. (2013). Differential object marking in child and adult Spanish heritage speakers. *Language Acquisition, 20,* 109–132.

Moon, J. (2000). *Children learning English.* Oxford: Macmillan-Heinemann.

Moyer, A. (2004). *Age, accent and experience in second language acquisition.* Clevedon: Multilingual Matters.

Müller, N. & Hulk, A. (2001). Crosslinguistic influence in bilingual language acquisition: Italian and French as recipient languages. *Bilingualism: Language and Cognition, 4(1),* 1–21.

Mullis, I.V.S., Martin, M.O., Kennedy, A.M. & Foy, P. (2007). *PIRLS 2006 international report: IEA's progress in international reading literacy study in primary schools in 40 countries.* Chestnut Hill, MA: TIMSS & PIRLS International Study Center, Lynch School of Education, Boston College.

Muñoz, C. (Ed.) (2006). *Age and rate of foreign language learning.* Clevedon: Multilingual Matters.

——. (2006). The effects of age on foreign language learning: The BAF project. In C. Muñoz (Ed.). *Age and rate of foreign language learning.* Clevedon: Multilingual Matters.

——. (Ed.). (2012). *Intensive exposure experiences in second language learning.* Bristol: Multilingual Matters.

——. & Lindgren, E. (2011). Chapter 5: Out-of-school factors: The home. In J. Enever (Ed.). ELLiE: *Early Language Learning in Europe.* London: The British Council.

——. & Singleton, D. (2011). A critical review of age-related research and L2 ultimate attainment. *Language Teaching, 44(1),* 1–35.

Murphy, V.A. (2000). Compounding and the representation of inflectional morphology. *Language Learning, 50(1),* 153–197.

——. (2010). The relationship between age of learning and exposure to the second language in L2 children. In E. Macaro (Ed.). *Continuum companion to second language acquisition.* London: Continuum.

——., Macaro, E., Alba, S. & Cipolla, C. (2014). Learning an L2 in primary school can facilitate the development of L1 reading skills. *Applied Psycholinguistics.*

Muter, V., Hulme, C., Snowling, M.J. & Stevenson, J. (2004). Phonemes, rimes and language skills as foundations of early reading development: Evidence from a longitudinal study. *Developmental Psychology,* 40, 663–681.

Myers-Scotton, C. (1997). *Duelling languages: Grammatical structure in codeswitching.* Oxford: Clarendon Press.

——. (2006). *Multiple voices: An introduction to bilingualism.* Oxford: Blackwell.

Nakamoto, J., Lindsey, K.A. & Manis, F.R. (2007). A longitudinal analysis of English language learners' word decoding and reading comprehension. *Reading and Writing,* 20, 691–719.

NALDIC (2011). *EAL and ethnicity in schools nationally and by LA, January 2011.* Report published by the National Association of Language Development in the Curriculum (NALDIC).

——. (2012). EAL statistics, available online at: <http://www.naldic.org.uk/research-and-information/eal-statistics/eal-pupils>. Accessed 04.06.13.

——. (2013). *EAL pupils 1997–2013.* NALDIC.

Namazi, M. & Thordardottir, E. (2010). A working memory, not bilingual advantage, in controlled attention. *International Journal of Bilingual Education and Bilingualism, 13(5),* 597–616.

Nation, P. (1990). *Teaching and learning vocabulary.* Boston, MA: Heinle and Heinle.

——. (2001). *Learning vocabulary in another language.* Cambridge: Cambridge University Press.

Nation, K. (2005). Children's reading comprehension difficulties. In M.J. Snowling & C. Hulme (Eds.) *The science of reading: A handbook,* Oxford: Blackwell, 248–265.

——. & Snowling, M. (1998). Semantic processing skills and the development of word recognition: Evidence from children with reading comprehension difficulties. *Journal of Memory and Language,* 39, 85–101.

——. & Snowling, M. (2004). Beyond phonological skills: Broader language skills contribute to the development of reading. *Journal of Research in Reading,* 27, 342–356.

——., Clarke, P., Marshall, C.M. & Durand, M. (2004). Hidden language impairments in children: Parallels between poor reading comprehension and specific language impairment. *Journal of Speech, Hearing and Language Research,* 47, 199–211.

——., Cocksey, J., Taylor, J.S.H. & Bishop, D. (2010). A longitudinal investigation of early reading and language skills in children with poor reading comprehension. *Journal of Child Psychology and Psychiatry, 51(9),* 1031–1039.

Nayak, G. & Sylva, K. (2013). The effects of a guided reading intervention on reading comprehension: A study on young Chinese learners of English in Hong Kong. *Language Learning Journal, 41(1),* 85–103.

Newport, E. (1990). Maturational constraints on language learning. *Cognitive Science, 14,* 11–28.

Newton, C. (2012). Between-word processes in children with speech difficulties: Insights from a usage-based approach to phonology. *Clinical Linguistics and Phonetics, 26(8),* 712–727.

Nguyen, H.T.M. (2011). Primary English language education in Vietnam: Insights from implementation. *Current Issues in Language Planning, 12(2)*, 225–249.
——. & Nguyen, Q.C. (2007). Teaching English in primary schools in Vietnam: An overview. *Current issues in Language Planning, 8(2)*, 162–173.
Nicoladis, E. (1998). Parental discourse and code-mixing in bilingual children. *International Journal of Bilingualism, 2*, 85–99.
——. (2006). Cross-linguistic transfer in adjective–noun strings by preschool bilingual children. *Bilingualism: Language and Cognition, 9(1)*, 15–32.
——. (2012). Cross-linguistic influence in French–English bilingual children's possessive constructions. *Bilingualism: Language and Cognition, 15(2)*, 320–328.
——. & Genesee, F. (1996). Bilingual communication strategies and language dominance. In A. Stringfellow, D. Cahana-amitay, E. Hughes & A. Zukowski (Eds.). *Proceedings of the 20th Annual Boston University Conference on Language Development*. Somerville, MA: Cascadilla Press.
——. & Krott, A. (2007). Word family size and French-speaking children's segmentation of existing compounds. *Language Learning, 57(2)*, 201–228.
——. & Secco, G. (2000). The role of a child's productive vocabulary in the language choice of a bilingual family. *First Language, 20*, 3–28.
Nicolay, A.C. & Poncelet, M. (2013). Cognitive advantage of children enrolled in a second-language immersion elementary school program for three years. *Bilingualism: Language and Cognition, 16(3)*, 597–607.
Nikolov, M. (2009). Early modern foreign language programmes and outcomes: Factors contributing to Hungarian learners' proficiency. In M. Nikolov (Ed.). *Early learning of modern foreign languages: Processes and outcomes*. Bristol: Multilingual Matters.
——. & Csapó, B. (2010). The relationship between reading skills in early English as a foreign language and Hungarian as a first language. *International Journal of Bilingualism, 14(3)*, 315–329.
——. & Mihaljević Djigunović, J. (2011). All shades of every color: An overview of early teaching and learning of foreign languages. *Annual Review of Applied Linguistics, 31*, 95–119.
Ó Baoill, D.P. (2007). Origins of Irish-medium education: The dynamic core of language revitalisation in Northern Ireland. *International Journal of Bilingual Education and Bilingualism, 10(4)*, 410–427.
Ó Muircheartaigh, J. & Hickey, T. (2008). Academic outcome, anxiety and attitudes in early and late immersion in Ireland. *International Journal of Bilingual Education and Bilingualism, 11(5)*, 558–576.
Oller, D.K., Eilers, R.E., Urbano, R. & Cobo-Lewis, A.B. (1997). Development of precursors to speech in infants exposed to two languages. *Journal of Child Language, 24*, 407–425.
Ordóñez, C.L. (2005). EFL and native Spanish in elite bilingual schools in Colombia: A first look at bilingual adolescent frog stories. In. A. de Mejía (Ed.). *Bilingual education in South America*. Clevedon: Multilingual Matters.
Organisation for Economic Co-Operation and Development (2003). *Where immigrant students succeed—A comparative review of performance and engagement in PISA 2003*. Report published by the OECD.
Orosz, A. (2009). The growth of young learners' English vocabulary size. In M. Nikolov (Ed.). *Early learning of modern foreign languages: Processes and outcomes*. Bristol: Multilingual Matters.
Páez, M.M., Tabors, P.O. & López, L.M. (2007). Dual language and literacy development of Spanish-speaking preschool children. *Journal of Applied Developmental Psychology, 28(2)*, 85–102.
Paradis, M. (1990). Language lateralization in bilinguals. *Brain and Language, 39*, 570–586.
——. (2007). Bilingual children with specific language impairment: Theoretical and applied issues. *Applied Psycholinguistics, 28*, 512–564.
——. (2010a). The interface between bilingual development and specific language impairment. *Applied Psycholinguistics, 31*, 227–252.

——. (2010b). Bilingual children's acquisition of English verb morphology: Effects of language exposure, structure complexity and task type. *Language Learning, 60(3)*, 651–680.

——. & **Genesee, F.** (1996). Syntactic acquisition in bilingual children: Autonomous or interdependent. *Studies in Second Language Acquisition, 18*, 1–25.

——., **Genesee, F.,** & **Crago, M.** (2011). *Dual language development and disorders: A handbook on bilingualism and second language learning 2nd Edition.* Baltimore, MD: Brookes Publishing.

——. & **Navarro, S.** (2003). Subject realization and crosslinguistic interference in the bilingual acquisition of Spanish and English: What is the role of the input? *Journal of Child Language, 30,* 371–393.

——., **Nicoladis, E.** & **Genesee, F.** (2000). Early emergence of structural constraints on code-mixing: Evidence from French-English bilingual children. *Bilingualism: Language and Cognition, 3(3),* 245–262.

——., **Nicoladis, E., Crago, M.** & **Genesee, F.** (2011). Bilingual children's acquisition of the past tense: A usage-based approach. *Journal of Child Language, 38,* 554–578.

Parkes, J. & **Ruth, T.** (2011). How satisfied are parents of students in dual language education programs?: 'Me parece maravillosa la gran oportunidad que les están dando a estos niños'. *International Journal of Bilingual Education and Bilingualism, 14(6),* 701–718.

Parsons, C. & **Lyddy, F.** (2009). The sequencing of formal reading instruction in bilingual and English-medium schools in Ireland. *International Journal of Bilingual Education and Bilingualism, 12(5),* 493–512.

Peal, E. & **Lambert, W.E.** (1962). The relation of bilingualism to intelligence. *Psychological Monographs: General and Applied, 76(27),* 1–23.

Pearson, B.Z., Fernández, S.C. & **Oller, D.K.** (1993). Lexical development in bilingual infants and toddlers: Comparison to monolingual norms. *Language Learning, 43,* 93–120.

Pearson, B.Z., Fernández, S.C., Lewedag, V. & **Oller, D.K.** (1997). The relation of input factors to lexical learning by bilingual infants. *Applied Psycholinguistics, 18,* 41–58.

Penfield, W. & **Roberts, L.** (1959). *Speech and brain mechanisms.* Princeton: Princeton University Press.

Philp, J., Oliver, R. & **Mackey, A.** (Eds.). (2008). *Second language acquisition and the younger learner: Child's play?* Amsterdam: John Benjamins.

Phyak, P. (2013). Language ideologies and local languages as the medium-of-instruction policy: A critical ethnography of a multilingual school in Nepal. *Current Issues in Language Planning, 14(1),* 127–143.

Pinter, A. (2006). *Teaching young language learners.* Oxford: Oxford University Press.

——. (2011). *Children learning second languages.* Basingstoke: Palgrave Macmillan.

Pires, A. & **Rothman, J.** (2009). Disentangling sources of incomplete acquisition: An explanation for competence divergence across heritage grammars. *International Journal of Bilingualism, 13(2),* 211–238.

Polinsky, M. (2008). Gender under incomplete acquisition: heritage speakers' knowledge of noun categorization. *Heritage Language Journal, 6(1),* 40–71.

——. (2011). Reanalysis in adult heritage language acquisition: New evidence in support of attrition. *Studies in Second Language Acquisition, 33,* 305–328.

Poon, A.Y.K. (2013). Will the new fine-tuning medium-of-instruction policy alleviate the threats of dominance of English-medium instruction in Hong Kong? *Current Issues in Language Planning, 14(1),* 34–51.

Poplack, S. (1980). 'Sometimes I start a sentence in English y termino en español': Toward a typology of code-switching. *Linguistics, 18,* 581–618.

Potowski, K. (2007). *Language and identity in a dual immersion school.* Clevedon: Multilingual Matters.

Proctor, C. P., Carlo, M., August, D., & **Snow, C.** (2005). Native Spanish-speaking children reading in English: Toward a model of comprehension. *Journal of Educational Psychology, 97,* 246–256.

Purkarthofer, J. & Mossakowski, J. (2011). Bilingual teaching for multilingual students? Innovative dual-medium models in Slovene–German schools in Austria. *International Review of Education*, *57*, 551–565.

Qiang, H., Huang, X., Siegel, L. & Trube, B. (2011). English immersion in mainland China. In A. Feng (Ed.). *English language education across greater China*. Bristol: Multilingual Matters. *TESOL Quarterly*, *33(2)*, 185–209.

Quay, S. (1995). The bilingual lexicon: implications for studies of language choice. *Journal of Child Language*, *22*, 369–387.

Richards, M. & Burnaby, B. (2008). Restoring aboriginal languages: Immersion and intensive language program models in Canada. In T. Fortune & D. Tedick (Eds.). *Pathways to multilingualism: Evolving perspectives on immersion education*. Clevedon: Multilingual Matters.

Rixon, S. (2013). *British Council survey of policy and practice in primary English language teaching worldwide*. London: The British Council.

Romaine, S. (1995). *Bilingualism, 2nd Edition*. Oxford: Blackwell.

Roth, F. P., Speece, D. L. & Cooper, D. H. (2002). A longitudinal analysis of the connection between oral language and reading. *Journal of Educational Research*, *95*, 259–272.

Rothman, J. (2007). Heritage speaker competence differences, language change and input type: Inflected infinitives in heritage Brazilian Portuguese. *International Journal of Bilingualism*, *11(4)*, 359–389.

——. (2009). Understanding the nature and outcomes of early bilingualism: Romance languages as heritage languages. *International Journal of Bilingualism*, *13(2)*, 155–163.

Ruíz de Zarobe, Y. & Jiménez Catalán, R.M. (Eds.) (2009). *Content and language integrated learning*. Bristol: Multilingual Matters.

Šamo, R. (2009). The age factor and L2 reading strategies. In M. Nikolov (Ed.). *Early learning of modern foreign languages: Processes and outcomes*. Bristol: Multilingual Matters.

Sarkar, M. & Metallic, M.A. (2009). Indigenizing the structural syllabus: The challenge of revitalizing Mi'gmaq in Listuguj. *The Canadian Modern Language Review*, *66(1)*, 49–71.

Saunders, W.M. & O'Brien, G. (2006). Oral language. In F. Genesee, K. Lindholm-Leary, W.M. Saunders & D. Christian (Eds.). *Educating English language learners: A synthesis of research evidence*. Cambridge: Cambridge University Press.

Sawyer, M., & Ranta, L. (2001). Aptitude, individual differences and L2 instruction. In P. Robinson (Ed.). *Cognition and second language instruction*. Cambridge: Cambridge University Press.

Schlyter, S. (1990). Introducing the DuFDE project. In J. Meisel (Ed.). *Two first languages: Early grammatical development in bilingual children*. Dordrecht: Foris.

Schmidt, R. (1990). The role of consciousness in second language learning. *Applied Linguistics*, *11*, 129–158.

Schwartz, M. & Katzir, T. (2012). Depth of lexical knowledge among bilingual children: The impact of schooling. *Reading and Writing*, *25*, 1947–1971.

Scovel, T. (2000). A critical review of the critical period research. *Annual Review of Applied Linguistics*, *20*, 213–223.

Selinker, L. (1972). Interlanguage. *IRAL*, *10*, 209–231.

Sen, R. & Blatchford, P. (2001). Reading in a second language: Factors associated with progress in young children. *Educational Psychology*, *21(2)*, 189–202.

Sharpe, (2001). *Modern foreign languages in the primary school*. London: Kogan Page.

Siân Hodges, R. (2012). Welsh-medium education and parental incentives—the case of the Rhymni Valley, Caerffili. *International Journal of Bilingual Education and Bilingualism*, *15(3)*, 355–373.

Siegel, L.S. (2011). Early English immersion in Xi'an China: An experiment in English language teaching. *Frontiers of Education in China*, *6(1)*, 1–7.

Simpson, J. & Wigglesworth, G. (Eds.) (2008). *Children's language and multilingualism: Indigenous language use at home and school*. London: Continuum.

Simpson, J.M. (2005). A look at early childhood writing in English and Spanish in a bilingual school in Ecuador. In. A. de Mejía (Ed.) *Bilingual education in South America*. Clevedon: Multilingual Matters.

Singleton, D. (2005). The Critical Period Hypothesis: A coat of many colours. *IRAL, 43,* 269–285.

Singleton, D. & Ryan, L. (2004). *Language acquisition: The age factor*. Clevedon: Multilingual Matters.

Skehan, P. (2002). Theorising and updating aptitude. In P. Robinson (Ed.). *Individual differences and instructed language learning*. Amsterdam: John Benjamins.

Smith, S.A. (2013). The nature of multi-word vocabulary among children with English as a first or additional language and its application to literacy. Unpublished Doctoral Dissertation. University of Oxford.

Snow, C. (1987). Relevance of a critical period to language acquisition. In M. Bornstein (Ed.). *Sensitive periods in development: Interdisciplinary perspectives*. Hillsdale, NJ/London: Erlbaum. pp. 183–210.

——. (2002). Second language learners and understanding the brain. In A. Galaburda, S.M. Kosslyn & Y. Christen (Eds.). *The languages of the brain*. Cambridge, MA: Harvard University Press.

——. (2010). Academic language and the challenge of reading for learning about science. *Science, 328,* 450–452.

——., Cancino, H., Gonzalez, P. & Sriberg, E. (1987). *Second language learners' formal definitions: An oral language correlate of school literacy*. (Tech. Rep. No. 5). Los Angeles: University of California, Center for Language Education and Research.

Södergård, M. (2008). Teaching strategies for second language production in immersion kindergarten in Finland. In T.W. Fortune & D.J. Tedick (Eds.). *Pathways to multilingualism: Evolving perspectives on immersion education*. Clevedon: Multilingual Matters.

Song, J.J. (2013). For whom the bell tolls: Globalisation, social class and South Korea's international schools. *Globalisation, Societies and Education, 11(1),* 136–159.

Sorace, A. (2011). Pinning down the concept of 'interface' in bilingualism. *Linguistic Approaches to Bilingualism, 1(1),* 1–33.

——. & Filiaci, F. (2006). Anaphora resolution in near-native speakers of Italian. *Second Language Research, 22,* 339–368.

Spada, N. (2011). Beyond form-focused instruction: Reflections on past, present and future research. *Language Teaching, 44(2),* 225–236.

——. & Tomita, Y. (2010). Interactions between type of instruction and type of language feature: A meta-analysis. *Language Learning, 60(2),* 263–308.

Stanat, P. & Christensen, G.S. (2006). *Where immigrant students succeed: A comparative review of performances and engagement in PISA 2003*. Paris: OECD.

Sternberg, R.J. & Grigorenko, E.L. (2002). *Dynamic testing: The nature and measurement of learning potential*. Cambridge: Cambridge University Press.

Stevens, F. (1983). Activities to promote learning and communication in the second language classroom. *TESOL Quarterly, 17,* 259–272.

Strong, M. (1984). Integrative motivation: Cause or result of successful second language acquisition? *Language Learning, 34(3),* 1–13.

Sua, T.Y., Ngah, K. & Darit, S.M. (2013). Parental choice of schooling, learning processes and inter-ethnic friendship patterns: The case of Malay students in Chinese primary schools in Malaysia. *International Journal of Educational Development, 33,* 325–336.

Swain, M. & Lapkin, S. (1998). Interaction and second language learning: Two adolescent French immersion students working together. *Modern Language Journal, 82(3),* 320–327.

——. (2000). Task-based second language learning: The uses of the first language. *Language Teaching Research, 4(3),* 251–274.

Swanson, H.L., Sáez, L. & Gerber, M. (2006). Growth in literacy and cognition in bilingual children at risk or not at risk for reading disabilities. *Journal of Educational Psychology, 98(2),* 247–264.

Szpotowicz, M. (2009). Factors influencing young learners' vocabulary acquisition. In M. Nikolov (Ed). *Early learning of modern foreign languages: Processes and outcomes*. Bristol: Multilingual Matters.

——. & Lindgren, E. (2011). Chapter 6: Language achievements: a longitudinal perspective. In J. Enever (Ed.). ELLiE: *Early language learning in Europe*. London: The British Council.

Taylor-Leech, K. (2013). Finding space for non-dominant languages in education: Language policy and medium of instruction in Timor-Leste 2000–2012. *Current Issues in Language Planning, 14(1)*, 109–126.

Tedick, D.J. (forthcoming). Bilingual/Immersion education and at-risk students. *Journal of Immersion and Content-Based Language Education*.

——., Christian, D. & Fortune, T.W. (Eds.) (2011). *Immersion education: Practices, policies, possibilities*. Bristol: Multilingual Matters.

Thomas, W.P., & Collier, V.P. (2002). *A national study of school effectiveness for language minority students' long-term academic achievement*. Santa Cruz, CA: Center for Research on Education, Diversity and Excellence, University of California-Santa Cruz.

Thordardottir, E. (2011). The relationship between bilingual exposure and vocabulary development. *International Journal of Bilingualism, 15(4)*, 426–445.

——., Rothenberg, A., Rivard, M.E. & Naves, R. (2006). Bilingual assessment: Can overall proficiency be estimated from separate measurement of two languages? *Journal of Multilingual Communication Disorders, 4(1)*, 1–21.

Tian, L. & Macaro, E. (2012). Comparing the effect of teacher codeswitching with English-only explanations on the vocabulary acquisition of Chinese university students: A lexical focus on form study. *Language Teaching Research, 16(3)*, 367–391.

Tinsley, T. & Comfort, T. (2012). *Lessons from abroad: International review of primary languages*. CfBT Education Trust.

Tomasello, M. (2003). *Constructing a language: A usage-based theory of language acquisition*. Cambridge, MA: Harvard University Press.

Tong, F., Lara-Alecio, R., Irby, B., Mathes, P. & Kwok, O. (2008). Accelerating early academic oral English development in transitional bilingual and structured English immersion programs. *American Educational Research Journal, 45(4)*, 1011–1044.

Tragant Mestres, E. & Lundberg, G. (2011). Chapter 4: The teacher's role: What is its significance in early language learning? In J. Enever (Ed.). ELLiE: *Early language learning in Europe*. London: The British Council.

Trofimovich, P., Lightbown, P., Halter, R.H. & Song, H. (2009). Comprehension-based practice: The development of L2 pronunciation in a listening and reading program. *Studies in Second Language Acquisition, 31*, 609–639.

Tse, S.K., Loh, K.Y.E., Lam, Y, H.R. & Lam, W.I.J. (2010). A comparison of English and Chinese reading proficiency of primary school Chinese students. *Journal of Multilingual and Multicultural Development, 31(2)*, 181–199.

Tsimpli, I.M. & Sorace, A. (2006). Differentiating interfaces: L2 performance in syntax-semantics and syntax-discourse phenomena. In D. Bamman, T. Magnitskaia & C. Zaller (Eds.). *Proceedings of the 30th Boston University Conference on Language Development*. Somerville, MA: Cascadilla Press.

Tsung, L.T.H. & Cruickshank, K. (2009). Mother tongue and bilingual minority education in China. *International Journal of Bilingual Education and Bilingualism, 12(5)*, 549–563.

Tupas, T.R.F. (2011). English-knowing bilingualism in Singapore: Economic pragmatism, ethnic relations and class. In A. Feng (Ed.). *English language education across greater China*. Bristol: Multilingual Matters.

Turnbull, M., Cormier, M. & Bourque, J. (2011). The first language in science class: A quasi-experimental study in late French immersion. *The Modern Language Journal, 95*, 182–198.

Tyler, A. (2010). Usage-based approaches to language and their applications to second language learning. *Annual Review of Applied Linguistics, 30*, 270–291.

Uchikoshi, U. (2006). English vocabulary development in bilingual kindergarteners: What are the best predictors? *Bilingualism: Language and Cognition, 9(1)*, 33–49.

Uysal, H.H., Plakans, L. & Dembovskaya, S. (2007). English language spread in local contexts: Turkey, Latvia and France. *Current Issues in Language Planning, 8(2)*, 192–207.

Vaish, V. (2012). Teacher beliefs regarding bilingualism in an English medium reading program. *International Journal of Bilingual Education and Bilingualism, 15(1)*, 53–69.

Verhallen, M. & Schoonen, R. (1993). Lexical knowledge of monolingual and bilingual children. *Applied Linguistics, 14(4)*, 344–363.

——. (1998). Lexical knowledge in L1 and L2 of third and fifth graders. *Applied Linguistics, 19(4)*, 452–470.

Verhoeven, L. (1990). Acquisition of reading in a second language. *Reading Research Quarterly, 25(2)*, 91–113.

——. (2000). Components of early second language reading and spelling. *Scientific Studies of Reading, 4*, 313–30.

——. & van Leeuwe, J. (2012). The simple view of second language reading throughout the primary grades. *Reading and Writing, 25(8)*, 1805–1818.

——. & Vermeer, A. (2006). Literacy achievement of children with intellectual disabilities and differing linguistic backgrounds. *Journal of Intellectual Disability Research, 50(10)*, 725–738.

Verspoor, M., Schmid, M.S. & Xu, X. (2012). A dynamic usage based perspective on L2 writing. *Journal of Second Language Writing, 21*, 239–263.

Vihman, M.M. (1985). Language differentiation by the bilingual infant. *Journal of Child Language, 12*, 297–324.

Volterra, V. & Taeschner, T. (1978). The acquisition and development of language by bilingual children. *Journal of Child Language, 5*, 322–26.

Vygotsky, L. (1962). *Thought and language*. Cambridge, MA: MIT Press.

Walker, D., Greenwood, C. Hart, B. & Carta, J. (1994). Prediction of school outcomes based on early language production and socioeconomic factors. *Child Development, 65(2)*, 606–621.

Wang, G. (2011). Bilingual education in southwest China: A Yingjiang case. *International Journal of Bilingual Education and Bilingualism, 14(5)*, 571–587.

Wang, L. & Kirkpatrick, A. (2013). Trilingual education in Hong Kong primary schools: A case study. *International Journal of Bilingual Education and Bilingualism, 16(1)*, 100–116.

Wang, Q. (2002). Primary School English Teaching in China—New Developments. *ELTED, 7*, 99–108.

Wei, L. (2000). Dimensions of bilingualism. In Li Wei (Ed.). *The bilingualism reader*. London: Routledge.

Werker, J.F., Weikum, W.M. & Yoshida, K.A. (2006). Bilingual speech processing in infants and adults. In P. McCardle & E. Hoff (Eds.). *Childhood bilingualism: Research on infancy through school age*. Clevedon: Multilingual Matters.

Wesche, M., Toews-Janzen, M. & MacFarlane, A. (1996). *Comparative outcomes and impact of early, middle and late entry French immersion options: Review of recent research and annotated bibliography*. Toronto: OISE/UT Press.

Wesely, P.M. & Baig, F. (2012). The 'Extra Boost': Parental involvement and decision making in immersion programs. *Bilingual Research Journal, 35*, 314–330.

White, L. (1989). *Universal grammar and second language acquisition*. John Benjamins.

Whiting, E.R. & Feinauer, E. (2011). Reasons for enrollment at a Spanish–English two-way immersion charter school among highly motivated parents from a diverse community. *International Journal of Bilingual Education and Bilingualism, 14(6)*, 631–651.

Wigglesworth, G. & Billington, R. (2013). Teaching creole-speaking children: Issues, concerns and resolutions for the classroom. *Australian Review of Applied Linguistics, 36(3)*, 234–249.

Wigglesworth, G., Simpson, J. & Loakes, D. (2011). NAPLAN language assessments for indigenous children in remote communities: Issues and problems. *Australian Review of Applied Linguistics, 34(3)*, 320–343.

Wiig, E.H. & Secord, W. (1992). *Test of word knowledge (TOWK)*. USA: The Psychological Corporation.

Wong-Fillmore, L. (1979). Individual differences in second language acquisition. In C.F. Fillmore, D. Kempler & W.S. Wang (Eds.). *Individual differences in language ability and language behavior*. New York: Academic Press, pp. 203–228.

——. (1983). The language learner as an individual. *On TESOL '82: Pacific Perspectives on Language Learning and Teaching*. Washington, DC: TESOL.

Yip, V. (2013). Simultaneous language acquisition. In F. Grosjean & P. Li (Eds.). *The psycholinguistics of bilingualism*. Chichester: Wiley.

——. & Matthews, S. (2000). Syntactic transfer in a Cantonese–English bilingual child. *Bilingualism: Language and Cognition, 3(3)*, 193–208.

——. & Matthews, S. (2007). *The bilingual child: Early development and language contact*. Cambridge: Cambridge University Press.

Zentella, A.C. (1999). *Growing up bilingual*. Malden, MA: Blackwell.

Index

(Page numbers annotated with 't', 'f' or 'n' refer to tables, figures, and notes respectively.)